Pruning,
Planting & Care

Written by
Eric A. Johnson
with
Scott Millard

Photography by
Scott Millard

Major Illustrations by
Don Fox

IRONWOOD PRESS
Tucson, Arizona

IRONWOOD PRESS

Publisher
Scott Millard

Associate Publisher
Eric A. Johnson

Business Manager
Michele V. M. Millard

Design production and indexing
Ed Allard

Proofreading
Mary Campbell

Printing 10 9 8 7 6 5 4 3 2

Printed in the United States

**Library of Congress
Cataloging-in-Publication Data**
Johnson, Eric A., 1913

Pruning, planting & care:
Johnson's guide to gardening
plants for the arid West /
written by Eric A. Johnson with
Scott Millard; photography by
Scott Millard; illustrations by
Don Fox

p. cm.

Includes index

ISBN 0-9628236-5-1 (pbk.)

1. Arid regions plants—West
(U.S.)   (2) Landscape plants—
West (U.S.)   3. Landscape
gardening—West (U.S.)
I. Millard, Scott. II. Fox, Don,
1959–   .   III. Title.
SB427.5.J64   1997
635.9′525′0978—dc21
97–849
CIP

The information in this book is
true and accurate to the best of
our knowledge. It is offered
without guarantees on the part
of the author and the publisher,
who disclaim any liability in
connection with the use of this
information.

Address inquiries to:
IRONWOOD PRESS
2968 West Ina Road #285
Tucson, Arizona   85741

Cover Photo
by Scott Millard
Landscape design by
Margaret West

Additional Photography
Charles Sappington, page 63,
bottom

Additional Illustrations
Naning San Pedro
page 4

Nancy Sappington
pages 82, 83, 85, 98 bottom, 106,
126, 130, 137

Bill Tollis
pages 75, 77, 80, 86, 87, 90, 91, 92,
93, 97, 98 top, 105, 108, 109, 111,
113, 114, 116, 117, 118, 121, 124,
128, 129, 132, 133, 134, 135, 138,
139, 142, 146, 147, 150, 153, 154

Special Thanks

The author and editor would like
to thank Ed Mulrean for his gen-
erous contributions to the information contained in this book.

Special thanks must also go to
Matt Johnson of the University of
Arizona Legume Program for his
valuable input.

Many thanks to Tohono Chul
Park in Tucson for access to their
facilities for many of the photographs used in this book.

Thank you to the following
individuals who contributed
their time in reviewing the text
and materials included in these
pages:

Russ Buhrow, Tohono Chul Park,
Tucson, Arizona

Ann Copeland, Coachella Valley
Water District, Coachella,
California

Bufford Crites, City of Palm
Desert, Palm Desert, California

Mary Rose Duffield, landscape
architect, Tucson, Arizona

Peter Duncombe, Las Vegas
Water District, Las Vegas,
Nevada

Ron and Maureen Gass,
Mountain States Nursery,
Glendale, Arizona

Allan Hollinger, arborist,
Bermuda Dunes, California

Robert Morris, horticultural specialist, University of Nevada,
Las Vegas

Janet Rademacher, Mountain
States Nursery, Glendale, Arizona

Greg Starr, nurseryman, Tucson,
Arizona

Dennis Swartzell, University of
Nevada, Las Vegas

Lauren Swezey, *Sunset* magazine

Dr. Jimmy Tipton, University of
Arizona, Tucson, Arizona

John White, extension specialist,
Albuquerque, New Mexico

Jack Zunino, landscape architect,
Las Vegas, Nevada

Additional Thanks

Charles and Lou Ann Basham,
Huntington Beach, California

Tom Doczi, landscape architect,
Palm Springs, California

Phil Furnari, nurseryman,
Bermuda Dunes, California

Tim Gallagher, Tohono Chul
Park, Tucson, Arizona

Ron Gregory, landscape architect,
Palm Desert, California

David Harbison, Coachella Valley
Water District, Coachella,
California

Glenn Huntington, The Living
Desert, Palm Desert, California

Warren Jones, landscape architect, Tucson, Arizona

John Krieg, landscape architect,
Palm Desert, California

Judy Mielke, Phoenix, Arizona

Michele V. M. Millard, Tucson,
Arizona

Zachary Millard, Tucson, Arizona

Linn Mills, horticultural
specialist, University of Nevada,
Las Vegas

Eric Moller, nurseryman, Palm
Desert, California

Bette Nesbitt, Tucson, Arizona

Kent Newland, water conservation specialist, Phoenix, Arizona

Robert Perry, landscape architect,
La Verne, California

Judith Phillips, Albuquerque,
New Mexico

Wayne Price, Cathedral City,
California

Christine E. Ten Eyck, landscape
architect, Mesa, Arizona

Larry and Deanna Waller,
Tucson, Arizona

Sally and Andy Wasowski, Taos,
New Mexico

Margaret West, landscape
designer, Tucson, Arizona

Locke Witte, Palm Desert,
California

James Wheat, landscape architect,
Mesa, Arizona

TABLE OF CONTENTS

Dedication

To the Plant Pioneers of the Arid West

As the story of landscaping and gardening in the West unfolds, the time has come to recognize those who have devoted their lives to the love of plants. This book is dedicated to these individuals.

Horticulture and landscaping history in the West and Southwest began in the 1700s as Spanish explorers and mission fathers introduced their favorite fruits —olives, grapes, citrus, figs— to the mission gardens in Arizona, California and Baja California.

By the 1800s, cattle ranchers landscaped their hacienda courtyards and ramadas with plants shipped to them from the eastern United States. Settlers brought seeds, bulbs and cuttings; local nurseries began growing plants better suited to the dry West.

Dr. Francesco Francheschi introduced many hundreds of species from other continents into Santa Barbara landscapes that thrived in the coastal and inland valley climates. Nurseryman **Peter Reidel,** also of Santa Barbara, was instrumental in growing and distributing plants after Dr. Francheschi returned to Italy.

Plant explorers Tracy Omar, left, and Matt Johnson, right, admire a Texas ebony tree in its native Chihuahuan Desert.

Kate Sessions introduced her share of tropical and dry climate plants to San Diego. These trees and palms have been important in shaping the look of gardens in coastal and inland valleys of California, as well as the low-elevation deserts. **Luther Burbank** is well known for his active role in hybridizing many important plants.

In the late 1800s and early 1900s, **John Armstrong** contributed to the Southern California landscape by supplying eucalyptus windbreaks and fruit trees for orchards as well as camellias, roses and ornamentals. In the late 1930s landscape architect **Garret Eckbo, Jay Gooch** and this book's author, **Eric A. Johnson,** worked together at Armstrong Nurseries in Ontario, California, developing new landscape programs.

Horticulturist and nurseryman **Theodore Payne** made a decided impact on plant palettes of the West by introducing over 500 coastal and inland valley California native plants to area gardens. Many also became popular in gardens overseas in Great Britain.

During the first half of this century, **William Hertrich** served as curator of the renowned 650-acre Huntington Botanic Gardens in San Marino. He traveled to many parts of the world to collect plants for the Huntington's Palm Garden, which included 450 species and varieties. Hertrich also made important contributions to the citrus and avocado industries.

Roland S. Hoyt deserves recognition for his superb book *Ornamental Plants for Subtropical Regions.* **Walter Anderson** of San Diego continues to provide his enthusiasm with introductions of new fruit tree varieties and ornamentals.

In the 1970s, agricultural and urban development throughout California and the Southwest began to test the limits of the region's water supplies. Less than a decade ago, drought conditions caused by low rainfall and snowpack in our mountains forced us to change our way of thinking about water use. State, city and water purveyors developed programs to conserve our liquid gold. The distribution of Colorado River water was pivotal during this period in Arizona and Southern California. The Central Arizona Project (CAP) brought water to Arizona. Water-efficient programs changed the way we think about water in agriculture, homes and landscaping. During the period from 1950 to the present, public and private botanic gardens and arboretums in Arizona and California benefited from the guidance of botanists such as **Dr. Mildred Mathias** of the University of California at Los Angeles and **Dr. Philip A. Munz, Dr. Lee Lenz** and **John Dourley** of the Rancho Santa Ana Botanic Garden in Claremont, California. Landscape architects **Ralph Cornell, Ken Smith, Robert Perry, Roland Hoyt, Morgan "Bill" Evans, Jacques Hahn,** nurseryman **Jim Perry** and horticulturist **Barrie Coate** deserve credit for their contributions. They worked with many institutions to develop landscape themes that utilized the new plants being introduced and grown in California. Landscape architect **Fred Lang** of Southern California was a dedicated environmental activist, promoting native plants as well as adapted plants from Mediterranean regions.

We must give credit to **Walter Doty,** former longtime editor of *Sunset* magazine. Walter guided the installation of demonstration gardens at the Los Angeles State and County Arboretum in Arcadia as well as the *Sunset* Magazine Demonstration Garden at the Arizona-Sonora Desert Museum in Tucson, Arizona, showcasing new uses for dry-climate plants. **Joe Williamson,** garden editor of *Sunset,* and **Lauren Bonar Swezey,** senior writer, contribute to the horticultural awareness in the West, providing information on new plants and gardening techniques.

In Tucson, the use of water-efficient plants has long been a way of life. Landscape architect **Warren Jones, Dr. Charles Sacamano, Matt Johnson, Dr. Howard Scott Gentry** of the USDA, horticulturist **Rodney Engard** and **Dr. David Palzkill,** botanist, deserve recognition for their efforts. Credit landscape architects **Mary Rose Duffield, Guy Greene** and **John Harlow, Jr.,** for developing new design trends, and **Dr. Mark Dimmitt** of the Arizona-Sonora Desert Museum with contributions to plant introduction programs. Nurseryman and plant explorer **Greg Starr** and nurseryman **Ralph McPheeters** contribute their experience and effort in introducing new native plants.

In 1906, **James Kellogg Wheat** opened his nursery in Phoenix. His son **Dewitt Wheat** was a pioneer in introducing water-efficient plants into the Salt River Valley. **Jim** and **Betty Wheat** carry on the tradition with their children **Libba** and **Kelly Wheat.** Also in the Phoenix area, the team of plant growers **Ron** and **Maureen Gass** remain leaders in plant exploration, introduction and production. Landscape architects **Steve Martino, Christine Ten Eyck** and **Carol Shuler** offer their talents with designs that emphasize native plants. **Judy Mielke,** landscape designer and author, is a rich source of information on southwest native plants.

The Boyce Thompson Arboretum in Superior, Arizona, with **Frank** and **Carol Crosswhite,** has provided us with many plant introductions.

Likewise, the Desert Botanic Garden in Phoenix continues to test arid plant introductions as well as providing homeowners with information on how to include native plants in today's gardens.

In the Coachella Valley, from Palm Springs to the Salton Sea, landscape architects **Mike Buccino, Wayne Connor, Tom Doczi, Ron Gregory, John Krieg, Ray Lopez, Michael Horton** and **Charles Shepardson** are establishing new directions on uses of water-efficient plants. The College of the Desert in Palm Desert under the direction of **Michael Watling** has developed programs to train future horticulturists.

The Living Desert Wildlife and Botanic Park, also in Palm Desert, offers educational programs and continues to test new plant introductions. The Coachella Valley Water District provides updated booklets and sponsors educational programs on using water-efficient plants.

In Las Vegas, Nevada, **Jack Zunino,** landscape architect; **Dennis Swartzell,** University of Nevada Las Vegas horticulturist; **Bob Morris** and **Linn Mills,** University of Nevada extension agents; and **Peter Duncombe,** horticulturist with the Las Vegas Water District, deserve credit. Each has worked to develop an understanding of water-efficient landscaping and use of native plants in the Mojave Desert.

New Mexico's gardens and landscapes have benefited from **Judith Phillips's** efforts. Her books such as *Natural by Design* help define a "sense of place" for gardeners and landscape professionals in the Southwest.

In Texas, the National Wildflower Resource Center, with **Lady Bird Johnson's** support, continues to raise our consciousness on the benefits of using wildflowers and native plants. **Sally Wasowski,** landscape designer and author, and her husband and photographer, **Andy Wasowski,** deserve acknowledgement for their books on growing native plants in Texas, the South, and California and the Southwest. **Lynn Lowry** is considered one of the most outstanding and productive plant explorers in Texas today. At Texas A&M University, **Benny Simpson** contributed greatly to the Texas native plant palette, particularly with his pioneering work with *Leucophyllum* species.

Many others have contributed to the horticultural heritage of the arid West. To these individuals, and to all listed here, thank you. Through your efforts you've helped make this special part of the world a better place to live.

Introduction

$\mathcal{G}$ardeners in the arid West face special challenges when it comes to planting and caring for our landscapes. First, there is the wide range of plants adapted to grow in our region. Tropicals, subtropicals, cacti and succulents, native trees and shrubs, flowering perennials, plus introductions from around the world beckon to us from nurseries and catalogs. It's tempting to give each a try in our gardens, and we often do. Then there are the climatic variables we face, with extremes of heat, cold, wind and humidity. Add in our warm weather and long growing seasons that encourage plants to grow vigorously, and it becomes a challenge to keep them within bounds. And, as the trend toward using new native plants continues, many of the old rules regarding plant care have changed. These factors, and others, require a *western attitude* when we plant, prune, fertilize and irrigate.

And that is the reason for this book. To provide us Westerners with the information in the following pages, I've relied on more than 50 years of personal experience as a grower, landscape designer, consultant and plant maintenance troubleshooter. I've also sought the advice of many experts. Landscape architects, arborists, wholesale growers, maintenance contractors and irrigation specialists have generously contributed their expertise.

Growing and caring for plants is often as much art as it is science. It becomes your observations and experience in your garden that enable you to make the right choices to keep your plants healthy. You can begin by understanding the natural progression of the gardening seasons in your region, so pruning, planting and maintenance tasks are in sync with the ebb and flow of plant growth. Keep a written record of activities in your garden: planting dates and methods, flowering periods, methods and times of weed control, times when plants were pruned, and how much and when they were watered. Become an amateur naturalist by observing native plants and note when they flower, drop their leaves or otherwise change gears. Keeping track of such matters will allow you to see and feel when it's time to reach for the pruning shears or when to sow your wildflower seeds.

Native and adapted dry-climate plants have an amazing will to grow. After they become established in a garden setting, they often thrive to such an extent that they outgrow their typical height and spread. But with a well-conceived garden design and proper plant selection, the result can be a rich tapestry of growth that requires less maintenance and water as each year passes. I hope this book helps you reach this goal.

Uncovering Some New "Gardening Truths"

When we garden today, we adhere to some of the same tried-and-true methods our grandmothers and grandfathers used years ago. At the same time, the plants we grow and the ways we grow them are constantly changing. Through research and experience, we turn to new methods that are better than the old ones. University extension agents, landscape professionals and experienced gardeners continually seek to set the record straight on the mysterious science-art of plant care. In fact, we sometimes discover that garden practices we've followed as a matter of habit may have caused more harm than good!

The methods used to plant and care for a landscape can be complex, even confusing. But there are a few recent discoveries that make it easier to grow long-lived healthy plants. These *garden truths* are explained in this book. But I hope you take this phrase with a grain of salt. It could turn out that we, too, have been fooled by Mother Nature. In the future we may discover a new and different method of planting or pruning. Or we may find out it's better to simply step back a little more often and leave plants alone!

In addition to the basic information provided in the following, there are some important items to consider in each of the book's chapters. Some of them are recent developments. The highlights are discussed here.

Pruning

This chapter begins with a pruning philosophy, namely, have a purpose before you pick up loppers or shears. Without a goal firmly in mind, you're probably going to do more harm than good. Similarly, you'll learn "preventive pruning" practices, which is a fancy name for the simple act of *planning, planning, planning*. The great majority of pruning problems and ongoing high maintenance are caused by poorly selected or ill-placed plants. Be certain of a plant's mature height and spread, and don't cheat on spacing. Plants can fool you, and you're soon surprised at how quickly they grow in our long, warm, growing seasons. Planting too close to structures, walkways, existing plants or too close to each other is a blueprint for a maintenance disaster. See page 14 for more tips on avoiding this common problem.

Everyone has seen trees that have been severely pruned, looking like they just got a close-cropped haircut. Topping a tree ruins its natural form and reduces its lifespan. The simple advice is, don't prune trees severely or let anyone prune with a heavy hand for you. Selectively thin branches to maintain the tree's health and beauty. In general, prune no more than 20 percent of the tree's canopy at one time.

Probably the most crucial pruning period in the life of a tree is the first two years after planting. Your goals are to develop good, long-term form and at the same time increase the *caliper*—the trunk's thickness and strength. Increasing trunk strength shortens the amount of time that trees need to be staked. These two goals can come into temporary conflict with one another. Our natural tendency is to prune lower branches right after planting to develop the desired upright form and canopy. But trunk strength is increased when lower branches are left in place, so they can feed the trunk. Leave lower branches in place for two to four years, then remove them. For more on this subject, see page 16.

When to prune can be as much a mystery as how. It is not as simple as "wintertime is pruning time." Many plants, particularly flowering trees and shrubs, should be pruned right after flowering for best results. The Master Flowering and Pruning Chart on pages 67 to 74 is a guide to learning when, providing flowering periods and the best period to prune. The chart also lists the minimum temperature tolerance of the plants described in this book.

Planting from Containers

The planting process has been revamped recently. Here are the important truths: Dig the planting hole the *same depth* as the container. Plant about one inch higher than the level of the plant in its nursery container. *Don't* dig the planting hole deeper and then add backfill. The plant may settle and sink. This could allow moist soil to come in contact with the trunk, which can cause a host of serious problems.

Make the width of the planting hole three to four times the diameter of the rootball, and use the soil on site as backfill around the rootball. The loose soil in the upper soil area allows the roots to get a good start in becoming established. In most cases, don't add soil amendments to the planting hole. Adding amendments creates a defined soil area different from the surrounding native soil. This can cause the roots to stay confined to this small area, actually retarding plant growth. Like most things in gardening, there are some exceptions. Pure sand and extremely rocky or poor soil may be improved if organic matter is added to the soil. See the drawings on page 28.

Plant Care

Watering plants properly is one of the trickiest maintenance items to explain to home gardeners. Perhaps it is because we can't see beneath the soil where the roots are located, so we don't know exactly where and how much to water. The many variables in climate, soils, seasons (winter compared to summer) and age of plant increase the complexity. But a new gardening truth has emerged: The roots that absorb water, the *feeder roots*—have been discovered to grow a considerable distance away from the tree—up to six times the diameter of the tree's canopy beyond the drip line. Very few (if any) feeder roots exist near the trunk, which is where many people apply their water! Irrigating the feeder root area (see below) makes the best use of water applied and increases the growth rate and health of the tree.

Drip-irrigation systems can be designed to anticipate this extended root growth. Placing emitters well outside the perimeter of the young tree's canopy at the time of planting anticipates future water needs as the tree roots grow outward. See illustrations, page 36.

Surface mulching to improve plant growth is an old garden truth that is gaining new value. Tests have shown that a 2- to 3-inch layer of mulch over the root zone (beneath the canopy and beyond) reduces moisture loss so that plants grow much faster than those without mulch. Compost is excellent for this purpose. To learn how to make your own compost, see page 40.

The Plants We Grow

Like our garden practices, the plants we use in today's gardens are a blend of old and new. In this book you'll find standbys such as *Bougainvillea* described along with relative newcomers such as *Agastache cana*, bubblegum plant. It is surprising how well the oldtimers and the new additions work together. It's a matter of using good design principles in combining plants according to mature size and water use as well as blending similar colors and textures.

The *legume family* in particular offers a varied group of plants well suited to the arid West. Many legumes are tolerant of high temperatures and low humidity and are drought tolerant once established. Few pests and diseases bother legumes. Numerous legumes are able to *fix* atmospheric nitrogen and grow well without supplemental fertilizers. Legumes come in a wide variety of shapes, sizes and forms and can fulfill many functions in the landscape. In addition, several of the shrubs have controlled growth habits, requiring minimum pruning. For these reasons, you'll find the legumes well represented in our Gallery of Dry Climate Plants, pages 65 to 156.

Water Where the Feeder Roots Grow

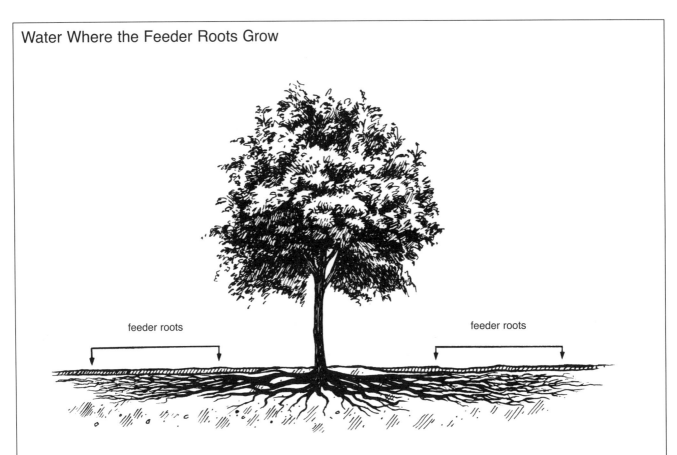

feeder roots   feeder roots

Watering plants in the area of their feeder roots encourages rapid, healthy growth. The area inside the drip line and up to three times the canopy diameter as shown contains the greatest portion of feeder roots.

Covering this area with a 2- to 3-inch layer of organic mulch during warm periods of the year slows moisture loss through evaporation and reduces heat in the upper soil layers, improving the plant's health and growth rate.

Climate and How It Affects Pruning, Planting and Care

Climate is the "big picture" of plant care. Sunshine, high and low seasonal temperatures, rainfall, wind, soil and other elements create the unique gardening environment that exists in your own yard. When you become a climate-wise gardener you garden with what nature provides, planting, pruning and maintaining plants according to the progression of the seasons. Understanding your climate will allow you to select adapted plants and locate them in the proper exposure and garden location. Doing so avoids serious problems such as cold damage or sunscald and helps ensure plants will grow to their potential.

The Sun

The amount of sunshine your garden receives depends on several factors. These include light intensity during the seasons; the direction of exposure (going from highest to lowest: south, west, east, north), and the amount of shade from plants and structures. Extreme sunshine and heat can adversely affect the growth of plants, even kill them. High temperatures, intense sunlight and less-than-adequate water supply stress plants and make them more susceptible to pests and diseases. This is particularly true of plants introduced to hot, arid regions from more temperate climates. Such plants are even more likely to fail if located in south or west exposures, where sunlight and high temperatures are most intense.

In most regions of the arid West (the cool California coast is an exception), it's a good idea to avoid the heat and delay planting most plants in late spring and summer. During this time higher temperatures and low humidity greatly increase water need and plants undergo serious stress. The ideal time to plant is early fall, when air temperatures are moderate yet the soil is warm to encourage rapid root growth.

If you must plant in summer, pay careful attention to the water needs of plants. They may need water every day (or even twice a day) when it is hot. Temperatures higher than 90F take a toll on newly planted plants. Signs of high-temperature damage are browning at edges and tips of mature leaves and wilting of new growth. Plants in fast-draining sandy soils are highly susceptible to heat damage because water drains quickly. High temperatures also increase the temperature of the upper layer of soil to the extent that roots near the soil surface are killed. Shallow-rooted annuals and perennials are particularly susceptible. If they are not watered thoroughly at planting time, death can come quickly. The direct sun on new tender leaves can also cause them to burn. Adding an organic mulch—a thick layer of material over the plant roots—cools soil temperatures and slows evaporation of moisture from the soil.

The sun and high heat affect other garden chores. Avoid heavy pruning during summer. Exposing shaded bark of trunks and limbs to direct sun can burn plant tissues and can be fatal to plants. When temperatures reach over 90F, it's also too warm to apply many treatments, such as oil sprays for pest control. Doing so causes leaves to burn.

In coastal gardens, insufficient sunshine and heat can be a problem. Conditions are often too cool, cloudy and foggy for plants such as *Leucophyllum* species that require heat to produce flowers. If you live along the coast, select plants adapted to your conditions. Locate plants that require heat in the sunniest locations—exposures facing south and west. Reflected heat and light from light-colored walls also increase temperatures.

Cold Temperatures

Every plant has a low-temperature tolerance. When the temperature drops below this point for a certain period of time, plant tissues are damaged. If the cold is severe or prolonged, the plant could be killed. How long cold temperatures last and how quickly they drop affect the extent of the damage. The faster they drop, the more severe the injury. Cold that lasts for an hour or less may not hurt plants, but if it stays cold for several hours, severe damage is likely. Coldest temperatures often occur just before sunrise. The cold tolerance for each plant in this book is provided with the individual descriptions and in the Master Flowering and Pruning Chart on pages 67 to 74.

If the plant is under stress due to lack of moisture or if it has recently been planted, it is more susceptible to cold injury. The time of year matters as well. When temperatures drop in late spring shortly after new, tender growth has emerged, damage will be much more severe than if new growth had an opportunity to gradually adjust to cooler temperatures. You can help plants adjust in early fall by inducing dormancy. Do this by gradually reducing water applied and cease applications of fertilizer.

Unusual cold waves occur infrequently, dropping temperatures well below normal lows. These "fifty-year freezes," also called *polar waves*, are pervasive, damaging or destroying plants that would otherwise be cold-hardy. A polar wave occurred in 1990, when temperatures in Las Vegas dropped to 6F and to 15F in Palm Springs.

If severe cold is forecast, takes steps to protect valuable plants. Move tender plants in containers under a patio overhang or dense tree canopy to protect from the cold. One of the most common ways to protect plants is to cover them with some type of material. Old blankets, burlap or plastic tarps work well. (See text and illustrations, pages 40 to 41.)

Rainfall

With the exceptions of the northern California coast and higher-elevation regions, the West does not receive abundant rainfall. The amount that falls can fluctuate greatly from year to year. For example, Yuma, Arizona, has recorded annual rainfall as little as less than 1 inch and as much as 11 inches!

Mountain ranges in the West help determine the regions where rain is distributed. Warm, moist air rises and cools rapidly when it comes in contact with abrupt changes in elevation. The result is condensation and rainfall. After moisture has been "wrung" from the clouds, little remains for areas beyond. This is called the *rain shadow effect*. A large-scale example exists in Nevada, where the Sierra Nevada Mountains stand in the way of coastal storms carrying the moisture-laden air. The same situation occurs in Southern California's low-desert region. The San Jacinto Mountains near Palm Springs block rains from reaching the Coachella Valley.

Throughout much of California, rainfall comes during two primary periods, winter and spring, followed by a warm, dry summer and fall. The lowlands along the coast from Santa Barbara to San Diego are typical. Other regions of the world with this type of climate include South Africa, Chile, western Australia and the Mediterranean. Many plants native to California and similar *Mediterranean climates* have natural adaptations that allow them to become dormant or semidormant during these warm, rainless periods. Because of such adaptations, many California natives may not tolerate regular summer water in a home garden. Too much water in summer can encourage root diseases. Be ready to adjust your watering practices, including cutting back on drip-irrigation scheduling, during summer. Newly planted plants are exceptions to this rule. Provide them with regular water until plants are established.

In southern Arizona, in New Mexico and occasionally in Southern California, summer rains come in the form of intense storms, originating to the south and southeast in the Gulf of Mexico and Gulf of California. These highly localized storms, often no more than three miles across, are capable of dumping large quantities of water in a short time. The rain that falls can do more harm than good due to erosion from runoff and the strong surface winds that accompany the storms. High summer temperatures also cause the moisture to evaporate rapidly. Often when it appears that a rainstorm has moistened the soil, the benefit to plants is negligible. So don't be fooled by the rain and stop irrigating plants. Dig down into the soil to see how far moisture has penetrated. Often, the soil is moistened only on the surface.

Humidity

In a low-humidity climate, the rate of evaporation of moisture from plants and soil surface can be quite rapid. Low humidity also causes rainfall to evaporate rapidly, to the extent that little actually accumulates in the soil. Low humidity, in combination with hot, dry winds, high temperatures and intense sunlight, causes plants to dry out very quickly. During these conditions, pay close attention to the appearance of your plants. The opposite occurs in high-humidity regions, such as along the coast. Moisture is retained in the air and around plants. This decreases water need but encourages certain diseases, such as blackspot and mildew. Gray-foliaged plants tend to be less susceptible to these problems.

Wind

Many areas of the West experience high winds—often in spring, occasionally in fall. In much of Southern California, Santa Ana winds sweep through mountain passes into San Bernardino, Riverside, the San Fernando Valley, and Ventura and Orange counties. In California's Coachella Valley and in high desert areas, winds 40 miles per hour are common and occasionally gust up to 60 mph or more. Las Vegas and Lancaster experience winds throughout the year, particularly during the spring.

Wind storms can turn into sand storms in many of these areas. Sand blown at a high velocity can seriously damage plants. In some instances the windblown sand builds up in watering basins and landscaped areas. Planting living windbreaks and providing protection such as fences or walls, especially for newly planted plants, is necessary in wind-prone regions. When accompanied by high temperatures, wind dries out plants rapidly, causing them to require considerably more water. Deep watering, which encourages deep roots, also helps prevent plants from being blown over. An extensive root system also draws on a larger reservoir of moisture in the soil. Water "deep and wide" out beyond the tree's dripline to develop extensive roots. However, avoid heavy irrigation just prior to strong winds. The moist soil can cause trees to blow over. Staking new trees is often necessary in windy regions, but don't leave stakes in place more than a year or two. Thin canopy-shaped trees prior to the windy season so breezes can pass through branches rather than catch, "umbrella-style."

Microclimates: The Small Climates

Variations in climate occur from street to street, from the bottom to the top of a slope, or even among different areas around your house. These small differences in climate are called *microclimates.*

Cold air flows down hillsides during the evening hours, lowering temperatures in its path. If the flow of air is blocked by a hedge, wall or other barrier, the air forms a pool like a pool of water, causing temperatures to drop even lower. For this reason, avoid placing cold-tender plants in low-lying areas. Areas that stretch laterally across slopes—above valleys but below the crest, especially if they face toward the sunny south—are *thermal belts.* Temperatures in a thermal belt remain as much as 10F warmer compared to the valley bottom below. If you garden in a thermal belt, you may be able to grow more cold-tender plants than typically recommended for your climate.

The lay of the land, paved areas, structures and size and placement of existing plants create a wide range of growing conditions, from full shade to reflected sun and heat. Every home lot is different, and conditions evolve as plants on site grow and create more shade.

It's possible to modify home microclimates to suit the plants you want to grow, perhaps increasing penetration and reflection of sunlight during cooler winter months and reducing the effects of the hot summer sun. Build overhead structures, install latticework panels or use shade cloth to filter the sun. Deciduous trees, which drop their leaves in fall, shade planting beds in summer. In winter, the branches are bare, allowing more sunshine. Better yet, select plants that are adapted to the growing conditions that exist. Plants in the right environment grow faster and maintain their health because they are not stressed. Study the information provided in the Gallery of Dry Climate Plants to determine which plants are best for the unique growing conditions of your landscape.

Planting with Microclimates in Mind

Microclimates on a Large Scale
Cold air travels like water, flowing down slopes and canyons, settling in low spots. Valley floors and along rivers or dry washes are among the coldest locations. If the flow of air is blocked by a hedge, wall or other barrier, the air forms a pool, causing temperatures to drop even lower. Sloping ground, where cold air drains away, is usually the best place to plant cold-tender plants. These areas are called thermal belts. See text, above.

Microclimates on a Small Scale
A southern or western exposure can be an advantage or a drawback, depending on the climate where you live and the plant in the exposure. Cold-tender plants near a south-facing wall benefit from reflected heat during the day. As shown above, the heat stored in the wall is released, increasing temperatures around the plant. Roof overhang provides additional protection. But in hot-summer areas, some plants suffer from the additional heat and reflected light. Know a plant's limitations and cold and sun requirements before selecting its location in the garden.

Pruning

Correct and timely pruning can enhance the beauty, health and value of most landscapes. Poor pruning can permanently ruin plants, turning an attractive outdoor scene into an eyesore. To prune successfully, you need to understand the growth habits and unique horticulture of each plant. It's worth repeating: *Pruning can do as much harm as good.* If you are unsure if you are doing the right thing, put down the pruning shears, shelve that chain saw and get some professional guidance. Plants represent a considerable investment in time and money and can greatly increase the value of your home. Hasty, uninformed pruning by you or an unskilled worker can quickly turn your investment into a liability in more ways than one.

Fortunately, extensive pruning is not required for most plants when they are carefully selected and placed in the right locations. This is particularly true of a naturalistic landscape. When considering the placement of landscape plants, become knowledgeable as to their mature height and spread. If in doubt, it is best to mildly exaggerate the mature size rather than underestimate. Placing plants where they have ample room to grow and managing their growth will significantly reduce the amount of pruning they require.

Locate plants carefully around structures, play areas and existing plants. Position trees so that upon reaching maturity they will provide the desired shade, privacy and screening. Also envision how mature trees will fit in with other components and uses of the landscape. Think ahead when locating shrubs, ground covers and accent plants near sidewalks, medians, streets, neighbors and other traffic areas. If plants have sharp thorns or spines they can be extremely dangerous. Place them too close to these areas or too close to each other and you'll be forced to battle plants with shears and clippers for as long as they live.

More and more arborists, municipalities, maintenance contractors and concerned home gardeners are using the theme of *preventive pruning* to control plant growth—first by selecting plants that are naturally dwarf and slower growing, and second, by selecting and placing plants thoughtfully so they will be allowed to grow to their natural height and width.

Developing a Pruning Philosophy

The natural growth habits of most native and introduced plants are normally far more attractive than the will imposed on them by unknowing gardeners. Generally speaking, the basic goal of pruning (when pruning is required) should be to reveal and showcase the plant's natural beauty and form. This usually involves little more than routine removal of crossing or wayward branches and pruning of off-balanced growth and dead or diseased twigs. If your home landscape has natural, native plants on site, consider removing a few of the lowest branches on selected trees and large shrubs. Careful thinning helps bring out the beauty of the trunk or trunks and primary branch framework. Such pruning should not drastically change the shape or height of the plant but rather accent or emphasize its natural character. It's also a good idea to leave some trees and shrubs unpruned so branches drape and trail to the ground, providing cover and shelter for birds and animals.

Periodic light thinning is the most desirable method of pruning. Some landscape professionals use the term *lacing out* to describe a light thinning of a tree's interior. For some trees and shrubs, thinning prior to seasonal winds and rainstorms reduces the potential for wind damage. With fewer leaves and branches the wind passes through the tree rather than catching in the canopy. Thinning can prevent uprooting of trees (professionals call this *wind throw*) due to wind storms. Young plants are particularly susceptible to life-threatening wind damage. They haven't had enough time to develop deep, wide-spreading roots that will anchor them in the ground.

Do not remove more than 20 percent of tree's canopy during the summer. If too many branches are removed at this time, the once-shaded bark is suddenly exposed to the intense sun, causing sunburn damage. The injured area becomes susceptible to infestations by

Four Simple Pruning Methods

ONE: Complete Renewal Method

Many perennials, grasses and small shrubs grow best when they are cut back severely at the end of their growing season or flowering season. This is often done just prior to the new spring growth surge, so that plants are "renewed," growing and flowering vigorously each year. Use hand pruners, pruning shears, hedge clippers or loppers to prune away dead or tired growth.

TWO: Two-Step Naturalistic Method

Use this method to control the size of shrubs yet maintain a more natural shape. Step One: Roughly prune back branches and stems to create a globe shape. Step Two: Cut every other branch back to the first large V. Vary cuts about 6 to 9 inches long. This gives shrubs an informal, natural look and opens up the interior to sunlight, helping develop new flowering wood.

THREE: Selectively Thin Method

This is the method used to control and train growth in trees, particularly when they are young—the first three or four years after planting. Rather than heading or topping growth, which can cause long-term problems, branches and stems are cut back flush to a supporting branch.

FOUR: Leave-It-Alone Method

This is perhaps the best pruning method of all. With time, most trees and shrubs develop into highly attractive plants if left to their own devices. Dead or diseased wood should be removed to keep the plant healthy, but otherwise, just stand back and admire what nature can do on its own.

wood-boring insect pests. Also avoid shearing or heading back glossy-foliaged shrubs such as *Photinia*, *Ligustrum* or *Rhaphiolepis*. Doing this will only stimulate excessive branching.

How to Cut? Where to Cut?

Depending on the size of the stems, use bypass-type pruning shears, loppers or pruning saw. If shears twist and turn when you try to cut through a branch, use loppers. In general, use hand pruners for branches up to 1/2-inch diameter, loppers for branches 1-inch diameter and a pruning saw for larger limbs. Avoid using bow-type saws; the blade is difficult to control. For delicate work such as pinching off new growth, use your fingers or pruning shears.

Where to cut depends partly on how you want the plant to look—bushy and compact, or airy with an open structure, for example. Age of plant is also a factor. Make major cuts first, then work on details. Always remove a branch or stem so it is flush with a side branch, leaf or dormant bud. Never leave a stub. Angle the cuts so they're parallel to the remaining branch. Step back and survey your progress every so often so you don't remove desirable branches.

Heavily pruned plants may develop *suckers* or *watersprouts*. These overly vigorous shoots are unwanted and should be removed as you see them.

Preventive Pruning

One of the best things you can do to reduce time you spend caring for your plants, as well as help ensure their beauty and health, is a program I call *preventive pruning*. The best time to practice preventive pruning is when you begin the plant selection process—at the garden's planning stage. Study the plants that interest you, and learn their mature height, spread, flowering habit, water needs and pruning requirements. The chart on pages 67 to 74 will help you make your selections. Even if you are planting only a few permanent landscape plants, taking the plant's vital statistics into consideration early on can prevent a lot of headaches.

You'll find preventive pruning tips throughout the Gallery of Dry Climate Plants, pages 65 to 156. As mentioned, proper spacing, selecting the right plants for the right locations and planting correctly prevents many common problems. The basic principles of preventive pruning are simple:

Select plants according to height, spread and shape so they can grow naturally in the allotted space with minimal pruning. Space them far enough apart to avoid crowding. This means that when a plant has a mature spread of 6 feet, plants should be located 6 to 8 feet apart.

Often, correct spacing leaves the newly planted area looking sparse. It's tempting to "cheat" and place plants closer together. This is especially true of arid land plants, many which are rather puny and unassuming in their nursery containers. But don't let them fool you. Avoid planting closely and you'll be rewarded tenfold with attractive plants that will require much less maintenance in the years to come. If the void between plants is bothersome, plant temporary annuals or perennials among the landscape plants, then remove them as the primary plants fill in.

Select plants that are naturally dwarf, reaching knee- or waist-high at maturity. These plants naturally require less pruning and shearing. Dwarf selections are noted in the plant descriptions.

Planting plants that have casual growth habits reduces pruning. Such plants will look attractive even when left alone. Many of the plants described in this book fall under this category.

Selecting plants that are hardy to cold for your climate region is an excellent *preventive pruning method*. If

---

When and How to Hire an Arborist

Some pruning jobs are best left to professionals. But it can be confusing when it comes time to hire the right company or firm to perform work in a safe, competent manner. Membership in professional organizations such as the International Society of Arboriculture or the American Society of Consulting Arborists tells you the individual is educated and up-to-date on the latest techniques. *Certified arborists* are professionals who have passed extensive examinations covering all aspects of tree care. Certification is not a measure of standards of practice, but it does mean that the individual has achieved a level of knowledge in the art and science of tree care that he or she must continue to keep membership current.

Before hiring, ask for proof of insurance. You could be liable for damages or injuries caused by uninsured tree care personnel.

Ask for references, especially if the work will be complicated, such as removal of a large tree. It's also wise to get more than one estimate if major work will be performed.

Ask for a written contract. Determine start and completion times, responsibility for clean up and hourly rate should extra work be required.

Be wary of tree and yard care companies that go door to door soliciting work. Most established, reputable companies are far too busy (due to references from satisfied customers) to seek employment this way. Be aware, too, that experienced, qualified arborists will not perform certain jobs. For example, they will not top trees, remove excessive live branches or use climbing spurs without just cause.

important structural branches are damaged by severe cold they must be removed, affecting the appearance and health of the plant. If cold damage is extensive, the plant could be killed or damaged to such an extent that it becomes an eyesore and must be removed. Some plants are slow to exhibit the effects of freeze damage. Branches that appear to be dead could produce leaves late in the growing season. Delay pruning suspect branches until the beginning of summer.

Watering correctly reduces excessive growth. Develop an irrigation program for your garden—applying the right amount of water when and where it is needed. A drip-irrigation system is an excellent way to control how much water to give your plants. See pages 33 to 36.

Applying too much fertilizer or fertilizing too often can cause plants to grow too rapidly, which naturally increases pruning amount and frequency. Follow all label directions as to proper dosage and use. Note that certain plants in the *legume* family can fix atmospheric nitrogen from the air and do not require supplemental fertilizer. Such plants are noted in the Gallery of Dry Climate Plants.

Growth Management

A somewhat extreme version of preventive pruning is a maintenance practice called *growth management*. It involves limiting water and fertilizer to significantly slow plant growth. This naturally reduces the need to prune and thin plants. With time, usually several years, some trees and shrubs may evolve from growth management to become *naturalized*. This means they can be left to grow on their own and will survive with little or no supplemental irrigation. For species that cannot be naturalized, limiting irrigation and fertilizer will reduce growth and pruning. However, use this method with caution, after you've gained an understanding of your plant's cultural needs.

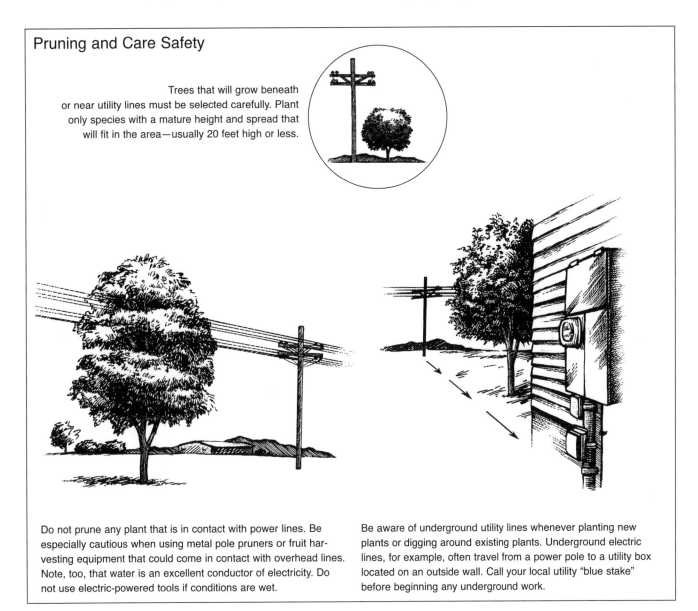

Pruning and Care Safety

Trees that will grow beneath or near utility lines must be selected carefully. Plant only species with a mature height and spread that will fit in the area—usually 20 feet high or less.

Do not prune any plant that is in contact with power lines. Be especially cautious when using metal pole pruners or fruit harvesting equipment that could come in contact with overhead lines. Note, too, that water is an excellent conductor of electricity. Do not use electric-powered tools if conditions are wet.

Be aware of underground utility lines whenever planting new plants or digging around existing plants. Underground electric lines, for example, often travel from a power pole to a utility box located on an outside wall. Call your local utility "blue stake" before beginning any underground work.

Pruning Trees

Trees are the most valuable elements of a landscape, for many reasons. They add structure, form and character. Many add seasonal color and shade. They provide the framework from which to build a balanced, pleasing landscape. Deciduous trees provide shade in summer, then allow the sun to shine through their branches in winter. Evergreen trees are in leaf all year and serve as windbreaks and screens for privacy.

When you plant trees, be aware that they require more care when young and less and less as they mature. Arid land trees have different requirements compared to trees grown in temperate climates with abundant rainfall. Water use, pruning and fertilization are well defined for each species. Refer to the Gallery of Dry Climate Plants.

Pruning Young Trees

When pruning young trees—those three to four years old—the goal is to establish strong *girth* or *width* in a single-trunk tree. The stronger the trunk, the more apt it will be able to grow without stakes. If you are growing a multitrunk specimen, your goal should be to develop three to four strong leaders.

To develop strong trunks, do not remove lower branches. They "feed" the trunk in this area and protect bark from sun damage. Leave these lower branches in place for a few years. They can then can be pruned up for a more refined look or to allow for pedestrian traffic beneath. Thin the interior to establish the desired branch spacing. Your goals should be to reduce the potential for wind damage while also increasing penetration of light. Remove branches that are dead, weakened, injured, diseased or damaged.

Protect the trunks of young trees from high heat and intense sunlight. If trees produce heavy canopy growth, this is often enough to shade the trunk. Unfortunately, most side branches on single-trunk trees grown in containers are removed at the nursery. Low side branches are often left on multitrunk trees. If trunks require protection from sunburn, apply white

---

Pruning Young Trees

Leave lower branches on young trees for first three years after planting. They help nourish the trunk to make it stronger. It's acceptable to reduce branch length if clearance if needed.

Thin branches of young trees to develop a proper framework. Avoid heading, also called topping. It will create a less-attractive structure and shortens life of the tree.

If possible, remove branches when angles are too narrow or too wide. These are weak and tend to split or break easily.

When selecting branches that are the proper angle for greatest strength, think 10 o'clock (left) and 2 o'clock (right).

latex paint diluted by half with water. Commercial tree trunk paints are also available.

To thin young trees as well as mature trees, selectively remove branches. You want to improve structure, control unwieldy branches, "lift up" lower branches by removing them from the trunk and thin the interior to decrease wind resistance. Improving branch spacing also preserves the tree's natural shape.

Don't prune too much at one time, especially during summer in hot climates. Pruning removes leaves, branches, buds and stored energy, all of which benefit the tree and are needed for proper growth. Removing too many branches also increases susceptibility to pests, slows growth, undermines health and stimulates excessive sprouting. I once inspected carob and mesquite trees in a parking lot in Palm Desert, in Southern California's Coachella Valley. The trees were exposed to reflected heat and sun, with temperatures reaching up to 120F! More than two-thirds of the trees had long deep scars, the length of their lower trunks,

caused by sun scald. The damage was a result of overzealous pruning. Too many side branches had been removed too soon, exposing the bark to the intense sun and causing it to burn and split.

Topping Tall Trees: Avoid!

In the West, certain trees such as *Brachychiton populneus*, bottle tree, tall-growing *Eucalyptus* species, and *Populus* species, poplar, are commonly planted where their height and vigorous root systems create serious problems.

In many situations the ultimate height, spread, rate of growth and pruning needs were not matched to the site. In addition, if large trees are not maintained regularly, major problems tend to develop. Aging branches can break and fall, damaging structures and automobiles, with the potential to cause injury or even death. The situation is often aggravated when urban development and housing moves into former agricultural areas where large-growing trees were planted as windbreaks to protect crops.

Pruning Mature Trees

Remove lower branches on trees three to four years after planting to allow for pedestrian traffic beneath. Continue to thin interior to maintain form and so wind can pass through branches.

Heading branches as shown is not usually recommended. It results in lightly attached new growth from each cut, as shown in inset. With time, tree form is ruined. Severe heading is called *topping*.

step one   step two

step three   Ouch!

Pruning large branches requires three steps, as shown. When making final cut, cut outside branch *collar* to allow branch to heal.

One-step pruning of large branches (far right) can cause severe damage, resulting in breaking and tearing of trunk, often killing tree.

If trees are pruned and growth is directed in the formative period, from one to five years after planting, future growth can be controlled. Waiting until trees have matured makes resolving problems difficult and expensive if professional tree care personnel are called in to do the job. Cutting the tops off trees—*topping*—merely aggravates the problems. Such trees produce sucker growth and watersprouts, which are lightly attached to the exterior of trunk tissue. Over a period of time, these branches can become a dangerous liability.

Root Pruning: From an Arborist's Viewpoint

In their search for water, the spreading roots of mature, vigorous trees have been known to destroy concrete curbs, walks, walls and driveways. In the process, the buckling and heaving of paved areas creates unsafe conditions for pedestrian and vehicle traffic. Select suitable, noninvasive trees that will be located near paving. To alleviate an existing problem you can either remove the tree or control the roots. If the tree has value such as providing shade, privacy and beauty, consider root pruning.

Root pruning of large trees should be performed by certified arborists. They have the expertise and equipment to perform this task. Such a procedure should be done over a period of time and performed in increments. Typically one side is pruned during one growing season. The roots are cut at the edge of walks or curbs. A trench approximately 6 inches wide and 18 inches deep is dug, and a plastic root barrier 18 to 24 inches wide is positioned and backfilled with soil. The top growth of the tree will be affected when roots are removed. It is necessary to maintain a balance between roots and top growth or the tree could die. Arborists are trained to do this critical work.

Pruning Shrubs

Attractive shrubs can make the difference between an average garden and a spectacular one. Unfortunately,

Prune Gently

To avoid sunburn damage, prune no more than 20% of tree's canopy at one time. Some trees benefit from a protective whitewash of 50% latex paint, 50% water on lower trunks and branches.

Root Barriers

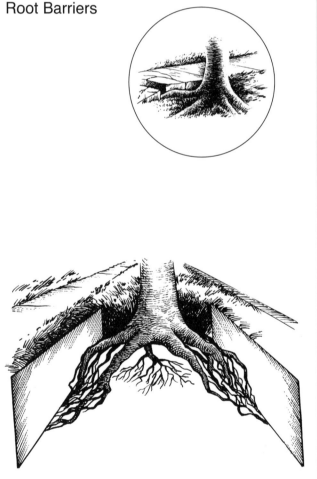

Trees planted near sidewalks or drives can cause damage, raising and breaking paving materials, creating a hazard. Installing a root-pruning barrier at planting time helps prevent damage.

many gardeners wield their pruning shears without mercy, turning their shrubs into gumdrops, lollipops and poodles. These contrived shapes create a high-maintenance situation that actually shortens the lifespan of the shrub.

A well-situated shrub left to its own devices usually requires little pruning. Most may need only pinching or pruning once or twice a year to look attractive. You'll also want to remove dead, diseased, frost-damaged, or weak wood to encourage flowering, fruiting and to promote new bushy growth. Only a few shrubs, discussed in the Gallery of Dry Climate Plants, require drastic pruning to rejuvenate growth.

A common problem with many shrubs is that little thought is given at planting time as to their mature size. Too often, tall-growing and broad-spreading shrubs are located next to walkways or close against houses and buildings—areas they'll outgrow in just a few years. As a result, they must be sheared regularly to fit the small spaces. Not only is shearing a tiresome chore, it can ruin the plant's form and eliminate (or reduce) its flowers. If you are at this stage it's usually best to cut your losses and start over with a different, smaller plant suited to the space.

Before you buy, learn how large a shrub ultimately grows so you can give it plenty of room. Learn its growth habit. For example, if it spreads broadly, it is a poor choice for a narrow space. Does it need full sun or partial shade? The climate where you live will make a difference. Get to know its flowering cycle. Some flowering shrubs should be pruned in winter or early spring. Others should be pruned after they finish blooming. Pruning at the wrong time could eliminate all flowers. See the chart on pages 67 to 74. Finally, gradually train shrubs when they are young plants so drastic measures won't be necessary later on.

Pruning Native Shrubs

How you approach pruning native shrubs depends on where the plants are growing. Are they in a garden

Two-Step Naturalistic Pruning: Shrubs

Use this method to control the size of shrubs yet maintain a more natural shape. This gives shrubs an informal appearance and opens up the interior to sunlight, helping develop new flowering wood.

Step One: Use hand pruners to cut back branches and stems, creating a rough globe shape.

Step Two: Cut every other branch back to the first large "V." Vary length of cuts randomly from 6 to 9 inches long.

environment, where, if left alone, they could not thrive without help? Or are plants in a natural area, with random spacing that allow them to grow as nature intended?

Native plants in a garden environment usually require a minimum amount of pruning to keep them in balance. Pruning guidelines are noted for each species in the Gallery of Dry Climate Plants. Regularly thin twiggy growth and dead branches and remove suckers to increase light and air circulation. This can be done any time. Do avoid serious pruning sessions during summer.

In a naturalistic landscape, the ideal approach is to allow plants to grow undisturbed to their normal height and spread. In other words, after plants are established, leave them alone.

Dry climate plants such as *Leucophyllum* species, Texas ranger, *Cassia* species, *Ruellia peninsularis* and petite varieties of *Nerium*, oleander, do well with a once-a-year pruning method, typically done after flowering. I call this the *two-step naturalistic method.* The beauty of pruning in this manner is its simplicity.

First, plants are pruned into an informal, rounded form or to a desired size. Second, every other branch is cut back to the first large "V." These cuts are usually made 6 to 9 inches back. This gives shrubs an informal, natural look and opens up the interior to sunlight, helping develop new flowering wood. See the illustrations on page 19.

Renovating an Overgrown Shrub

Often, when large shrubs with strong branch frameworks are allowed to grow unchecked, they become too dense, wild or rangy-looking. Typical plants of this type include *Vauquelinia,* Arizona rosewood; *Callistemon,* bottlebrush; *Myrtus,* myrtle; *Xylosma, Juniperus,* juniper; and *Rosmarinus,* rosemary.

To maintain a shrub form, continually thin out older growth. It's best to do this gradually each season before branches become too thick and woody. This will avoid the "stubbed" look.

Occasionally, an overgrown shrub can be trained into a multitrunked tree. Choose three to five nicely shaped, well-positioned trunks. Using a pruning saw,

Pruning Perennials and Small Shrubs

"Deadheading" spent blooms during the flowering season encourages plants to produce more flowers and keeps planting areas looking neat.

When the bloom season has passed, cut back stems and branches for renewed growth the following spring.

Pruning Grasses

Many grasses benefit from being cut back severely each year. Cut to 6 inches above ground during dormant season late in winter. Plants will produce healthy new growth the following spring.

remove all other branches to ground level. Thin out crossing and crowded branches with loppers or a saw and prune off twiggy growth along the lower stems. If necessary, thin out some of the upper foliage. If you're forced to prune plants severely, check them often for suckers or watersprouts during the growing season. Prune them off as you notice them.

Pruning Roses

How much you prune roses depends on the type of rose, time of year and use in the landscape. Hybrid teas and grandifloras are pruned the most severely as the buds begin to swell in late winter. Both are pruned similarly, except grandifloras can support more flowering canes.

Begin by removing dead or damaged canes. Cut back dead or broken branches so they are flush with the base of plant. Remove all suckers. These are vigorous canes that originate from rootstock below the bud union. Select three to six evenly spaced canes. Try to leave the center of the plant open. Generally, reduce overall height by one-third to one-half.

Floribundas have more twiggy growth than hybrid teas, especially near the center of the plant. Prune so there are small, evenly spaced canes. Remove all dead wood and canes that cross.

Deadheading spent flowers is an ongoing process. (See illustration, page 20.) It encourages a steady supply of new blooms during the flowering season.

For a complete guide to growing roses, refer to the Ironwood Press book, *The Natural Rose Gardener*, by Lance Walheim.

Pruning Frost-Damaged Shrubs

If shrubs have been damaged by cold, wait to prune until new growth has emerged in spring. A stem that has dropped its leaves may still be alive and healthy. Starting at the top of the plant, look for the first sprouting bud along the stem. Prune the stem to just above the bud. After removing all of the frost-damaged wood, the plant may need additional pruning to restore its shape. If it is severely damaged, shape after the first growth flush has filled in.

Many factors can influence hardiness to cold. These include duration and intensity of the freeze, maturity of the plant, whether the plant is growing or dormant and if it has had an opportunity to gradually adjust to colder temperatures so tissues are *hardened off*. Where the plant is located in the landscape also has an effect. Often, plants are provided some protection by nearby plants and buildings. In the Gallery of Dry Climate Plants, we've provided each plant's known or estimated hardiness to cold, listed in degrees Fahrenheit. Also see methods for cold protection, pages 40 to 42.

Pruning Perennials

Many small shrubs (called subshrubs), ground covers and perennials benefit from being cut back after bloom. This induces plants to bloom again later in the season, or causes them to produce vigorous new growth for more flowers the following season. Use pruning shears to make cuts close to the remaining branch or stem. Make major cuts first to maintain the desired structure and form of the plant.

If your goal is an informal garden appearance, avoid shearing plants. Rather, selectively thin excess interior growth and wayward branches. This way you can maintain the plant's natural form and still control its growth. Do not prune basal growth so the plant's trunk is bare. Allow branches to drape and trail to the ground. To reduce a plant's height, cut vertical growth down to and flush with a laterally growing stem or branch. To reduce a plant's width, cut side growth and lateral branches to upright-growing stems.

Some winter-dormant perennials and shrubs such as *Rudbeckia, Helianthus* and many ornamental grasses can be pruned back close to the plant's basal growth late in fall or early winter. New growth will emerge the following spring. If plants are damaged by frost, wait until the following spring and remove dead wood after new growth begins.

Certain species develop woody growth at the center of the plant, which reduces flower production and fresh, healthy growth. Maintain a schedule of cutting plants back by one-third or more every year or two before the heavy wood has a chance to develop. *Rosmarinus* and *Lavandula* are both susceptible to becoming woody and benefit from this procedure.

As with roses, deadheading, removing flowers that are well past their prime, should occur throughout the blooming season. It keeps plants looking their best. And when dead flowers are removed, the plant's energy goes into producing more flowers rather than producing seed. Flowers with long stems should have the stems removed as well to maintain the plant's appearance. Plants that produce flower spikes, such as *Penstemon* and *Salvia,* should be cut back to the first set of leaves. This often induces the plant to produce new flowers where the leaves meet the stem.

Staking—Some perennials cannot stand up to wind and rain on their own and will sprawl over the bed. Providing stakes or other supports keeps plants upright, in control and attractive. The type of support used depends on the plant. Staking must be done early, before the plant shows signs of needing support, or the stalk or clump will be damaged by the next strong wind or rain. Staking early allows the plant to grow around the support and mask it with leaves. The underpinning should not be visible.

Pruning by the Seasons

When to prune depends largely as to why you are pruning. Light corrective pruning and removing dead wood can be done almost any time. Major pruning is best done during the dormant season. Here are some guidelines. Timing for individual species may differ.

Winter

During winter, growth slows and plants gradually become dormant. In mild climates they are semidormant. Pruning when plants are not actively growing is the most common timing, resulting in vigorous new growth the following spring. Typically, it's best to prune after the coldest part of winter has passed. Some plants, such as mesquites, ashes and sycamores, may bleed when the sap begins to flow. This is not harmful and will cease when the tree leafs out.

Prune trees or shrubs that bloom in summer or fall on current year's growth in winter. Examples are crape myrtle, pomegranate and roses.

Plants that freeze or go dormant during the winter such as *Caesalpinia gilliesii*, *C. pulcherrima* and *Salvia leucantha* should be pruned back in late winter to within 1 to 1-1/2 feet from the crown or base. See photos, pages 57. In warm-winter areas, *Caesalpinia gilliesii* and *C. pulcherrima* may remain green and alive, but pruning helps keep plants compact and in control plus encourages fresh, healthy, new growth.

Late winter is also the time to thin the canopies of young, fast-growing trees such as *Prosopis* hybrids, mesquites, and many *Acacia* species. Left unpruned, the dense canopies can catch the strong spring winds, causing trees to blow over.

Spring

Plants such as azalea, camellia, *Cassia*, *Cordia boissieri*, *Calliandra eriophylla*, *Justicia*, *Photinia* and *Sophora* species develop flowers on the previous year's growth. Prune after bloom period is completed. If you find their seed pods unattractive, remove them at this time. To increase side growth for a more compact plant, pinch off vigorous vertical tips.

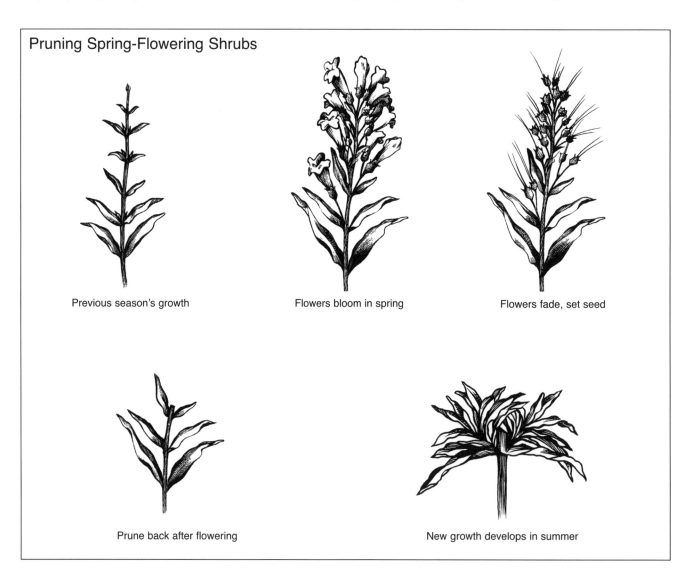

Pruning Spring-Flowering Shrubs

Previous season's growth

Flowers bloom in spring

Flowers fade, set seed

Prune back after flowering

New growth develops in summer

Prune frost-tender shrubs as they come out of winter dormancy in spring: lantana, bougainvillea, cape honeysuckle, hibiscus, justicia, natal plum and plumbago usually need severe pruning to control growth. If plants are damaged by frost, they may need pruning later in the season, depending on climate and how late in the year frost occurs.

Hardy, nonblooming shrubs grown for their dense foliage can be pruned lightly any time. Remove long

of a tree or branch by reducing the total leaf surface. This reduces the amount of food manufactured and sent to the roots, and slows development of next year's crown growth. Don't prune so much that branches are exposed to the intense sun.

Summer is also the time for minor corrective pruning of fast-growing shrubs such as bougainvillea, cape honeysuckle and hibiscus. Dead limbs can be seen more easily, as well as limbs that hang down too far under weight of leaves.

Many shrubs benefit from periodic pinching during the growing season to maintain their shape. Remove spent blooms and seed pods. You may have to sacrifice a few flowers of summer-blooming varieties to keep plants in control.

Fall
Decay fungi spread their spores profusely in the fall. Fresh pruning cuts are an invitation, so avoid pruning now. Cuts seem to heal slower when performed at this time. Wait for the winter season to prune.

Previous season's growth

Prune back early in spring

New growth comes on late spring to summer

Flowers bloom on new growth

Planting

The great majority of landscape plants are planted from containers, available in a range of sizes at the nursery. Container plants are relatively inexpensive and are easy to plant. Some plants can also be planted as *bare root* while they are dormant. Roses are typically sold and planted this way. Other plants can be started as seeds, such as wildflowers and many vegetables and flowering annuals. But planting from containers extends the planting season to practically year-round, although some periods are decidedly better than others.

With some container-purchased plants, you get a preview of what the plant and flowers will look like. Be aware, however, that when immature, many native and adapted plants look deceptively scrawny in their containers. Don't judge their potential by a few stems and leaves. But you should be selective when purchasing plants. Avoid a plant that has been growing in the container too long, with roots extending out the container bottom. Plants should have a robust, healthy appearance. As a rule, select a small plant with vigor rather than a larger, less-robust specimen.

Fall is the preferred planting time in most regions of the arid West, with some exceptions. During fall the soil is still warm, promoting root growth, while air temperatures are moderate so new plants are not stressed by cold or heat. As fall progresses into winter and spring, the now-established roots are quick to respond to the warmer weather and produce healthy top growth.

Spring is the second-best planting period. In hot-summer regions, plant as early in the season as possible so plants begin to establish before heat comes on. In cold-winter regions, some fall-planted plants will be susceptible to cold damage. Plant in spring after danger of frost has passed. In moderate climates such as along the coast, planting can be done year-round. But more water will be required to establish plants set out during late spring to summer due to the warmer temperatures.

If in doubt about the proper time to plant for your region, remember this simple rule: Plant any time you can usually count on four weeks or more of mild weather to follow. This will allow plants to begin to establish before stress—in the form of either heat or cold—comes on.

Preparing for Planting

Before you begin to dig your planting holes, be sure your plants are going into locations where they are sure to thrive. Picking planting sites requires attention to two basic factors: Will the plant grow well in your chosen spot? And is there enough space for the plant or plants to grow to mature size without hindrance from other plants, sidewalks or structures? This is the essential philosophy of *preventive pruning,* discussed on page 14. Careful plant selection will eliminate potential pruning and shearing problems.

Most plants require at least six hours of sun each day, but some plants do well in shade. (The specific requirements for plants are provided on pages 65 to 156.) However, sunlight is highly variable, depending on your climate and the time of day plants are exposed to the sun. Morning sun (eastern exposure) is much less intense than afternoon sun (southern or western exposure). In addition, six hours of sunlight is not nearly as intense in a cool coastal region as in the sunny desert. Garden plants in the low desert cities, for example, are almost always appreciative of afternoon shade, or the shade supplied by a canopy tree.

The many small climates around your garden, *microclimates,* provide planting opportunities. For example, if sunshine is lacking, a warm south wall, particularly if it's light in color, reflects heat. More likely, however, this site would be too hot, reflecting light and heat to an extent that it damages plants. An overabundance of heat can be tempered by providing shade in the form of trees or structures such as lath panels. For more information on microclimates, see page 11.

Nearby trees and shrubs provide mixed blessings. They do produce desirable shade, turning a too-hot western exposure into a tolerable planting area. Then again, roots of many trees and shrubs can compete with new plants for water and nutrients. Be prepared to compensate with additional moisture and fertilizer.

Soil and Planting

One of the most-important aspects of growing plants is providing them with the right soil. The question soon becomes: Should I improve the soil or leave it alone? The current thinking is that most plants native to arid regions do best in the natural, unimproved soil that exists on site. On the other hand, some introduced, high-water-use plants (from non-arid regions of the world) or garden variety plants such as lawn, annuals, vegetables and some perennials grow better in an improved, highly organic soil.

Soils are highly variable from one geographic region to the next, as well as from landscape to landscape on the same street. Many housing developments today are built on compacted soils that have been excavated and moved around and are in far from a natural state. In addition, most western soils are low in organic matter. This is because natural vegetation is sparse in low-rainfall regions. Leaves, stems and other plant parts are not available in large quantities to decay and create organic material. The long periods of intense heat also cause organic matter to dissipate quickly. For plants with substantial root systems (trees and many shrubs) it is usually best to leave the planting hole unamended. Studies have shown that when backfill soil is amended, plant roots have more difficulty growing into the surrounding native soil. This interface problem can result in slow development and establishment of plants. (See page 27 for more information.)

Primary Soil Types

Soils in the arid West include heavy clay soils, such as those found in coastal California; sandy soils, common to the arid regions of Southern California and the alkaline, caliche-plagued soils of Nevada, Arizona and New Mexico. Some regions are blessed with loam soils, a balanced mixture of materials high in organic matter. Many regions are variable, and soil type can differ from neighbor to neighbor.

Sandy soils—These are composed of a high percentage of large particles, and water drains through quickly. Moistened sandy soil will crumble and fall apart when squeezed in your hand. In desert regions the particulates that make up sandy soils cause them to blow easily in heavy winds. Nutrients, particularly nitrogen, are *leached*—washed down from plant roots—by this rapid drainage. Sandy soils absorb water at a rate of 2 inches or more per hour. They warm up more quickly in the spring than clay soils and are also the easiest to work with, allowing plant roots to develop freely.

Clay soils—Small, tightly compacted particles, heavy, dense and sticky when wet, describe clay soils. If you squeeze moistened clay soil in your hand, it will "ribbon" through your fingers. Moisture moves through clay soils slowly. When you apply water, it tends to create puddles and pools rather quickly. Clay soils absorb water at a rate of less than 1/4 inch per hour. Do not dig or cultivate clay soil when it's wet, or you will be sorry. Large, hard clods will form when the soil dries and become almost impossible to work. Clay soils can develop a crust on the surface, which repels water. Roots grow more slowly in clay soils, and the considerable resistance and the fact that oxygen does not penetrate as deeply makes it more difficult for plants to develop a deep root zone.

Loam soils—These are ideal soils for plant growth. They are a balanced mixture of clay, sand and organic matter, and are generally well draining. Loam soil is crumbly in your hand. Organic material in loam creates variable spaces among the soil particles, which help hold moisture and nutrients in the root zone longer to the benefit of plants. Loam soils absorb water at the rate of 1/4 inch to 2 inches per hour. They can crust over like clay soils, repelling water.

Granitized alluvial soils—These are less common and are found at the bases of mountains and hills, fanning out due to forces of water runoff. They are coarse, "young" soils, still in the process of breaking down from large particles to small ones. Alluvial soils drain well and roots penetrate if given plenty of moisture. When dry, they are difficult to work. For some

plants, adding organic matter to these soils improves them by increasing their moisture- and nutrient-holding capacity.

Problem Soils

Hardpan and caliche are serious problem soils in the West. Hardpan is generally found in heavy clay soil areas where the land has been farmed for long periods. Calcareous soils (caliche) are formed from mineral deposits that create cementlike layers—practically impenetrable if more than a few feet thick. The solution may be drastic—creating raised beds or drainage "chimneys" in planting holes with pickaxe, power auger or jackhammer. (See illustrations below.) In fact, it's not a bad idea to check the depth and workability of the soil when shopping for a new home or property to avoid serious long-term problems.

Saline or salty soils are common on converted farmlands. Soils are salty due to years of regular use of salt-based fertilizers. Water supplied from the

---

Soil Type: How It Affects Planting and Care

Sandy soil is loose and gritty

Clay soil ribbons through your fingers

Loam soil crumbles in your hands

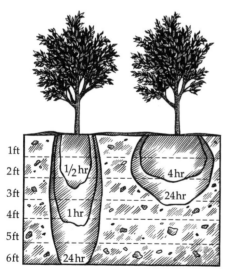

Soil type affects how water moves through the soil. Note differences between sandy loam, left, and clay loam, right. It takes much longer to irrigate clay soils deeply. How much moisture spreads differs as well. Sandy soils have a narrower profile.

If planting in caliche or hardpan soils, it may be necessary to build a drainage chimney. A soil auger (inset) can be used to dig through caliche or hardpan to reach well-draining soil.

Colorado River is also high in salts. Leaching out saline soils by applying water slowly for several hours helps wash soil salts down and away from the plant's root zone. This is a common practice in many desert regions where soil salts are high. Leach your soil every six months or so, perhaps more often during summer.

Improving Soils

If you need to improve your soil, add organic matter. As mentioned, this is recommended for lawns and vegetable and annual gardens. It's also a good idea if soil is so poor or rocky or sandy that organic matter is necessary to get plants started. Well-aged animal manures, leaf mold, ground bark products and home-made compost are common amendments. Shredded oat hay or alfalfa hay work well, particularly in sandy soils.

As a guide, about one-quarter to one-third of the soil in a planting bed should be organic matter. If you work a bed to a depth of about 8 inches, add a layer of organic matter about 2 to 3 inches deep over the area. Dig thoroughly into existing soil, blending it so there are no streaks or layers of material. Avoid an abrupt "begin and end" situation from improved soil to native soil. The soils should make a gradual transition from one to another so plant roots won't "stop" when the soil composition changes.

Organic matter mixed into sandy soils increases the nutrient- and water-holding capacity. If your soil is sandy to the point of being a sand dune, it will blow around in high winds. Plant windbreaks or install a fence or wall to protect plants and to keep soil in place. Organic matter improves the drainage and workability of heavy clay soils.

As mentioned, not all plants require an improved soil. Some have natural adaptations that allow them to grow better in poor, sandy or rocky soils. Most plants adapted to arid regions do require good drainage, however. Refer to the Gallery of Dry Climate Plants.

Planting Trees and Shrubs

In the last few years horticulturists have begun to rethink traditional planting methods. Questions have been raised about the size, shape and depth of the planting hole, the value of adding organic amendments and the value of post-transplant pruning. Dr. Jimmy Tipton, with the Department of Plant Sciences at the University of Arizona, has developed some recommendations that home gardeners and landscape professionals should consider when planting.

The traditional planting method required a hole be dug slightly larger and deeper than the dimensions of the box size or container being planted. The shortcomings of this method are many:

1. The plant may sink lower than desired, so that the trunk comes in contact with the soil, exposing it to soil-borne diseases.

2. A deep planting hole does not necessarily encourage deep rooting. Trees planted in this manner have been dug up and examined, with the observation that roots have not extended deep into the hole.

3. Availability of oxygen in the root zone in a deep hole may be limited.

The currently accepted method of planting is to make the hole no deeper than the depth of the rootball and three to five times as wide as the rootball. For a 5-gallon container, this would be an area of 3 to 4 feet wide by about 1 foot deep. The wider rootball area encourages root growth because the majority of active tree roots are found within two feet of the soil surface. The planting hole is dug so that it is rough and uneven on the sides and bottom. This method creates a better interface between backfill and existing soil. It also creates conditions that encourage lateral root development. The bottom of the planting hole is left undisturbed. This helps avoid settling, which can cause problems if moist soil comes up against the trunk later on.

Backfill, the soil that is placed around the rootball in the planting hole, is left alone and is not amended with organic matter. Studies have shown that organic amendments in the backfill tend to restrict root spread and thus reduce top growth. Often the organic matter is not thoroughly blended with the native soil in the planting hole, creating air pockets. When dealing with heavy clay soils, sand can be added to the backfill to increase the rate of water penetration and improve drainage.

The development of new roots is stimulated by and dependent upon the growth of leaves and stems. The old practice of reducing top growth right after planting can actually delay establishment. Such pruning is considered unnecessary and can actually slow plant development.

Not all planting locations can accommodate this planting method. For example, there may not be sufficient room when planting trees along narrow street medians. In such an instance, dig a long, narrow planting hole, which also helps encourage lateral root growth.

When planting trees in compacted or heavy clay soils, there is an alternative method that might work in some situations. Dig the planting hole three to five times the width of the rootball but only as deep as

Planting Step-by-Step

1. Plant on a cool, cloudy day, or if sunny, wait until late afternoon. Dig planting holes before you purchase plants and check for sufficient drainage. This also premoistens soil in the rootball area. Space plants far enough apart and far enough away from sidewalks and structures to allow them to develop to their mature size.

2. Dig a hole three to four times as wide and <u>the same depth</u> as the rootball. Do not disturb soil at bottom of hole. Fill planting hole with water and allow to drain. Fill again. Water should drain in about 24 hours. If it hasn't, try another site or create a drainage chimney. See illustration, page 26.

3. Remove plant gently from container. If soil mass is rootbound, use a knife or pruning shears to slice the outside of the rootball and splay it open. Set in planting hole so that top of rootball is about 1 inch above the surrounding soil level. Add soil dug from planting hole around the rootball, gently pressing soil around roots. Add time-release fertilizer tablet so it will be about 6 inches below soil surface at perimeter of rootball. Water thoroughly to settle soil.

4. Build a soil basin to hold the water. Make it 3 to 4 inches high and extend it just beyond the outer edge of the rootball. Be prepared to extend the basin as the plant grows. Or, if using drip irrigation, provide sufficient emitters and proper gallonage. (See chart, page 34.) Stake plant only if necessary. Add 3- to 4-inch layer of mulch over the root area to conserve moisture.

Plants are available for purchase in a range of container sizes. Typical are, from left to right, *1-gallon, 5-gallon, 15-gallon* and *boxed specimens.* Plants in smaller-size containers establish most quickly and are less likely to be rootbound. Plants from

larger containers provide more immediate impact in the landscape. Check to be sure roots are not twisting or circling in the container. Boxed trees often require professional help to install.

half of the rootball depth. Large trees planted from boxes are the best candidates for this method. Mound uncompacted topsoil over and above the rest of the rootball. Gradually taper the slope of the mound to prevent erosion runoff. This creates a rooting area where half the soil is now actually above the original soil line, providing the necessary drainage.

Planting and Plant Competition

Plant spacing reduces competition between roots and helps provide proper amounts of water use, air, sunlight and atmospheric gases. It is key in developing plant growth. This is true no matter what the size of your garden. Follow these methods to allow healthy development.

Space plants according to their normal, mature, growth patterns.

Irrigate with a drip-irrigation system. Use emitters with different gallon-per-hour output to provide the proper water required for each type of plant.

Control plants by pruning them according to their seasonal growth cycles. See Master Flowering and Pruning Chart, pages 67 to 74.

Plant in soil that drains properly. Soil types that drain well allow plants to develop adequate roots. If soil does not drain well, plant in another site. If this is not possible, consider creating your own drainage by using the "chimney method" as shown on page 26.

The Art of Establishing Plants

Every plant has a certain time and water requirement before it adjusts to the shock from planting and an adequate root system begins to develop. This period may range from one to three months for perennials and six months or more for five-gallon, containerized shrubs, vines and trees. Boxed trees may require up to one year; field-grown trees and palms (those with unconfined root systems) may require two years. Generally, the larger the rootball, the longer the establishment period and need for regular moisture.

Planting Bare-Root Plants

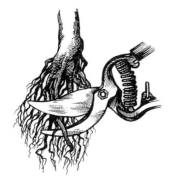

1. Keep roots moist if not planting right away. Before planting, trim off any broken or discolored roots.

2. Dig hole about three to four times diameter of roots. Test for drainage, as discussed on page 28. Dig just deep enough so that plant will be planted at same depth or slightly higher than it was grown at the nursery. Build cone in center of hole from backfill soil.

3. Spread roots out over the cone of soil. Check planting depth as mentioned in step two. Look for soil stain on the trunk or stem to determine previous planting depth.

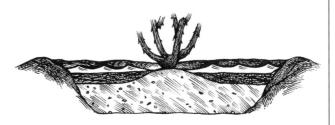

4. Add backfill soil around roots, firming gently. To keep canes from drying out, cover one-third of their height with soil or organic matter. Remove this covering when you see signs of new growth.

The size of a plant and when it is planted have a significant effect on its survival and how soon it becomes established. Tests have demonstrated that 1-gallon and 5-gallon size plants have excellent survival rates and are recommended for most plantings. Plants in the 15-gallon to 24-inch box size take longer to adjust to their their new, in-ground homes.

When you plant affects establishment. Trees planted in winter—December through February—require approximately 9 to 12 months before they are established. They will not produce top growth for about three months, but roots are slowly developing. Spring planting—March through May—allows roots to develop as the soil warms up. Top growth develops even more rapidly than roots. Summer planting is the most-stressful. Temperatures well over 100F stress plants as they try and supply moisture to foliage and branches, hindered by a limited root system. However, some desert species do better in summer. Apparently, the warmer soil temperatures encourage root growth.

Staking Trees

In nature, trees grow well without being staked or supported throughout their early development. Staking becomes important in a landscape setting because newly transplanted trees either lack sufficient trunk strength to resist winds or don't have enough roots to provide needed anchorage and stability.

The goal of staking should be to allow trees to quickly develop trunk diameter and trunk strength. The extent of staking may depend on tree strength and crown density, expected wind conditions, car and foot traffic, type of landscape planting and level of maintenance. All staking practices have an effect on subsequent growth and development of the tree. Staked trees may grow taller and produce less caliper near the ground and more near the top of the tree. They also tend to develop smaller root systems and offer more wind resistance (because the trunk is not free to bend), and they are subject to trunk damage

Staking Trees

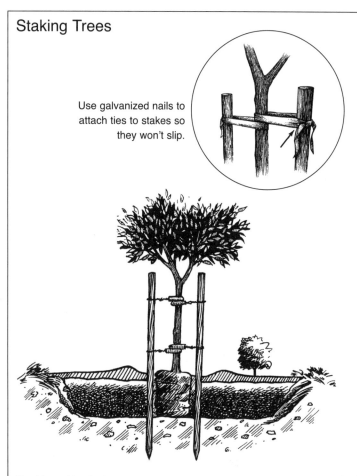

Use galvanized nails to attach ties to stakes so they won't slip.

Double staking is the most common method currently used. It employs two stakes with tie loops from each post to the trunk. Ties are arranged opposite one another to allow support and some "give." An imaginary line drawn between the two stakes should be at a right angle to the strongest winds.

Anchor staking holds the trunks of newly transplanted trees steady, preventing movement of the rootball. Even small movements of the rootball can severely damage new roots growing into surrounding soil, lengthening the time it takes for the tree to become established.

due to rubbing and girdling from stakes and ties. All of these factors tend to make a tree less able to survive on its own when it is staked too long.

With these points in mind, consider staking a short-term aid that helps trees become established. Actual staking methods vary widely. Durability of the materials, ease of installation, appearance of the tree, branch structure and size of the container or box that the tree is growing in are factors. In general, staking may be necessary for one to two years, depending on the plant species and rate of growth.

Materials used to stake trees include wood or metal stakes and ties that link the trunk to the supporting posts. Stakes should never come in contact with tree trunk or branches. Any material used as a tie should contact the trunk with a broad, smooth surface and have enough elasticity to "give," preventing injury. Polyethylene tape and wire covered with a section of garden hose are common materials. Use brightly colored ties. They serve as visual reminders that they remain on the tree, so you'll check them more frequently. Plus they are easier to find when it's time to remove them. If ties are not removed, they can cause girdling of the branches or trunks. (See photo, page 50.) A figure-eight tie looped between the stake and trunk is flexible and provides extra protection from injury to the trunk from the tie or the posts.

Posts should be strong enough to withstand the anticipated winds for your region. As mentioned, tie materials should provide support yet give slightly. This also allows tree to sway in mild winds and develop strength and proper caliper.

Staking should not be a standard practice applied to all newly transplanted trees. Stake only after careful consideration of the site, the species of tree and anticipated wind conditions. Generally, trees with low branches, multiple trunks or a natural, shrublike growth habit do not require it. After trees are established, remove all stakes and ties to prevent future damage to the tree.

Planting Seed, Step by Step

When you sow seed over a large area, it can be hard to tell where it is distributed. To see where seed is applied, mix one part seed with three parts light-colored sand. Broadcast this mixture. For more even coverage, divide seed to be applied into two equal batches. Apply one batch going north and south; apply the second batch perpendicular to the first, going east and west. Some fertilizer spreaders are handy if you are sowing seed over a large area. If you've grown flowering plants the previous year, collect and save the dry seedheads. The following season, shake out the seeds where you want flowers to grow.

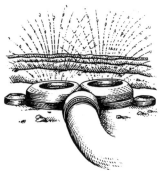

1. Sow seed by hand, use a fertilizer spreader or shake out seeds from seedheads saved from the previous-year's crop.

2. Rake or press seed into soil. Double rake to ensure good seed-to-soil contact but don't bury seed too deep.

3. Water the seeded area directly after sowing. Use a sprinkler that emits a fine spray pattern to avoid puddling and soil erosion.

Plant Care

*G*ardening has gone through many changes over the past 20 years. Landscape architects have developed new design concepts that are increasingly sensitive to their regions. More and more often, they are including native plants in their designs, providing a subtle but undeniable *sense of place*. Other changes are initiated by plant explorers and growers, who continue to introduce new plants. Many of these plants are discoveries of superior natives; others are selected through breeding programs. The space we have available to garden has changed as well. Homes are being built on smaller lots, so more dwarf plants and smaller-scale plantings are being used.

These factors influence how we garden, but it is Mother Nature and our inherent western climate that becomes the great equalizer. Recurring droughts, increasing cost of water and shortages do not let us forget that this is the *arid* West. As a result, a traditional landscape mainstay, the grass lawn, is gradually being replaced or reduced in size and stature. In the newly available garden space you'll see native and adapted shrubs, ground covers, perennials, succulents and cacti. The result are gardens composed of an interesting blend of the traditional and the new.

The methods we use to water, fertilize and control pests and diseases have changed as well to meet the needs of this evolving western landscape. Drip irrigation systems have become more reliable, inexpensive and easier to install. In home gardens and in commercial applications, they help control plant growth while maintaining plant health.

One of the amazing things about plant care is how much better our plants grow if we maintain *a sense of balance*. Keeping plants growing healthy with the right amounts of water and fertilizer and pruning at the right time (or not pruning at all) encourages pests to look elsewhere for their hosts. Likewise, we're discovering that alternative methods of controls deserve a try before we reach for an arsenal of chemicals. Avoiding indiscriminate chemical sprays allows the pest's natural predators to live in our gardens, taking care of uninvited guests so we don't have to. In the following pages you'll learn how to use these new gardening tools and techniques to make your garden grow better, naturally.

Watering

Learning to water correctly comes with practice and some green-thumb sense of your own plants. Being in tune to the changing water needs of plants as spring rapidly steams into summer, is just one example. Miscalculate with too little or too much water and your plants can suffer or even die.

Watering Newly Planted Plants

The most-important watering period, even more important than summer watering, begins right at planting time. Newly planted plants, even if they are low-water natives, require moist soil. (*Larrea tridentata*, creosote, is one exception, requiring less.) Regular irrigation is necessary while plants are adjusting to their new environment, which is often in a soil or even climate that is markedly different from their nursery growing grounds. Any prolonged dry period will prevent roots from developing uniformly, and plant growth and performance can be permanently affected by being stunted. Many California native plants that typically do better without regular water during summer should receive regular applications during this season to develop healthy root systems.

Schedule daily irrigations for newly planted plants. If the weather is cloudy, skip a day or two. If it is windy, the upper 1 to 2 inches of soil or mulch can dry out very quickly. Apply water slowly in an area around the plant's rootball. If you are not using drip irrigation, build a basin to hold the water. Do not use a sprinkler to apply water, especially if it's windy. Water is wasted due to uneven applications and evaporation. Continue to monitor soil moisture by checking the soil regularly for several weeks. Installing a drip irrigation system with an automatic timer is highly recommended. You can control exactly how much water is applied, as well as where and how often. See chart on page 34.

The amount of water you should apply depends in part on soil type, exposure and prevailing weather. Daily waterings of new plants may last only a week along the coast yet could be required for several weeks in hot, inland valley and desert areas.

If plants are located on slopes, water in intervals to help prevent soil erosion. Do this by watering for a determined period, such as five minutes, allowing water to soak in. Repeat later with another five-minute watering, and so on, until moisture has soaked deeply into the soil.

After plants adjust to planting and produce new growth, gradually space out waterings, perhaps to two or three applications per week. Irrigations will be fewer along coastal areas and more frequent in the hot deserts and inland valleys. If heat increases to 85F or more or if winds are excessive, check each day for moisture in the top several inches of soil. Water if soil is dry. Using a shovel or trowel, dig down into the soil to see how deep moisture is reaching. The top few inches of the soil surface should be kept moist, but do not allow it to remain wet at any time. Most plants prefer the soil to dry out partially between waterings, which allows necessary oxygen to reach plant roots. High temperatures in combination with wind may mean you'll have to water once or even twice per day.

Developing an Efficient Irrigation Program

After plants are established, which usually means living through a complete summer season, you can begin a program of watering efficiently. Knowing the exact amount of water the many kinds of plants in your landscape require is difficult. Zoning plants by water requirement, called *hydrozoning*, groups plants with similar moisture requirements, such as high, moderate and low. This helps avoid overwatering or underwatering plants within the same area of the landscape. Zoning plants is necessary in designing and operating a drip irrigation system properly.

To develop your program, you'll need to become accustomed to the differences (and benefits) of *irrigation duration* and *irrigation frequency*. Controlling the duration—how long each irrigation lasts—is important, because a long, slow irrigation allows water to soak the entire root zone. Frequency—how often you water—can vary according to the age of the plant, exposure, time of year, extent of the root zone and soil type. The more shallow the root system (as with new plants), the more frequent the irrigation. The rule, then, is to change your irrigation program as the plant grows and changes, gradually reducing the frequency and increasing the duration of irrigations. This helps plants develop deep and wide root systems, whether they are new plants or established plants that you want to wean from a high-water diet.

It helps to know when your plants show the first signs of stress so you can quickly adjust watering schedules to prevent loss of growth, injury or even death. Here are some additional key points to help you water plants efficiently:

Know your soil type—Soil type affects how deeply water penetrates, how quickly it gets into the root zone and how long it remains there. Basic soil types are described on pages 25 to 27. Most plants, particularly those native to arid climates, require good soil drainage. Generally speaking, 1 inch of rain or irrigation in sandy soil will go about 1 foot deep. For water to reach 2 feet deep, you'll need to apply water slowly for about an hour without runoff. Clay soils are dense and compact; an inch of water penetrates to only four or five inches. For water to reach two feet deep, for example, you'll need to irrigate slowly for about two hours. Loam soils, depending on the organic matter content, fall somewhere between these two extremes.

Check for soil moisture—How deep water penetrates your soil will help guide your watering schedule. Dig down after an irrigation to see how far moisture has penetrated. Or push a long, steel rod or screwdriver into irrigated soil. The rod will come to a stop when it reaches dry soil. You can also use a tool called a soil sampler to pull a narrow core of soil from the ground, showing the depth that moisture has penetrated.

Doing this lets you see when the soil is dry and plants will soon need water—before they become water-stressed.

Know when plants show signs of water need—Plants show when they need water if leaves change in appearance from shiny to dull. Green leaves turn to blue or gray-green. Leaf tips turn brown. Drastic signs are when new plant growth wilts or droops, leaves curl and flowers fade quickly and drop prematurely. Older leaves become brown, dry and fall off.

Put water where it's needed—As plants grow, their roots grow and extend mostly out, away from the trunk. The roots that absorb water, *the feeder roots*, tend

Irrigation Guide: Established Trees and Large Shrubs *Plants 15 to 20 feet high and as wide*

| | WATER USAGE OF PLANTS | | | |
MONTH	HIGH	MEDIUM	LOW	TIMES PER WEEK
January	7.9 gal	5.3 gal	3.7 gal	1
February	11.5 gal	8.0 gal	5.6 gal	2
March	13.3 gal	11.5 gal	8.0 gal	2
April	22.5 gal	15.7 gal	11.0 gal	3
May	27.0 gal	19.0 gal	15.5 gal	4
June	31.7 gal	23.3 gal	15.7 gal	4
July	31.7 gal	22.3 gal	15.7 gal	4
August	26.3 gal	18.5 gal	13.0 gal	4
September	24.0 gal	16.7 gal	11.9 gal	3
October	16.7 gal	11.5 gal	8.0 gal	3
November	10.2 gal	7.5 gal	5.0 gal	2
December	6.5 gal	4.5 gal	3.0 gal	1

Irrigation Guide: Established Shrubs and Ground Covers *Plants 4 to 6 feet wide or less*

| | WATER USAGE OF PLANTS | | | |
MONTH	HIGH	MEDIUM	LOW	TIMES PER WEEK
January	0.7 gal	0.5 gal	0.3 gal	1
February	1.0 gal	0.7 gal	0.5 gal	2
March	1.5 gal	1.0 gal	0.6 gal	2
April	2.0 gal	1.5 gal	0.9 gal	3
May	2.3 gal	1.7 gal	1.0 gal	4
June	2.7 gal	2.0 gal	1.3 gal	4
July	2.7 gal	2.0 gal	1.3 gal	4
August	2.3 gal	1.7 gal	1.3 gal	4
September	2.0 gal	1.5 gal	0.8 gal	3
October	1.5 gal	1.0 gal	0.6 gal	3
November	1.0 gal	0.7 gal	0.4 gal	2
December	0.7 gal	0.5 gal	0.3 gal	1

If you have a drip-irrigation system, here's how to calculate how long to water. With 1-gallon emitters, multiply the gallonage rate times 60 minutes. For example, 0.3 x 60 = 18, or 18 minutes.

This chart was developed by the Coachella Valley Water District, where summers are hot and rainfall is typically less than 4 inches per year. Soils are commonly fast-draining sandy soils. If you live where temperatures are cooler and receive more rainfall, adjust accordingly. No matter where you live, irrigation amounts and frequencies illustrate how the water needs of plants change as the seasons progress.

to be concentrated at the plant's *drip line*—the area where rainwater drips off leaves to the ground—and beyond. Researchers now believe that roots can extend up to three times wider than the drip line in sandy soils, up to two times in clay soils. Apply water in this area—inside the drip line area and beyond. (For a guide to how far beyond, see text and illustration, page 8.) This helps ensure plant roots are getting the most benefit from the moisture you're supplying.

The depth to water depends on the type of plant and its root depth. This varies considerably, depending on plant type. Soil type is also a factor. Roots in sandy soils penetrate deeper than in clay or loam soils.

Plant roots that go deep in the soil are better insulated against heat and cold and have a greater reservoir from which to draw water when it is not provided on a regular basis. This makes them more drought tolerant. Shallow-rooted plants have none of these advantages. The upper soil layers dry out most quickly. Evaporation of moisture from this upper soil layer can be reduced by adding a 2- to 3-inch layer of mulch over the root area. (See page 39.)

Water when evaporation rates are low—When wind moves across plants, it not only disperses water elsewhere, it increases transpiration by moving water vapor away from the leaf surface. Low humidity also increases transpiration. High heat such as that at midday during summer greatly increases loss due to evaporation. Water during the cool times of day—evening or early morning—when there is little or no wind. During periods of hot, dry winds, construct temporary windbreaks around valuable plants to reduce moisture loss.

Install drip irrigation—A drip irrigation system offers many benefits: Water is applied to the root zone of plants and is not wasted on surrounding soil, walkways and hardscapes such as patio surfaces. Water is applied at the soil surface so the wind is not able to blow the water away or cause it to evaporate. Drip avoids overwatering and water loss due to wasteful runoff, which often occurs with traditional sprinkler systems. Evaporation through sun and heat is lessened much more efficiently than with hose-end sprinklers or hand-held waterings.

Drip saves time: no more evenings or mornings spent watering plant after plant, hoping you're supplying the right amount of water. (Chances are you're not.) It's as simple as turning on a spigot for a period of time. If you have a timer, which is highly recommended, plants are watered automatically. Plants receive the right amount of water so they grow faster and are healthier. Water goes deep into the root zone of plants on a regular basis. Plants are not stressed due to overly dry soil and are given the right amount of water to grow to their potential. (It's also possible to *slow* plant growth after they're established by reducing water via the drip system.) A drip system can be adjusted to suit the seasonal needs of plants, increasing watering duration or frequency during summer and decreasing during winter. Changing the gallonage of the emitter delivering water to plants is another way to increase or decrease the water flow.

Practice water conservation—Check outdoor spigots for leaks, and don't water when it rains or during heavy winds. Turn off automatic sprinklers and irrigation systems if rain is forecast. Use a rain gauge to see how much rain has fallen. When watering from a hose, use a watering nozzle with a shutoff valve. They allow you to shut off the water flow when you want, conserving water. "Harvest" water by utilizing rainwater runoff from the roof or gutters. Channel runoff to plants, or locate plants near downspouts. Add a watering basin to catch the runoff, and plants will receive a good soaking with each substantial rain.

Winter Watering
Many reference materials on gardening in arid regions discuss summer irrigation practices. But little information is provided on how much to water plants in winter. Even less is written about the detrimental effects of excessive winter irrigation, which can harm certain plants. Unlike many deciduous trees that drop leaves in response to shorter fall and winter days, some popular arid trees drop leaves in response to cold temperatures. As a result, some trees may remain in full leaf during the winter months when winters are warm or when planted in protected microclimates. Although leaves are present, little if any growth occurs. In a natural setting most landscape plants can survive through winter on rainfall.

A winter irrigation schedule must be sensitive to the same environmental factors that influence summer irrigations: soil type, age of the plant, frequency and amount of rainfall, the tree's immediate physical environment (sun, shade, proximity to structures), the irrigation demands of understory plantings and weather conditions (unseasonably warm or higher than average rainfall). Every landscape has a different set of variables so there are no hard and fast rules for irrigation schedules. Still, there are some general guidelines. Review the recommendations in the chart, opposite, with your particular landscape and conditions in mind. Adjust up or down if your garden is warmer or cooler or in an inland region as compared to a location along the coast.

Established trees may require little supplemental irrigation. Dig or probe soil periodically to see if it is moist. Some plants are more tolerant of moderate overirrigation. Refer to the individual descriptions.

In winter it is actually safer to err on the side of slightly underirrigating plants. This is because the detrimental effects of overirrigation usually do not become apparent until the following spring, after serious damage to the roots has already occurred.

The Connection Between Irrigation and Pruning
In the arid West, the long growing season and short winter or dormancy season place heavy demands on plants. Plants given regular moisture in our warm, mild climates grow rapidly. More plant growth means more pruning, increasing maintenance time and expense. The additional plant trimmings and debris accelerate the filling of municipal dumps. Using less water reduces pruning maintenance. Less moisture also reduces weeds and curtails or eliminates some insect and plant disease problems.

Established plants three years or older don't seem to suffer if winter water is cut back by half or more. Gardeners following this method have realized savings in water use and time spent pruning.

In studies comparing naturalistic landscaping to traditional turf and garden layouts, the naturalistic designs show a significant cost difference in water and maintenance. For example, in Palm Desert, California, a naturalistic garden consisting of native and adapted plants covering 32,000 square feet required 0.19 cents per square foot to maintain. Care included water, fertilizer, labor and general maintenance of plants. This compared to 0.32 cents per square foot required to care for a similarly sized turf and landscape garden. Over the course of a year, the savings were significant, with the naturalistic landscape requiring $4,100 less in maintenance costs.

Drip Irrigation

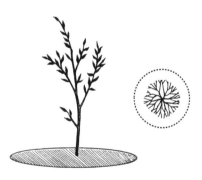

A newly planted tree or shrub should receive sufficient moisture from one or two emitters as long as rootball area and just beyond receive regular moisture through at least one growing season.

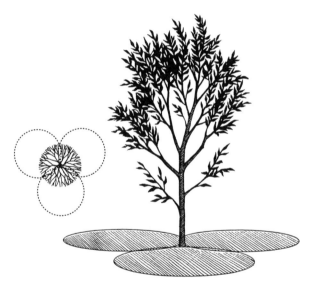

Older plants, two to five years old, generally do fine with three emitters. Note how moisture is being distributed well beyond the drip line in the area where feeder roots grow. If spray heads are used, be sure they face away from trunks to prevent problems with diseases. Place emitters halfway between base of tree and edge of canopy.

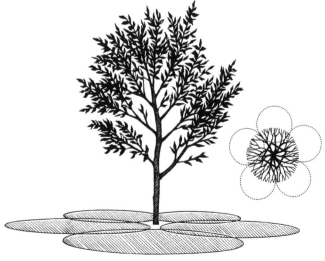

Well-established plants may need five emitters or more, depending on their size. The same principle applies as above: The goal is to apply moisture to the root area where feeder roots are located, while avoiding spraying the trunk. See illustration, page 8.

Fertilizing

The supply of plant nutrients in western soils is generally adequate to meet the needs of native trees and shrubs. However, many plants respond to increased soil fertility with more vigorous growth and better foliage color. The most important nutrients for plant growth are nitrogen, phosphorus and potassium. If you purchase a packaged fertilizer, the ratios listed on the bag, such as 16-6-8, describe the percentages of nitrogen, phosphorus and potassium, respectively.

Nitrogen is the nutrient usually lacking in most soils. Plants use a lot of it and it is easily leached out of the root zone, particularly in sandy soils. Plants use large amounts of nitrogen as they form protein, chlorophyll, enzymes and structural tissues.

Nitrogen has the quickest and most profound effect on plant growth. Applications of large amounts of nitrogen fertilizer can result in excessive vegetative growth. Such growth may make plants more subject to wind damage or severe cold injury.

Phosphorus is essential for the development of roots (particularly lateral and fibrous roots), flower and fruit formation and seed maturity. Only a small amount of the phosphorus in native soils is in a form that can be absorbed by plants. Even when soluble forms of phosphorus are added to soils they become chemically bound up and are largely unavailable to plants. To get phosphorus into the tree's root area, dig holes around the drip line, pour fertilizer containing phosphorous into holes and water well. Follow all product label directions. See illustration, page 38.

Potassium, or potash as it is sometimes called, is involved in the formation of starch within plants and seeds. It increases plant resistance to temperature extremes and diseases. Unlike phosphorus, potassium is readily available in all but the most sandy soils and is rarely required as a soil additive in arid western landscapes.

Minerals used by plants in large amounts including nitrogen, phosphorus and potassium are called *macronutrients*. Minerals needed in extremely small amounts are *micronutrients*. These include copper, zinc, boron and manganese. Although overapplication of certain macronutrients can stimulate excessive growth, high concentrations of micronutrients can be toxic or fatal to certain plants. For this reason, read and follow all product label directions carefully. Don't assume a little bit more will help the plant grow that much better; it will probably do more harm than good.

The most common fertilizer formulations are *dry* (granules or crystals), *liquid* and *slow release*. Dry fertilizers are easy to handle and simple to apply selectively to individual plants in the landscape. For best results, use a product created as a *homogeneous* formulation. This means each granule of the product has the same nutrient concentration. For example, each granule would contain 20% nitrogen, 20% phosphorus and 20% potassium). *Blended* fertilizers are composed of separate nitrogen, phosphorus and potassium granules that are mixed together.

Liquid fertilizer formulations can be applied directly to individual plants as a foliar spray or soil drench or through an irrigation system. Slow-release fertilizers, in tablets, pellets or granular form, are specially formulated or coated to inhibit the solubility of the nutrients. They are applied to the surface of the soil or come in the form of large tablets, which are buried in the soil around the plant rootball. Nutrients are released slowly from these formulations when the tablets become wet. It is necessary to place the fertilizer in the right location and to water sufficiently to release the nutrients so the plant roots can absorb them. These are effective when used with drip irrigation and when feeding plants growing in containers.

When (or if) to Fertilize

Some plants, particularly those native to dry regions, do not require fertilizers to stay healthy. They actually grow better without them, especially if you use fast-acting chemical or liquid fertilizers, which encourage rapid, excessive, soft growth that is more susceptible to disease and insect attack. Among this group of plants are many of the *legumes*. Numerous legumes are able to fix atmospheric nitrogen and do not need supplemental fertilizers. Many of the plants featured in this book are legumes. (Refer to the plant descriptions to determine their nutrient requirements.)

If your soil is sandy or otherwise low in organic matter, you may need to add additional nitrogen due to its poor nutrient content. If in doubt as to whether a plant needs fertilizer, use one-fourth or less of the amount recommended on the product label, then watch how plants respond. Add more if performance remains below par.

If your plants are not growing properly and you think it could be a nutrient problem, add compost or fertilizer. If things do not improve, test your soil to find out if something might be out of balance. Private soil-testing labs will test your soil for a fee, or you can analyze your soil with a test kit available at nurseries or through mail-order catalogs.

A soil analysis will also measure the pH—acidity-alkalinity—of the soil. The pH scale ranges from 3.5 (the most acid) to 9.5 (the most alkaline); 7 is neutral. Soils in the arid West tend to be more alkaline. Soils in the East are more on the acid side.

The vast majority of native plants in the arid West evolved in nutrient-poor soils and are adapted to grow in them. The lack of rainfall and the limited availability of nutrients moderate the growth of plants. But when native and adapted species are planted in home landscapes, conditions change. Water and fertilizer become effective tools for managing plant growth and health. Apply fertilizer formulations that contain nitrogen and phosphorus immediately following transplanting. This promotes rapid vegetative growth and contributes to new root development. Fertilizing when plants are actively growing in summer is also effective. Fertilizers applied in the cooler months, when little if any growth occurs, have no immediate effect on establishment. For dormant plants, apply when buds are begin to open.

Fertilizing established trees and shrubs present different challenges. After trees and shrubs reach the desired size, you can reduce or eliminate nitrogen to slow the growth rate. Slower growth of maturing trees helps reduce the risk of wind blow over and severe branch damage, common occurrences in summer wind storms. In addition, early fall applications of nitrogen can encourage vegetative growth that is more vulnerable to cold damage in winter.

Cold-hardy garden perennials can be fed twice a year—early in spring just prior to new growth and again in early summer. Water fertilizer in immediately after applying, and wash it off leaves. Applying compost as a mulch and digging it into the soil around plants will also supply some nutrients to plants. Organic fertilizers, such as cottonseed meal or composted manure, are less likely to overfertilize or burn plants but they can add salts to soils.

Cacti and succulents generally do not need fertilizer; however, a light application of a balanced fertilizer early in the growing season stimulates growth of established plants. Apply to soil about 2 feet away from plants, and scratch into the soil surface. Avoid fertilizing or irrigating cacti in the fall. The new tender growth may come on just as temperatures drop in winter, making plants more susceptible to cold injury.

Some Fertilizer Basics

Many people think of fertilizers as plant food. A more accurate analogy would be to consider them as plant *vitamins*. Fertilizers are typically a combination of inorganic elements such as nitrogen, phosphorus, iron or copper. Plants need these minerals to manufacture essential complex molecules like proteins, starches and structural tissues. Ideally, fertilizers are applied to soils to supplement minerals that are in short supply, or to supplement those that are present in a chemical form that cannot be absorbed by the plant. Fertilizers can stimulate rapid growth, promote root development, encourage flower and fruit development and help plants resist diseases and survive temperature extremes. Caution: don't overfertilize. Follow product label recommendations.

If you purchase a packaged fertilizer, the ratios listed on the bag, such as 16-6-8, describe the percentages of nitrogen, phosphorus and potassium, respectively. Nitrogen is the nutrient usually lacking in most soils. Plants use a lot of nitrogen and it is easily leached out of the root zone.

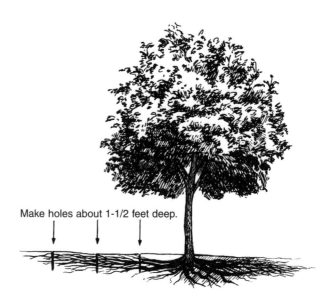

Make holes about 1-1/2 feet deep.

When applying phosphorus or potassium, place it in holes dug 1 to 1-1/2 feet deep in the root area. Water well. Fill holes with soil or sand. If applying nitrogen fertilizer sprinkle the recommended amount according to the product label around the plant's dripline area and beyond. Cultivate lightly into the soil and water well.

Mulches

Covering the bare ground around plants with a layer of material—usually organic—has many advantages. Tests have shown that mulches help plants grow faster. A 3-inch layer of mulch helps controls weeds that compete for moisture and nutrients. It also slows evaporation of soil moisture, moderates soil temperatures, spruces up the look of things and adds organic matter to the soil as it decays. Leaf mold, shredded leaves, straw, homemade compost, composted animal manures, pine needles, grass clippings and ground bark are common organic mulches. Where you live helps determine what's available.

Inorganic mulches such as rock, pea gravel and decomposed granite also conserve moisture and reduce weeds, but they do not break down to improve the soil. They are often used as a ground covering around plants in place of lawn or living ground cover.

When applying mulch around trees and shrubs, place it beneath the plant's canopy, and beyond. Make the layer 2 to 3 inches thick. Keep materials from coming in contact with the trunk.

In mild-winter areas, apply mulch after temperatures warm in spring. Leaving the soil bare during winter and early spring allows the soil to warm, which encourages plant growth. Apply mulch before heat gets too intense to reduce moisture loss through evaporation and to modify the soil temperature around the root zone.

In extremely cold areas, a mulch can protect plant roots. Apply mulch to soil *after* the soil freezes, so it will remain frozen until the spring thaw. This way the soil does not alternate between freezing and thawing, which can literally "heave" plants from the soil, exposing their roots and killing them.

Controlling Weeds

The best time to control weeds is before they gain a foothold in your landscape. Advance planning to combat weed growth is an important but all-too-often bypassed step when gardening. Eliminating or controlling weeds creates a less competitive environment for seedlings and young plants. Water and nutrients benefit only your landscape plants, as you intended, not the weeds.

If you are looking for nonchemical means of controlling weeds, a simple, preliminary plan of action will prevent them from taking over. If you can, prepare or treat planting areas (see following text) a few months prior to planting. Treat in late summer for fall planting and in late winter for spring planting. If you don't remove the weeds' seedheads, the cycle of heavy annual weed growth continues. Get in the habit of pulling weeds when you see them, especially when they are young and have yet to form seedheads. But don't drop them back on the ground; this allows them to reseed. Throw them in the trash or add to your compost pile.

Major weed invasions—This is a nonchemical method of control that can be used if you've had serious problems with weeds in the past. It works on the principle that you rid the planting area of weeds by encouraging them to germinate and grow and then kill them all at once.

Using a shovel or rototiller, dig down about 6 to 8 inches, turning the soil over. Grade and level the soil, raking it smooth. Apply enough water so it will reach several inches deep. Now wait and watch the weeds grow. Continue light applications of water for a few more weeks, until weeds develop into young seedlings. (The rate of growth will depend on warmth and day length.) Remove weeds with a hoe or rake, or pull them, roots and all, before seedheads develop.

Here's another method, usable only in warm weather. Till and water as above, then cover the proposed planting area with clear plastic. This "cooks" the weeds. Leave cover in place for several weeks, securing the perimeter with rocks. The heat kills weeds and weed seeds near the soil surface.

Minor weed invasions—If your soil is generally free of weed seeds, follow this "less-is-more" method. The idea is to disturb the soil as little as possible, so fewer weed seeds germinate. Test your soil for proper drainage beforehand. (See page 26.)

Do not rake or dig the soil. Get rid of weeds as they appear, pulling by hand.

Chemical Control of Weedy Grasses

Common Bermudagrass and nutgrass are two of the most troublesome weeds in the arid West, seeming to take hold in all irrigated areas, especially those watered with spray heads. Pulling by hand or trimming is seldom effective. Spraying the chemical glyphosate (a common trade name is *Roundup*) on the grass when it is actively growing—late spring to early fall—is one of the most reliable treatments, but repeat sprays will probably be required. A new chemical spray, *Manage*, also shows some promise as being effective on nutgrass. It was recently registered for use in California. Check in other states for availability. Treatment for the two sprays are similar. Spray on a windless day, and do not allow spray to fall on landscape plants. Protect surrounding plants by shielding them with sheets of cardboard. Avoid watering after applications. Follow all product label directions.

Plants and Cold Temperatures

The ability of a given plant to tolerate freezing temperatures is called *cold hardiness*. A variety of factors influence how much cold a plant can tolerate: maturity of the plant, duration and intensity of freezing temperatures, protection provided by other plants and structures, whether the plant is actively growing or dormant and hardened off to cold, and genetic characteristics of the plant. Many common arid land trees such as hybrid mesquites and some acacias will grow as long as temperatures and cultural practices encourage growth, regardless of daylight hours. Such trees are especially prone to frost injury from sudden cold fronts or rapid drops in temperatures. Their tissues have not had time to harden off prior to the cold.

Hard freezes pose special challenges. A survey was conducted by William Kinnison in 1978 at Central Arizona College after a hard freeze that reached 24F to 15F. Results were published in *Desert Plants*. His study showed that *Acacia aneura, A. berlandieri, A. craspedocarpa, A. stenophylla, Prosopis chilensis, Pithecellobium flexicaule* and *P. mexicana* survived the freeze. Warren Jones reported on the effects of the same freeze in northern Sonora, Mexico (also published in *Desert Plants*), in which *Lysiloma microphylla* var. *thornberi* were damaged by temperatures below 25F; *Olneya tesota* were damaged at 20F.

Trees and shrubs planted in lawns that are overseeded with winter grasses create special problems. An overseeded lawn requires large amounts of water and fertilizer during a season when many trees and shrubs should receive little of either. It's best to keep low-water plants out of turf areas altogether.

Protecting Plants from Cold

When the days of hot summer weather draw to an end in September or October, it signals the time to prepare landscape plants for the approaching winter. Begin by gradually reducing irrigations and stop all applications of fertilizer. Avoid late-season pruning. It may encourage flushes of new growth that will be tender to cold. In most instances it's best to wait until winter before beginning to prune.

Mulches

Mulches improve the growing environment of your plants. In a recent study conducted by the University of Arizona, trees provided with a 3-/12 inch layer of mulch produced trunk growth almost 150% greater than trees grown without a mulch.

Remove mulches during winter and early spring so the soil will warm, which encourages plant growth. Apply mulch before heat gets too intense in midspring to reduce moisture loss through evaporation and to cool soil temperatures around the root zone, improving root growth.

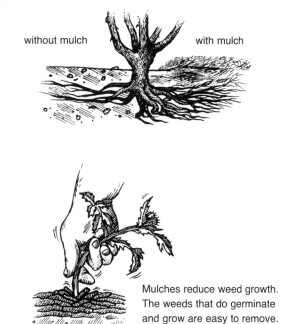

without mulch   with mulch

Mulches reduce weed growth. The weeds that do germinate and grow are easy to remove.

Compost as Mulch

Compost is decomposed organic matter high in nutrients. Fully decomposed compost looks much like rich, dark soil. A backyard compost pile serves a dual purpose. First, it recycles yard and kitchen waste that would only serve to speed the filling of public landfills. In some communities, 50 percent or more of solid wastes are composed of leaves, trimmings and clippings. Second, compost is a superior mulch or soil amendment that is free for the making.

If maintained properly, a compost pile will seldom cause odors or attract flies to bother you or your neighbors. Keep the pile neat with fencing or build a simple bin to contain it. Concrete blocks stacked together work well. Some gardeners make three bins: one to hold fresh, raw material, another for the composting process and another for the finished product.

What you can compost—Leaves, grass clippings (allow them to dry before adding), weeds, trimmings, kitchen refuse such as fruit peelings, coffee grounds and vegetable leavings can all be used. To increase the volume and to add nitrogen to the pile, necessary for the decomposition process, add horse, goat, cow or chicken manure. Be aware that some manures add salts, particularly cattle and horse manure. If your soil tends to be saline, do not use them.

What you shouldn't compost—Avoid materials that compound the problems of western soils. These include salted foods and salt-laden plants such as tamarisk, as well as bones and eggshells—they add unwanted calcium. The same is true of wood and barbecue ashes; they tend to make soils more alkaline. Don't add foods cooked in oil or fat or use meat scraps—they attract animal pests. Bermudagrass and nutgrass can be invasive. Also, avoid using plants or lawn clippings sprayed with pesticides or herbicides.

Prevention in the form of appropriate selection of plants hardy to your region remains the most effective method of avoiding cold injury. Hardiness information on plants is supplied in the Master Flowering and Pruning Chart on pages 67 to 74. Here are a few steps to take to minimize damage.

Cover plants—With a simple covering of blankets, burlap or plastic, heat stored in the soil from the daytime sun is trapped under the cover to keep the tree several degrees warmer than outside air temperatures. Support the cover with some type of framework so it doesn't come in contact with the foliage. Otherwise, leaves that touch the cover may be damaged. Permeable covers can be left on trees during the day if temperatures are moderate. Nonpermeable plastic covers should be removed to prevent excess heat buildup. Some gardeners use spotlights or string outdoor Christmas lights on trees then protect them with a cover. (See photo, page 60.) Be careful when using electricity outdoors, especially if rain is forecast.

Protect young plants—Recently planted plants are particularly susceptible to cold. They require special protection. Because they are small, they are easy to protect by covering them. It is also helpful to provide extra protection around the trunk. Various types of insulating trunk wraps are available in nurseries and garden centers. It is also easy to make your own from newspaper, carpet scraps or other thick material.

Apply water—Turn on sprinklers at the bases of trees and slowly fill basins with water. As the water cools it releases heat, increasing air temperatures around a plant by at least one or two degrees. In extremely cold weather, the sprinkler water may freeze on the tree, covering it with ice and providing additional insulation. However, ice can build up, causing branches to break due to the weight. Likewise, too much water may waterlog poorly drained soil. To be effective for cold protection, the water must be turned on several hours before temperatures reach a critical level and kept running until the danger is over.

Protecting Plants from Cold

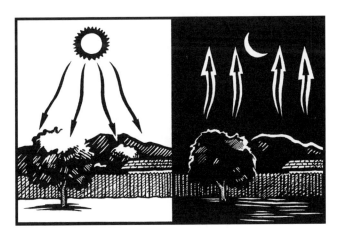

On clear, still nights, heat stored in the ground during the day escapes to the open sky. Severe freezes are much more likely with these conditions if temperatures drop. If it's cloudy, clouds act as a layer of insulation, preventing heat stored in the ground during the day from escaping.

Covering tender plants at night if freezing temperatures are forecast is an effective method of cold protection, most practical with young trees or shrubs. PVC plastic pipe is inexpensive and makes a suitable framework for a cover. Frame keeps cover off foliage, preventing damage. Adding a string of outdoor Christmas lights further increases temperatures around plant. If the cover is nonpermeable, remove it each morning. Heat buildup from the sun can damage plants.

Maximize heat stored in the soil—During the day, the sun shines on the soil, causing it to warm. At night the heat is slowly released, raising the temperature of the surrounding air. By maximizing the amount of heat stored in the soil during the day, more heat will be released at night. Bare, firm soil stores the most heat, so keep the area around your plants free of weeds and remove mulches during winter. Also, wet soil holds more heat than dry soil. Apply water to trees several days prior to cold weather.

Use chemical cold protection—Materials have been developed in recent years that, when sprayed on a plant, may provide some frost protection. Some of these materials are *antitranspirants,* which form a thin, waxy coating on plant leaves. Others are more like bactericides, which usually contain copper-based compounds. In either case, these chemicals help prevent the formation of ice crystals in leaves and may add a few degrees of protection.

Wait to prune if cold damage does occur—If plants are damaged by cold, don't prune leaves or stems—yet. Wait until late spring—after new growth has emerged. In spring you can more accurately detect which branches are actually damaged after new growth has emerged. (See photos, page 60.)

Extremely cold winds and intense sun can damage plants, producing symptoms that are similar in appearance to freeze damage. If the soil is frozen it may prevent moisture from moving through roots and up to branches of the plant. Remove dead wood and heavy sucker growth to prevent stimulating excessive or unwanted new tender leaves and branches that could lead to additional frost damage the following winter.

Identifying and Solving Plant Problems

Clean, healthy plants growing in well-draining soil seldom have serious problems with diseases or insects. This is especially true of native plants, as long as they are planted and cared for properly. In addition, a naturalistic design rarely suffers from pests or diseases due to the diversity of plant species and the wide spacing between plants. When plants are overfed, crowded or stressed by heat or drought problems tend to occur with more frequency.

Step One: What Is the Problem?
It's usually easy to tell *when* plants are not healthy. It is far more difficult to determine *why* they are not growing vigorously and what to do to correct the situation. Sources of problems could range from insects, such as grubs in the soil, diseases, soil conditions, fertilization (too much or too little), herbicide injury, too much or too little water, or extreme weather conditions (freezing, excess rainfall, wind damage or sunburn). Using the wrong control strategy can be expensive and even contribute to the problem. For example, plants with root rot often exhibit wilting symptoms. Viable roots to extract water from the soil have been killed. Applying additional water to treat the wilt symptoms saturates the soil, creating conditions that encourage the disease! An accurate diagnosis of the problem is critical.

A photographer's hand-held magnifying lens (10 to 14 power) is one way to inspect plants for pests and diseases. Be sure to closely examine the undersides of leaves. Inspect plants every week or so to prevent infestations from developing too extensively.

Before beginning any treatments, review the current status of the entire landscape. Have any cultural practices changed recently or recently completed, such as irrigation, fertilizer, pest control or pruning? Have climactic conditions followed seasonal norms, or is the weather in transition, such as winter changing to spring? How are the general health and vigor of neighboring landscapes? Have you seen similar symptoms in past years? Answering these and similar questions may help you zero in on the problem. At the least, it could eliminate some of the possibilities and provide valuable information to a plant care professional.

The overwhelming majority of plant problems are caused by incorrect cultural practices. These include over- or underwatering, overfertilizing, excessive pruning and shallow or deep planting. Environmental conditions such as soil type, soil drainage, incompatible plant mix, heat and sun exposure add to the list. However, be reasonably certain that the changes you make will remedy the problem before making changes in major cultural practices.

If you discover that the problem is caused by an insect pest, consider following the principles of Integrated Pest Management (IPM). It is a program that promotes maintaining a balance between pests and beneficial insects. In home garden situations, landscape plants do not require a regular preventive spray program to control pests. In fact, frequent use of strong pesticides may actually make problems worse by killing natural predators and parasites.

Occasionally, particular insects or diseases may become serious enough that controls are required to save the plants. IPM takes a common-sense approach, calling on natural or least toxic methods first. Stronger measures are used only when the survival of a plant is threatened. To be successful using IPM, you need to know which pests are common to your area, learning their life cycles. Most are vulnerable to control measures at certain stages of their lives. You must also learn to accept some pest damage. Your goal is to achieve a balance of natural organisms, both good and bad.

Pest Prevention

Keeping plants healthy with proper water and fertilizer prevents them from being bothered by many insects and diseases. Overfertilizing, for example, produces lush growth that attracts many insects. Overwatering can promote certain soil-borne diseases. Simply hosing off plants with a strong spray of water will control some common pests, such as aphids or spider mites.

Providing shelter and food sources for beneficial insects (such as ladybugs and lacewings) in and around the landscape helps maintain an ongoing population of the "good bugs." This is necessary for them to be effective over the long term. Doing so means eliminating use of pesticides. Chemical sprays kill the good bugs as well as the bad ones.

Alternative Pest Controls

Gardeners are becoming more concerned with the safety of the pesticides they use around their homes and gardens. At the same time, pesticide registrations are constantly changing. Each year there are fewer effective chemicals available. Luckily, the availability of alternative, less toxic control measures and how they can be effective is increasing. Here are some of the most common.

Biological pest controls—These take advantage of living organisms that prey on plant pests. *Bacillus thuringiensis*, commonly called Bt, is a bacterium that attacks and kills moth and butterfly larvae (caterpillars) but is harmless to humans. Bt is sold under several trade names. It is effective in controlling many caterpillar pests and leafrollers.

Beneficial insects—These are natural enemies of plant pests. Many beneficial insects, such as lacewings and ladybugs, occur naturally and can be encouraged to populate your garden and devour pests. Planting alternative food sources, such as plants in the Umbelliferae family (dill, queen Anne's lace, parsley), will attract and shelter beneficial insects. Ceasing use of potent pesticides helps ensure that beneficial insects stay around to take care of the pests.

Some beneficial insects can be purchased and released in your garden to help control insect pests. Among the most effective are Aphytus wasps. Other beneficials include predatory mites, which feed on spider mites and sometimes attack thrips.

All beneficial insects require specific conditions to be most effective. Timing of release is important, as is the presence of alternative food sources, as mentioned previously. Before buying and releasing beneficial insects, understand their food and shelter requirements, and which pests they are likely to attack.

Botanical insecticides—These are commercially available products derived from plant parts. Common botanical insecticides include pyrethrum, neem, rotenone, ryania and sabadilla. *Pyrethroids* are synthetic pyrethrums. *Pyrethrins* are natural products derived from pyrethrum. In general, these are considered broad-spectrum insecticides, which means they kill many types of pests. Some are more effective against certain pests than others. Once they are applied, they break down quickly. Because their effectiveness lessens with time, repeat applications are often necessary. Even though these are natural controls derived from plants, botanical insecticides are potent sprays that can be poisonous or cause allergic reactions in people. Follow label instructions as carefully as you would with chemical controls.

Insecticidal soaps—These are products that interfere with the membrane activities of many types of pests, including aphids, scale and spider mites. You can purchase them premixed, or make your own soap spray. Mix 2 tablespoons of mild, unperfumed household dishwashing soap in a gallon of water. Thoroughly spray the solution on the entire affected plant. Allow it to remain for an hour or two, then rinse the plant with clean water. Do not use soap sprays on plants that are stressed for moisture or spray during periods when temperatures are over 90F; the spray will burn plant leaves.

Horticultural oils—These work because their coating action smothers insects and their eggs. Summer oils are highly refined and can be used during the growing season. They are especially effective against scale insects. Important: Don't use summer oils on days when temperatures will rise above 85F or when atmospheric humidity will remain below 30 percent. Doing so might burn plants.

Safe Use of Pesticides

Before you use any pesticide, make sure you have correctly identified the pest. If necessary, take samples of the pest or afflicted plant part to a local nursery or cooperative extension office. Once identified, make sure the pest (and plant you are trying to protect) are listed on the product label.

After you've selected the product for control, follow the instructions on the label exactly. You are risking your health and the health of your plants (and are breaking the law!) if you don't. Do not spray on windy days. Do not spray if plants are in need of moisture or leaves may burn. Wear rubber gloves when handling concentrates, and store pesticides in original labeled containers where they are safe and out of the reach of children. Clean sprayers away from plants after use.

Common Insect Pests

Ants—Ants feed on the sugary substance called *honeydew* that is secreted by many insect pests, including aphids, scale and whiteflies. In the process, they fend off natural predators that normally feed on the pest and reduce its numbers. So to control pests such as aphids, it helps to control the ants.

The best way to control ants is to keep them out of plants. Prune branches so that leaves do not touch the ground, then place a barrier around the trunk. Sticky materials, such as the product Tanglefoot, smeared on a strip of paper and wrapped around the trunk, prevent the ants from climbing it. Applying poisonous ant baits around the base of plants also control them.

Aphids—Aphids are common and widespread pests. These tiny, pear-shaped insects suck plant juices, preferring succulent new growth on the tips of branches and twigs. Young leaves that curl and become distorted are signs of aphids. Aphids come in a variety of colors including green, brown and red. Like whiteflies and scale, aphids secrete honeydew, which attracts ants. Honeydew often develops a black fungus called *sooty mold*. After aphids are controlled, the mold goes away. It is also easy to remove with insecticidal soap sprays.

Aphid populations are usually kept in check by a variety of natural predators and seldom require sprays for control. Predators usually show up on their own shortly after the aphid population surges and quickly reduce their numbers to acceptable levels. If aphid outbreaks are severe or if young trees are being attacked, try spraying the foliage with a strong jet of water or apply an insecticidal soap. It may also be necessary to control ants.

Scale—Armored scale, which is protected by a red, brown or black waxy, oyster shell-like cover most of its life, is the most difficult to control. Soft

Some Nonchemical Pest Controls

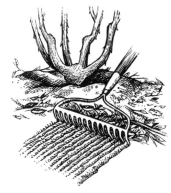

Many pests and diseases can be prevented with regular garden cleanup, eliminating hiding places and breeding grounds.

Pests such as aphids and spider mites can usually be controlled by hosing them off with a strong stream of water. Or, spray with a dilute solution of dish soap, 2 tablespoons to 1 gallon of water.

Trichogramma wasps parasitize the eggs of more than 200 kinds of moths and butterflies.

Ladybird beetles (ladybugs) and their larvae feed on a variety of pests, including thrips and aphids.

Lacewings and their larvae are effective beneficial insects, feeding on many common pests.

scales such as cottony cushion scale and brown soft scale are usually controlled by natural predators.

Scale insects are most susceptible to sprays when in their "crawler" stages. This is when the shells have not yet matured completely and the insects are moving slowly (crawling) on the branches. Summer oils can be effective at that time, as can strong chemicals such as chlorpyrifos and Sevin. Repeated releases of predatory wasps may help control scale, depending on which type is infesting plants.

Slugs and snails—Slugs, and especially snails, feed on foliage and fruit of all types of plants. The easiest way to control them is to exclude them from plants. Wrap the trunk with strips of copper, which neither slugs nor snails will cross. In parts of southern California, decollate snails, which prey on pest snails, are another control. Check with your cooperative extension office to see if they can be used in your county. Trapping snails in trays of beer and under boards also works. Poisonous snail baits are widely available in nurseries and garden centers. Be cautious using these baits if you have children or pets.

Spider mites—Spider mites are small, spiderlike pests that are most troublesome in hot, dry climates. Plants stressed for water are more susceptible. Infested plants have stippled, yellowing leaves. Undersides of leaves often have fine webbing. In most cases, natural predators keep spider mites at bay. In fact, using strong chemical controls almost always makes spider mite populations worse by killing off natural predators. To combat spider mites, wash leaves free of dust, release predatory mites or spray with insecticidal soap or summer oil. Do not use oil sprays if temperatures reach above 85F.

Thrips—These are minute (barely visible with the naked eye) insects that feed on plant leaves. Leaves become twisted and distorted and may drop from branches. In most home gardens, natural predators keep thrip damage to a minimum so spraying is not recommended. In fact, using strong chemicals usually makes problems worse by killing the predators.

Whiteflies—Whiteflies are tiny white flies that suck the juices from leaves and tender stems. They are usually controlled by a variety of naturally occurring beneficial insects and are rarely a serious problem. Like scale and aphids, they secrete honeydew that attracts ants and leads to sooty mold. Heavy infestations usually follow use of strong pesticides.

To control whiteflies, avoid spraying potent pesticides that will kill beneficial insects. Spraying plants with insecticidal soap or summer oil may help reduce whitefly populations. A strong blast of water from the garden hose also disrupts their feeding and dislodges eggs and pupae. Whiteflies are attracted to the color yellow and can be trapped by placing commercially available yellow sticky traps near infested plants. Encarsia wasp is a beneficial insect that attacks whiteflies. Keeping the area around plants clean helps reduce infestations.

Acacia whiteflies feed by scraping at the undersides of leaves, causing a blotchy, yellowing appearance. The insects appear to be dark gray or black because of a large dark spot on the body. They reproduce rapidly and cause significant leaf loss.

Ash whiteflies are 1/8-inch-long pests found in great numbers on the undersides of ash (*Fraxinus* species) leaves. Spray with an insecticidal soap.

Uncommon Insect Pests

The following pests and diseases are not always prevalent throughout the arid West but cause serious problems in certain regions or afflict certain plants.

Eucalyptus longhorn borer—Dark-colored, 1-inch beetle that is becoming a common pest of *Eucalyptus*. Certain species are believed to be more susceptible, including *E. globulus, E. viminalis, E. diversicolor, E. saligna* and *E. nitens*. Signs are oval holes in trunks and branches. Entire trees decline and sometimes die. Leaves remain attached. Regular irrigation practices help prevent. Also avoid pruning May to October when beetles are most active. Seal pruning cuts if pruning is necessary. Infested *Eucalyptus* firewood can help spread the pest, so avoid transporting. No known treatment at this time.

Agave weevil—Grubs and weevils attack the center of agaves, especially the century plant. By the time you notice damage, it is too late. It is best to treat annually during spring to prevent infestations. Apply a soil drench on and around the plant with a solution of diazinon. Follow all label directions.

Flatheaded borers—These pests commonly invade sunburned or otherwise damaged areas along the trunks and branches of trees. Borers are typically more active during periods of drought. The olive-gray adults lay eggs under the bark of damaged areas. Larvae are cream colored and legless and mature to 1 inch long. Maturing larvae feed on dead wood, producing small tunnels called *galleries* filled with what looks like sawdust. This damage occurs beneath the bark and can go unnoticed for long periods. Because the insects are hidden within the wood they are well protected from chemical sprays applied to the tree's surface. Larvae do not attack adjacent healthy, undamaged wood.

Grape leaf skeletonizer—These yellow and black worms that are about 1/2 inch long can quickly defoliate your grapevines. In spring, capture and destroy 1/2-inch, blue-black, slow-moving moths that look similar to wasps; they lay the eggs on the grape leaves. Damage from the worms is easily noticed as the grape leaves literally become skeletons of their former selves. Remove and destroy the worms. Avoid touching the worms because they can cause some skin irritation.

Oleander leaf scorch—Recently discovered bacterial disease believed to be spread by glass-winged sharpshooter, a native leafhopper insect. Symptoms are brown leaf tips, with dieback spreading to branches, then to the entire plant. The bacteria shuts down the plant's water-conducting system, eventually killing the plant. Currently, older plants, 20 to 30 years old, are most affected. In addition to oleanders, other plants may be susceptible. At this time there is no cure. Contact your local cooperative extension service for help with this disease.

Palm borers—These have become a serious pest, attacking *Washingtonia* species, *Brahea armata*, blue fan palm, as well as date palm. How to identify their damage and treatment are discussed as part of the *Washingtonia filifera* description, page 153.

Palo verde borers—These root borers are rarely seen above ground. Adult beetles are typically black, 4 to 6 inches long, with antennae nearly as long as their bodies. Adults are most active in early to midsummer. Immature larvae feed on roots of *Parkinsonia aculeata*, Mexican palo verde, and other trees. Larvae spend up to three years underground feeding on roots. Over 7 to 10 years, palo verde borers will gradually kill a tree. Most adult borer females lay eggs from spring through summer.

Roundheaded borers—Larvae are cream to white in color. Like the flatheaded borers, limited to damaged wood or weakened trees. An exception is the mesquite twig girdler, which girdles and kills small twigs of mesquite trees. The females then lay eggs in the section that is killed, and the larvae develop within the wood. Holes typically observed on trees are the exit

Some Common Pests

Aphids feed on young, tender leaves, often causing them to become distorted. Beneficial insects are effective controls.

Spider mites are tiny pests that cause stippling and yellowing of leaves. Some mites also produce telltale webs.

Thrips are minute pests that distort leaves. The damage is similar to that caused by aphids, above.

Whiteflies are tiny mothlike insects that fly up in a cloud when disturbed.

holes where the mature adults have chewed their way out of the tree. These exit holes are sometimes later occupied by many other noninjurious insects.

With the exception of the palo verde borer, most borers complete their life cycles from egg to adult in about a year. Landscape trees located near areas of mature, undisturbed desert trees are more likely to be attacked by tree borers. Naturally occurring native desert trees can harbor populations of pest insects that can easily migrate into nearby landscape plantings. Keep your native trees as healthy as possible to reduce infestations.

White grubs, sometimes encountered during excavation of the roots of dead trees, usually are not tree borers. These are often the larvae of the common June beetle, which feed on decomposing organic matter.

Palo verde scale—This is a previously unidentified pest of palo verdes recently observed in the Phoenix metropolitan area. To date, it does not appear to cause injury to the trees. Young trees, three to five years old, may require sprays to control foliar insect pests. The damage from these insects can slow growth. Allowing

moderate populations of these insects to survive will help support populations of a number of beneficial insects such as lady beetles and parasitic wasps.

Diseases

Planting plants correctly and keeping them healthy prevents most diseases. Occasionally, disease problems do occur. Here are some common diseases that afflict plants in the arid West:

Armillaria root fungus—Identified by general withering and yellowing of leaves. Commonly infects oaks. Look for small, white, striated fans in between grooves on bark. It is encouraged by moist conditions during summer months. Prevent by not disturbing soil level around trunk, and leaving natural litter around trunk. Avoid spraying trunks with lawn sprinklers. Water deeply and infrequently. For control, contact your state or county extension service.

Texas root rot—Common in former agricultural areas in the Southwest. (Also called *cotton root rot* in some regions.) It is a fungus that attacks and kills the roots

Some Uncommon Pests

Flatheaded borer—Olive-gray adults lay eggs under the bark of damaged areas. Larvae are cream colored and legless and mature to 1 inch long.

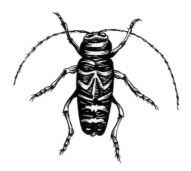

Roundheaded borer—Adults grow up to 4 to 5 inches long. Larvae are cream to white in color and are legless.

Palo Verde borer—Adult beetles are typically black, 4 to 6 inches long with antennae almost as long as their bodies.

Eucalyptus borer—1-inch dark-colored beetles that leave behind oval exit holes in trees.

Palm borer—Reaches 2 to 3 inches long. Eats extensive tunnels throughout the trunk, eventually killing the tree. Exit holes in trunk indicate activity.

of many plants. It comes on when conditions are warm, moist and humid, such as during periods of summer rain. The fungus can sometimes be seen on the soil surface. It looks something like spilled pancake batter, often a cream to tan color. The plant shows symptoms similar to drought because a large portion of the root system has been destroyed. Unable to absorb water, plant leaves droop and become lackluster. Unfortunately, by the time you notice this, the root system is damaged to such an extent that the plant usually dies.

Treatment is not a sure cure. It involves modifying the soil pH (making it less alkaline) and adding organisms that will slow the growth of the fungus.

Loosen soil beneath the canopy of the plant. Apply the following in this area: 2 inches of composted steer manure; ammonium sulfate and soil sulfur, 1 pound each for every 10 square feet. Dig materials into soil to a depth of 6 inches. Water well. Then hope you've cur-

tailed the disease in time. If plant shows serious damage, you might have to prune top growth due to the extensive root loss. Before doing this, contact your cooperative extension service for advice.

Animal Pests

Rabbits, gophers, ground squirrels, moles and deer may find your plants a nice addition to their diets. Sturdy fencing sometimes keeps the smaller critters from eating your plants. But if they are determined to eat your landscape, often your only choice is to select plants they don't like to eat. What animal pests consider suitable fare can depend on what is available to them in the wild. In low-rainfall years when naturally available plant material is scarce, they may eat just about anything your landscape has to offer.

In regions plagued by high animal pest populations, growing plants from the lists below is one way to help keep your landscape intact.

Protecting Against Animal Pests

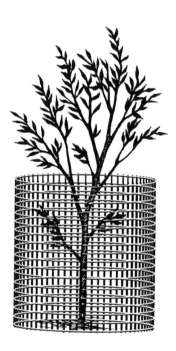

Protecting young plants from rabbits and similar animal pests can be crucial to their survival. Enclose each plant in a cylinder of 1-inch mesh chicken wire or 1/2-inch hardware cloth to a height of at least 2 feet. Bury wire about 6 inches deep to secure and to help protect against burrowing animals.

Rabbit-Resistant Plants

Carissa species
Centaurea species
Dalea greggii
Euryops pectinatus
Fallugia paradoxa
Gelsemium sempervirens
Geranium species
Myoporum species
Macfadeana unguis-cacti
Nandina domestica
Nierembergia species
Nerium oleander
Plumbago scandens
Rhapiolepis species
Rosmarinus officinalis
Salvia species
Santolina species
Thymus species
Vinca major
Westringia rosmarinifolia

Deer-Resistant Plants

Acacia species
Abelia grandiflora
Albizia species
Anosodontea species
Arctostaphylos species
Bougainvillea species
Buddleia species
Callistemon species
Cassia species
Cercis occidentalis
Cupressus species
Dodonaea viscosa
Elaeagnus species
Ficus carica
Gazania species
Gelsemium sempervirens
Heteromeles arbutifolia
Juniperus species
Lantana species
Myoporum species
Olea europaea
Pinus species
Rhus species
Rosmarinus species
Salvia species
Teucrium species

Step-by-Step Guide to Pruning and Care

The following pages feature color photos that demonstrate common pruning methods, from thinning a young tree to cutting back a frost-damaged shrub. You'll also see what happens "when bad things happen to good trees," with topping, incorrect pruning and other miscalculations made by well-meaning gardeners.

The section concludes with photos of landscapes throughout the arid West that demonstrate good design and plant selection and maintenance principles. See pages 62 and 63.

Photo below: Mature trees require little pruning to keep them healthy and attractive. Here a professional arborist is removing mistletoe to prevent it from spreading throughout the tree. With minimum care, this handsome specimen will thrive for decades to come.

Above: An attractive landscape begins with a well-
planned design. Proper
plant selection and spacing
allow plants to grow without
extensive pruning.

Right: It pays to check
stakes and ties often to
prevent serious damage.
Eventually these ties would
have girdled the trunk and
killed a valuable tree.

Below right: Examples of
proper pruning cuts. The
old cut (below left) was
made outside the branch
collar, which allowed the
cut to heal. With time, the
freshly made cut (top) will
do the same.

Far right: When pruning
large branches, it's necessary to use a three-step
process, as shown in the
drawings on page 17.
"One-step" pruning can
cause the branch to tear
down the length of the trunk,
making the tree
vulnerable to insect or disease infestations.

Pruning Young Trees

Above left: Mesquite tree before pruning. Goal is to thin branches and create an overall balanced structure for future growth.

Above right: Branches that cross over or rub another branch are removed.

Left: After pruning, the basic structure begins to show. Prune no more than 20 percent of foliage at any one time.

Above: a wind storm put an end to these *Eucalyptus,* but a poor planting location helped cause their death. Because they were near power lines, both were topped, causing extensive growth that acted as "sails" to catch the wind. Caliche soil also forced their root systems to remain shallow, preventing trees from anchoring.

Above right: Lack of soil area to anchor roots and heavy, umbrella-shaped canopy contributed to this loss. Thinning top growth to allow wind to pass through helps prevent trees from being blown over.

Right: The result of topping trees. The natural form is lost, and stubbed branches are unattractive. Topping stresses trees and shortens their life.

Left: An attractive landscape can add as much as 15 percent to the value of your home. This oak tree was photographed at the National Wildflower Research Center in Austin, Texas. NWRC staff applied dollar amounts to illustrate to visitors the value of a mature, well-cared-for tree.

Below left: This tree has been ruined by improper pruning.

Below: While researching this book, author Eric A. Johnson, right, with Scott Millard, left, came across some unusual plant specimens, such as this *Yucca*.

Step-by-Step Guide to Pruning and Care ■ 53

Above left: Mass planting of Texas rangers in early spring before pruning. Goal is to reduce size of plants, renew growth yet retain natural shape and appearance.

Above right: After pruning, shrubs are smaller, more controlled. Note that sides taper out at bottom to allow sunlight to hit base of plants.

Right: The following summer, the renewed plants put on a brilliant show of flowers.

Left: Many perennials and small shrubs can be cut back severely after flowering so they will regrow with greater vigor the following spring. This combination of *Salvia greggii,* red salvia, *Encelia farinosa,* brittlebush, and *Sophora secundiflora,* Texas mountain laurel, was pruned in early winter.

Below left: Shortly after pruning was completed. Dead flower stalks and tired, old growth have been removed.

Below: Plants regrow and bloom vigorously the following spring on new growth.

Zauschneria californica, California fuchsia, before pruning. Flowering period has ended.

Zauschneria californica, California fuchsia, after pruning. Note new growth that will regrow to produce next year's flowers.

Calylophus hartwegii before pruning.

Calylophus hartwegii after pruning.

Salvia leucantha, Mexican bush sage, before pruning.

Salvia leucantha, Mexican bush sage, after pruning.

Salvia greggii, red salvia, before pruning.

Salvia greggii, red salvia, after pruning.

STEP BY STEP GUIDE

For a more refined appearance, groom plants by removing dried seed pods. Above: pods and stalks of *Salvia clevelandii,* San Diego sage, are trimmed by using hand pruners.

Above right: With some plants, seed pods can be removed simply by shaking the branches.

Right: Tim Gallagher, groundskeeper at Tohono Chul Park, a botanical garden in Tucson, removes seed pods of *Tecoma stans* var. *angustata,* yellow bells.

58 ■ *Step-by-Step Guide to Pruning and Care*

Top, left and right: *Lecophyllum* species and *Simmondsia* are planted too close together. Rather than *shear* plants, individual branches are *thinned* to maintain natural shapes.

Center, left and right: Espalier training allows plants to be grown in small-space gardens. This pyracantha is pruned in late winter to control wayward branches, and to show off its red berries.

Left: Beware! Many plants have sharp thorns. Use leather gloves and goggles for protection when pruning.

Right: When covering plants to protect them from cold, keep the covering from touching foliage. This simple PVC pipe frame draped with clear plastic protects a young citrus tree. Christmas lights inside increases temperatures even more.

Below: If plants are damaged by cold, as with this *Hamelia patens,* wait until plant regrows the coming spring before removing damaged stems and branches. Often, branches that appear dead regrow.

Left: PVC pipe framework works well as a structure to hold screening, keeping birds from getting to harvests before you do.

Above: Plastic netting helps protect pomegranate fruit from birds.

Below left: In rabbit country, wire cages are a necessity to protect new plants.

Below: wide basins allow you to apply water where its needed: to the feeder roots. Organic mulch over the area slows evaporation and cools soil. See drawing, page 8.

Right: Claremont, California, is the home of this impressive *Quercus agrifolia,* coast live oak. *Heuchera* species makes an excellent understory plant beneath the wide-spreading branches.

Below right: A grass lawn can be an appealing part of the landscape, particularly as a cool oasis or play area. This smart design makes good use of backyard space with a small, well-bordered lawn that blends effectively with patio and elevated planter bed.

Bottom right: In Irvine, California, flowering *Bauhinia variegata,* purple orchid tree, makes a colorful scene with curved bed of *Hemerocallis,* daylily, and upright *Kniphofia uvaria,* red-hot poker.

Below: Ornamental grasses are some of the best low-water, low-maintenance plants. Many look exceptional when planted among boulders. This is *Muhlenbergia rigens,* deer grass.

Left: A landscape near San Antonio features *Quercus texana*, Texas red oak.

Above: These *Ferocactus* species in a Phoenix garden work well as accent plants. Also shown are purple- and pink-flowering *Verbena,* yellow *Baileya multiradiata* and red *Penstemon* (background.)

Below: Although this Palm Springs landscape is less than five years old, its design allows plants to grow and thrive with little maintenance.

Gallery of Dry Climate Plants

*T*he range of plants available to western gardeners today is surprisingly broad. In this book, more than 300 varieties are reviewed for their use in gardens, including their pruning and maintenance needs, water use, soil requirements, hardiness to cold and more.

The steadily increasing emphasis on water-efficient landscaping (some call it *xeriscaping*) is gradually altering the appearance of communities in the arid West. The plant categories include introductions from the Chihuahuan and Sonoran deserts of western Texas, New Mexico, Arizona, California, Baja and Mexico, but also a large selection hail from arid regions in Africa, Asia, Australia, the Middle East and Latin America.

Some of the best examples of the new trends in plants can be seen in the miles of median landscaping along freeways and streets. Here you'll see colorful native and introduced trees, shrubs and ground covers that use 50 to 60 percent less water than their traditional counterparts used in the recent past. Home gardeners as well are creating their own imaginative outdoor living areas with these "new" plants. For many adventurous gardeners, growing a new plant species is the thrilling part of gardening. It is a challenge; it is a learning experience. For most it is a pleasure, no matter the outcome.

In considering plants for an area as large and climatically diverse as the arid West, be aware that appearance, mature growth and cultural requirements vary according to climate and location in the garden. For example, recommending that a plant be grown in full sun may be suitable for many regions, but in hot desert areas and warm inland valleys, plants often do better with some afternoon shade. When possible, specific information has been provided. Ultimately, however, you as gardener and caretaker of your plants become the final judge. Observing your plants and reacting to their seasonal needs will go a long way in helping you supply them with what they need to grow and remain healthy.

Opposite: Gardens in the Arid West are not always composed of gravel and cactus. Proper plant selection and a thoughtful design have helped create this lush, inviting garden along the coast near Long Beach, California.

About the Plants in the Gallery

The plants included in this chapter are a blend of the old and the new. I've tried to provide information on plants that are, for the most part, consistent performers in a wide range of western climates. You'll also find a mixture of landscape plant forms, including trees, shrubs, ground covers, vines, grasses and perennials.

You may find shopping for particular plants a frustrating experience, especially if you are looking for recent introductions. Some retail nurseries will order plants for you if you know of a wholesale source. Even if they can't obtain certain plants for you, it's a good idea to communicate an interest in plants they don't have in stock. Perhaps they'll carry them (and similar plants) in the future.

Botanic gardens and arboretums are excellent resources for less-common landscape plants, especially natives. Many gardens hold plant sales once or twice a year. Contact the gardens in your area to find out if and when they sell plants to the public. (Refer to the listing of gardens on page 157.) Native plant societies are also often good sources of plants, and their members offer a wealth of information on plant growth and care.

A Few Thoughts on Landscape Design

Landscaping means different things to different people. Some seek a garden requiring the least amount of maintenance possible, and are content with a few cacti placed in a sea of gravel. Others are happy only with a sweep of lawn backed by smartly trimmed hedges, set off by formal flowerbeds. Others strive toward creating a naturalistic landscape, one in which appropriate plants are selected and placed to recreate the indigenous nature of a region.

Naturalistic gardens are appealing in that once they are given a few years to establish, they require much less care than traditional gardens. Designs are informal, without straight lines or adherence to symmetry. Plants, for the most part, are lightly pruned or left alone so they develop their natural character, much as they would in their native habitats.

A garden composed of native plants takes on the unique identity of the region and the community, while encouraging soil and water conservation. A naturalistic garden helps reduce water use by the very nature of its life cycle. In the arid West, where water is a precious resource, a naturalistic garden is right at home. A naturalistic garden also relies on a balanced approach to pest and disease control, avoiding use of chemical sprays. The diversity of plants and the elimination of sprays create a self-sustaining environment of food, cover and shelter for insects, butterflies, birds and animals.

A naturalistic garden is guided by the seasons and the will of plants to grow, flower and set seed. Such a garden can be more difficult to create than a conventional design composed of lawn, bedding plants, foundation shrubs and trees. In fact, a naturalistic garden may not be for everyone. Some may not enjoy the casual, seemingly haphazard appearance, feeling more comfortable in controlled surroundings.

But it is not necessary to abandon a traditional landscape for a naturalistic garden design. Many gardeners are blending natives with traditional garden plants into existing landscapes.

Even if you plan to design your own garden, no matter what theme you choose, it is wise to obtain guidance from a professional landscape architect or consultant. Study the wide range of low-water use plants and talk to experienced nursery personnel about the specific plants you'd like to grow.

Musings on the Plant Introduction Process
Greg Starr, plant explorer and nurseryman, Tucson, Arizona

Introducing a "new" plant to the landscape industry is a time-consuming process when done correctly. The word "new" is placed in quotes because such plants are not necessarily new to the world even though they are new to the landscape and nursery trades.

Several steps are involved in the introduction of new plants. The first is the collecting and testing of plants, which can be done in any number of ways. A grower can simply visit an area with a climate similar to his market area and collect whatever is growing there. Or a grower can target one specific plant. When collecting new plants, I like to bring back seed and not live plants. This serves two purposes. First and foremost is the minimal impact on the plant population. Second, seed-grown plants have more variation, enabling the grower to select plants that have better qualities.

Plants are grown and monitored for at least five years before growers learn enough about them for release to the landscape and retail nursery industry. Water use, insect and pest problems, growth rate, hardiness and planting exposure are evaluated. Only after these factors have been tested are growers able to determine whether or not the plants are well-suited for release to the landscape and nursery industries.

Master Flowering and Pruning Chart

The traditional time to prune is during the winter, when plants are dormant. But not all plants are pruned during this period. Flowering plants in particular require different timing. In the following you can see at a glance the flowering periods and corresponding best times to prune each plant described in this book.

Woody trees, shrubs, vines, some cacti and succulents generally have more predetermined growth and flowering schedules because they are less influenced by temperature and moisture. By contrast, annuals and perennials are greatly influenced by elevation, moisture and temperature. Because of these variables, flowering periods can vary by a week or two or more. Plants tend to flower later into summer in coastal regions. In hot desert areas, the color season can begin in late winter.

The climate extremes of the arid West likewise delay or accelerate the timing of pruning. For example, in hot desert regions, avoid pruning during the months of June to September to prevent serious sunscald injury to branches and trunks.

Cold hardiness of plants is also extremely variable. The cold tolerances supplied here came from many sources, including plant performance records following severe freezes in Las Vegas, Phoenix, Tucson, the Coachella Valley and other regions. Sometimes a range of temperatures has been supplied to reflect differences in cold hardiness from one region to the next.

Above all, it's important to remember that not all plants require pruning. Many plants, when given ample space and allowed to grow naturally, look attractive if left alone or with minor grooming. Refer to the individual plant descriptions before beginning any pruning task.

The Master Flowering and Pruning Chart is also an excellent aid to planning a garden. Use it to create color combinations, or to plan a design that includes plants that have a wide range of flowering periods.

Plant Name	Cold Tolerance	Flowering Season	Pruning Period
Acacia abyssinica	25F	March thru May	June
A. aneura	20F	March and June and September	October
A. berlandieri	15F-20F	February thru May	June
A. pendula	20F	February thru April	April
A. redolens 'Prostrata'	18F-20F	February thru April	April
A. rigens	20F	February thru April	April
A. salicina	22F	October thru December	March
A. saligna	22F	March thru April	May
A. schaffneri	20F	March thru April	May
A. smallii	10F-15F	January thru March	April
A. stenophylla	18F	October thru November	January
A. willardiana	20F-25F	March thru April	April
Agastache cana	20F	June thru September	February
Agave species	0F-20F	May thru August	September
Ailanthus altissima	0F	April thru May	January
Albizia julibrissin	0F-15F	May thru August	January
Aloe barbadensis	25F	March thru April	May
Aloysia triphylla	32F	May thru August	February
Ambrosia dumosa	10F-15F	April	February
Anisacanthus species	10F	February thru June	October
Anisodontea hypomandarum	25F-28F	Year-round	February

Plant Name	Cold Tolerance	Flowering Period	Pruning Period
Antigonon leptopus	32F	March thru October	December
Aquilegia chrysantha	10F	March thru May	December
Arbutus unedo	5F	May	February
Asclepias subulata	20F	May thru July	February
A. tuberosa	20F	July through September	February
Asparagus species	28F	May thru June	March
Atriplex canescens	0F	March thru May	July
A. lentiformis	10F-15F	March thru May	July
Aucuba japonica	8F-20F	April	February
Baccharis 'Centennial'	10F-15F	September thru November	February
Baileya multiradiata	20F	February thru November	January
Bauhinia blakeana	28F	May thru August	March
B. lunarioides	15F	March thru June	August
B. variegata	25F	February thru April	May
Beaucarnea recurvata	18F-20F	Only with old age	As dead leaves occur
Berlandiera lyrata	10F	May thru August	November
Bougainvillea species	28F-30F	February thru October	February and July
Brachychiton populneus	18F-20F	May thru June	February
Buddleia davidii	0F	April thru August	January
B. marrubifolia	15F	March thru July	February
Caesalpinia cacalaco	20F	September thru February	March
C. gilliesii	10F	March thru September	June and January
C. mexicana	20F	March thru October	June
C. pulcherrima	28F-30F	March thru October	November
Calliandra californica	20F-25F	March thru September	May
C. eriophylla	10F	March thru June; November	May
C. haematocephala	32F	Dec. thru Feb.; Sept. thru Nov.	April and August
C. tweedii	32F	March thru July	February
Callistemon citrinus	20F	March thru August	June
Calylophus hartwegii	15F-20F	March thru September	November
Carissa species	28F	March thru June	May
Cassia artemisioides	18F	December thru April	April
C. goldmanii	15F-18F	May thru September	October
C. nemophila	15F-18F	January thru March	April
C. phyllodinea	22F	January thru March	April
C. wislizenii	10F	May thru September	November
Ceanothus impressus	30F	April thru May	January
Cedrus deodara	5F	None	May
Celtis pallida	15F	June thru August	January

Plant Name	Cold Tolerance	Flowering Period	Pruning Period
C. reticulata	10F	June thru August	January
Cephalantus occidentalis	10F	June thru September	January
Ceratoides lanata	0F	June thru October; January	February
Cercidium floridum	24F	March thru May	June
C. hybrid 'Desert Museum'	15F	March thru May	June
C. microphyllum	15F	April thru May	June
C. praecox (Sonoran origin)	20F	March thru May	June
Cercis canadensis var. mexicana	10F	March thru May	December
Cercocarpus montanus	10F	March thru May	November
Chamaerops humilis	6F	July	August
Chilopsis linearis	0F to 5F	April thru September	November
Chitalpa tashkentensis	10F	April thru September	November
Chorisia speciosa	26F-28F	September thru November; June	February
Chrysactinia mexicana	15F	March thru September	February
Chrysanthemum leucanthemum	10F	June thru November	January
Chrysothamnus nauseosus	-20F	September thru November	December
Citrus sinensis	20F-30F	April thru May	March
Cleome isomeris	15F-20F	March thru May	January
Comarostaphylis diversifolia	25F-28F	March thru April	January
Condalia globosa	15F-20F	March thru April	January
Cordia boissieri	20F-22F	March thru October	August
Coreopsis lanceolata	10F	April thru September	July thru November
Cortaderia selloana pumila	10F	May thru September	January
Coursetia glandulosa	18F-20F	March thru May	January
Cowania mexicana var. stansburiana	0F	April thru June	January
Cuphea llavea	15F-20F	March thru September	June thru November
Cupressus arizonica	0F-5F	None	December
Dalbergia sissoo	20F-25F	April thru May	January
Dalea bicolor var. bicolor	5F-10F	September thru November	February
D. dorycnioides	10F	October thru December; March	April
D. frutescens	0F	September thru November	March
D. greggii	15F-20F	March thru May	February
D. lutea	17F-20F	October thru November	March
D. pulchra	0F-5F	October thru February	April
D. versicolor var. sessilis	10F	March thru May; Sept. thru Nov.	January
Dasylirion wheeleri	0F-10F	July thru August	October
Dicliptera suberecta	25F	February thru October	January
Dietes iridioides	15F-20F	March thru November	January
Dodonaea viscosa	10F	April thru May	October

Plant Name	Cold Tolerance	Flowering Period	Pruning Period
Dyssodia acerosa	5F	April thru September	October
D. pentachaeta	10F	March thru September	December
Echium fastuosum	32F	April thru May	October
Elaeagnus angustifolia	-20F	July thru August	January
Encelia farinosa	15F	March thru April	June
Eremophila decipiens	20F	February thru May	August
E. maculata	25F	March thru June	August
Ericameria laricifolia	10F-15F	September thru December	January
Eriogonum fasciculatum	0F	June thru August	January and February
Erythrina species	25F-30F	March	May
Eucalyptus ficifolia	25F-32F	May thru August	October
E. microtheca	5F-10F	April thru May	August
E. nicholii	12F-15F	May thru June	August
E. sideroxylon 'Rosea'	20F-25F	August thru January	February
E. spathulata	15F-20F	May thru July	September
E. torquata	17F-22F	April thru May	August
Euphorbia biglandulosa	0F	April thru July	September
Fallugia paradoxa	0F	April thru October	January
Feijoa sellowiana	15F-20F	May thru June	January
Ficus carica	20F-25F	May	January
Fouquieria splendens	5F	April thru July	No pruning
Fraxinus greggii	20F	July thru August	January
F. uhdei 'Majestic Beauty'	28F	July thru August	February
F. velutina	10F	July	February
F. velutina 'Rio Grande'	10F	July	February
Fremontodendron californicum	20F-25F	April	January
Gardenia jasminoides	20F-22F	May thru July	October
Gazania rigens	15F	March	January
Geijera parviflora	18F	February thru April	October
Gelsemium sempervirens	15F	January	March
Grevillea robusta	20F-25F	May	October
Hemerocallis species	18F	April thru May; August thru September	January
Hesperaloe funifera	15F	April thru August	October
H. parviflora	-5F	April thru August	October
Heteromeles arbutifolia	15F-20F	June thru July	March
Hibiscus moscheutos	15F	April thru August	November
H. syriacus	15F	April thru September	November
Hymenoxys acaulis	0F	April thru October	January
Hyptis emoryi	20F	April thru June	February

Plant Name	Cold Tolerance	Flowering Period	Pruning Period
Ilex species	0F	May	January
Jacaranda mimosifolia	28F	May or June	August
Juniperus species	0F	June	Winter
Justicia californica	28F	January thru April	January
J. spicigera	24F	January thru May	December
Koelreuteria bipinnata	0F	August	February
Lagerstroemia indica	20F	May thru July	January
Lantana species	28F	March thru November	February
Larrea tridentata	0F	March thru May	June thru July
Lavandula species	15F	June thru November	January thru February
Leucaena retusa	10F	March thru May	January
Leucophyllum candidum 'Silver Cloud'	10F	Summer with Humidity; Fall	Jan. thru Feb.
L. candidum 'Thunder Cloud'	10F	Summer with Humidity; Fall	Jan. thru Feb.
L. frutescens	10F	Summer with Humidity; Fall	Jan. thru Feb.
L. frutescens 'Compacta'	10F	Summer with Humidity; Fall	Jan. thru Feb.
L. frutescens 'Green Cloud'	10F	Summer with Humidity; Fall	Jan. thru Feb.
L. frutescens 'White Cloud'	10F	Summer with Humidity; Fall	Jan. thru Feb.
L. laevigatum	10F	Summer with Humidity; Fall	Jan. thru Feb.
L. langmaniae 'Rio Bravo'	10F	Summer with Humidity; Fall	Jan. thru Feb.
L. 'Rain Cloud'	10F	Summer with Humidity;Fall	Jan. thru Feb.
L. pruinosum 'Sierra Bouquet'	10F	Summer with Humidity, Fall	Jan. thru Feb.
L. revolutum 'Houdini'	10F	October thru December	February
L. revolutum 'Sierra Magic Mix'	10F	Summer with Humidity; Fall	Jan. thru Feb.
L. zygophyllum	5F-10F	Summer with Humidity; Fall	Jan. thru Feb.
Liatris spicata	15F	June thru August	December
Ligustrum species	15F	April thru May	October
Linum perenne lewisii	0F	June thru November	December
Liquidambar styraciflua	0F	May	January
Lobelia laxiflora	0F	June thru September	December
Lysiloma watsonii var. thornberi	25F	May thru June	January
Mahonia aquifolium	10F-15F	April	February
Malephora luteola	28F	April	March
Maytenus boaria	0F	May	January
Melaleuca quinquenervia	28F	April thru May	February
Melia azedarach	0F	April thru May	January
Mimulus cardinalis	0F	June thru August; October	January
Monarda didyma	0F	June thru August	September
Morus alba	0F	April	January
Muhlenbergia capillaris	0F	August thru December	February

Plant Name	Cold Tolerance	Flowering Period	Pruning Period
M. dumosa	20F	March thru May	June
M. emersleyi	10F	August thru December	January
M. lindheimeri	10F	August thru December	January
M. rigens	10F	August thru December	January
Myoporum parvifolium	24F	March thru May	December
Myrtus communis 'Boetica'	20F	April thru May	February
Nandina domestica	10F	April	February
Nerium oleander	18F-24F	March thru October	June
Nolina matapensis	5F-10F	June thru July	October
N. microcarpa	0F	June thru July	October
Oenothera missourensis	0F	March thru May; October	February
Olea europaea	15F	March thru April	February
Olneya tesota	20F-22F	May thru June	October
Parkinsonia aculeata	15F	April thru May	June
Passiflora edulis	28F	March thru August	March thru April
Pennisetum setaceum 'Cupreum'	18F-20F	March thru December	July or February
Penstemon baccharifolius	5F	May thru December	Remove spikes May-June
P. eatonii	18F	March thru April	Remove spikes May-June
P. parryi	18F	March thru April	Remove spikes May-June
P. superbus	5F-10F	April thru May	Remove spikes May-June
Perovskia atriplicifolia	0F	April thru September	January
Phlomis fruticosa	25F	June thru September	November
Phormium tenax	10F	May thru September	November
Photinia species	5F-15F	April-May	December-January
Pinus eldarica	0F	May	Winter
P. halepensis	15F-20F	None	January
Pistacia chinensis	10F	October (fall leaf color)	February
Pithecellobium flexicaule	20F	May thru June	February
P. mexicanum	10F-15F	March thru April	January thru February
P. pallens	20F	May thru June; August	February
Pittosporum phillyraeoides	10F	March thru April	May
Platanus wrightii	0F	October thru November (fall color)	February
Plumbago scandens	20F	April thru August	February
Populus species	10F-15F	October (fall color)	March
Portulacaria afra	32F	May thru June	July
Prosopis alba	15F	April thru May	February
P. chilensis	12F	April thru May	February
P. glandulosa var. glandulosa	0F	April	January
P. glandulosa var. velutina	0F	August thru May	February

Plant Name	Cold Tolerance	Flowering Period	Pruning Period
P. pubescens	0F	April thru May	February
Prunus caroliniana	20F	April thru May	February
Psilostrophe species	15F	March thru November	January
Punica granatum	20F	April	February
Pyracantha species	0F	April	February
Pyrus species	0F	January thru February	March
Quercus agrifolia	10F	April	October
Q. engelmannii	0F	March thru May	November
Q. fusiformis	0F	March thru May	March
Q. gambelii	0F	March thru May	March
Q. ilex	24F	March thru May	March
Q. lobata	-10F	March thru May	March
Q. muehlenbergii	0F	March thru May	March
Q. texana	15F	March thru May	March
Q. virginiana	10F	March thru May	March
Rhaphiolepis species	20F-24F	April thru May	November
Rhus glabra	18F-24F	April thru May	January thru February
R. lancea	15F-20F	April thru May	January thru February
R. microphylla	5F	April thru May	January thru February
R. ovata	5F	April thru May	January thru February
R. virens	5F	April thru May	January thru February
Ribes aureum	0F	March thru May	February
Romneya coulteri	10F	May-July	November
Rosa banksiae	10F	April thru May	February
Rosmarinus officinalis	10F	January thru March	April
Ruellia brittoniana	28F	June thru September	February
R. brittoniana 'Katie'	28F	June thru October	None
R. californica	28F	June thru September	February
R. peninsularis	26F-28F	May thru September	March
Salix babylonica	0F	April	February
Salvia chamaedryoides	15F	April thru October	February
S. clevelandii	20F	April thru June	February
S. columbariae	15F	April thru July	February
S. dorri var. dorri	20F	February thru May	September
S. farinacea	24F	March thru October	January
S. greggii	0F	March thru May; Aug. thru Nov.	January
S. leucantha	24F	February thru June; September	January
S. leucophylla	20F-25F	Sept. thru Jan.; March thru June	Feb. and July
Schefflera elegantissima	32F	March	April

Plant Name	Cold Tolerance	Flowering Period	Pruning Period
Schinus molle	25F-30F	July	February
Sequoiadendron giganteum	0F	None	March
Simmondsia chinensis	15F	April thru June	January
Sophora secundiflora	10F	March thru May	May
Tagetes lemmonii	28F	September thru February	March
Tamarix aphylla	0F	June thru July	March
Tecoma stans var. angustata	20F	March thru June; Aug. thru Oct.	February
Tecomaria capensis	28F	November thru March	April
Thevetia peruviana	30F-32F	April thru September	March
Trachycarpus fortunei	10F	July thru August	September
Tulbaghia violacea	20F-25F	March thru September	October
Vauquelinia angustifolia	10F	June thru August	September
V. californica	15F	April thru May	October
V. pauciflora	10F	May thru Junly	September
Verbena gooddingii	10F	March thru July; September	February
V. peruviana	24F	March thru July; September	February
V. rigida	15F	March thru July; September	February
V. tenera	20F	March thru July; September	February
Viguiera deltoidea	25F	April thru July	June
Vitex agnus-castus	20F	June thru October	January
Washingtonia filifera	18F	May thru July	June and July
W. robusta	25F	May thru July	June and July
Westringia fruticosa	20F	April thru July	January
Xylosma congestum	15F	Minimal show	February thru March
Yucca brevifolia	10F	June thru August	September
Y. elata	15F	May thru August	September
Y. recurvifolia	10F	May thru August	September
Y. rigida	0F	May thru August	September
Y. rupicola	15F	May thru August	September
Y. whipplei	20F	May thru August	September
Zauschneria californica	32F	April thru August	October
Zephyranthes candida	0F	May thru July; Sept. thru Oct.	November
Ziziphus jujuba	0F	May thru July	February
Z. obtusifolia	15F	May thru July	October

Acacia Species
Acacias

Acacias introduced from Australia once predominated in Southern California's coastal and inland valley gardens. Today, many species from Mexico, Africa, Texas and Argentina have become welcome additions to landscapes in the arid West. Worldwide there are over 1,000 varieties of *Acacia*. Some flower beginning in winter and spring; others flower in fall. Flower colors range from yellow (with orange or golden tones) to white and cream colored. Hardiness to cold is 10F to 25F. Most provide filtered shade with refined growth almost tropical in effect. Many are appropriate for courtyards and patios with a height and spread from 15 to 30 feet. All are legumes, and all require low to moderate water.

Acacia abyssinica
Ethiopian Acacia

Native to Ethiopia
Semi-evergreen
20 to 40 feet high, 20 to 30 feet wide
Full sun
Hardy to 25F
Low water use cool months, moderate in
    summer

Trees have open, flat canopies that create filtered shade with a tropical effect. Form can be too fragile for high-wind regions. Slow to rapid growth depending on water and high temperatures. Can achieve 20- to 30-foot spread in just a few years. White flowers bloom in spring. Spines are short or even nonexistent. Fruit pods are 3 to 5 inches long.

Pruning & Maintenance
Winter is ideal time to prune. Train for multitrunk effect. Remove crossing branches and sucker growth. Pods may be unsightly so remove them in summer. Cut back long vertical branches about one-third in youth to develop canopy. Self-fertilizing, so fertilization is not necessary. Irrigate deeply when watering.

Acacia aneura
Mulga Acacia

Native to Australia
Evergreen
20 feet high, 14 to 18 feet wide
Full sun
Hardy to 20F
Low to moderate water use

Mulga is one of the most abundant trees in its native Australia. Airy, lacy quality of the densely arranged, narrow, silver-gray leaves suggests the leaves of an olive tree. Dark reddish brown ascending branches create an umbrella form. In the landscape, plant as well-controlled hedge, small tree or screen planting. A welcome addition to the small-tree palette for courtyards or patios. Flowers are 3/4 inch, sulfur-yellow. They bloom in three to four cycles a year. Heaviest is in spring and in summer after rain.

Pruning & Maintenance
Prune lower branches after two to three years of growth to create a small-tree effect, or allow trees to develop a low, "skirted" profile. Avoid planting in saturated soils, in lawn or with high-water-use plants. Foliage becomes chlorotic when tree is overwatered. In youth, leaving lower branches intact can promote sturdier trunks. As plants age, light thinning after a flowering cycle encourages more flowering branches, but avoid pruning in summer. The 1/2-inch to 3/4-inch seed pod clusters mature after flowering and eventually drop, creating light litter. Grows in low-rainfall areas with clay soils. Moderate growth rate. Self-fertilizing.

Acacia berlandieri
Guajillo

Native to southwestern Texas and
    northeastern Mexico
Evergreen
10 to 15 feet high, equal spread
Full sun
Hardy to 15F to 20F
Low to moderate water use, good
    drainage essential

Lush green, lacy leaves and graceful curved branching patterns create the

Acacia species
Acacia

If you inherit native trees growing in your landscape, it's best to keep surface watering to a minimum. The roots of mature native plants are already deeply established. Too much moisture in the upper layers of soils can cause problems with diseases.

large fern effect often sought in oasis gardens. Like *Lysiloma watsonii*, fern of the desert, *A. berlandieri* produces fragrant, creamy white ball flowers in early spring. Use with larger, more frost-tender or deciduous shrubs. Tolerates partial shade.

Pruning & Maintenance

Because of shrublike habit and tendency toward multiple-trunk growth, young trees require delicate shaping and pruning to achieve desirable small-tree form. Gentle pruning necessary for low-growing shrublike structure. Plant with other shrublike plants at its base to minimize appearance of seed pod litter. A self-fertilizing legume.

Acacia pendula
Weeping Acacia

Native to Australia
Evergreen
15 to 25 feet high, equal spread
Full sun in coastal and inland valley
    areas, afternoon filtered shade in hot-
    summer regions
Hardy to 20F
Low water use on the coast, moderate
    water use in hot-summer regions

A slow-growing legume ideal for small planting areas. Weeping cascade of narrow, blue-gray leaves are actually flattened leaf stalks that grow to 4 inches long, clothing the pendulous branches. Small yellow puffballs appear sporadically in April and May. Plants are more at home along the coast but will grow in low-desert regions with increased irrigation and good drainage. Avoid planting in turf and where heavy winds occur.

Pruning & Maintenance

Minimal pruning required. Remove interior dead twigs or thin so wind can flow more easily through the branches. Prune up lower pendulous branches to allow space for shrub underplantings.

Acacia redolens 'Prostrata'
Prostrate Acacia

Native to Australia
Evergreen
1-1/2 to 2 feet high, to 15 feet wide
Full sun
Hardy to 18F to 20F
Low water use

Excellent on slopes for rapid coverage and erosion control. Impractical near foot traffic areas because of its wide spread. Several selected clones are more prostrate in form, such as 'Desert Carpet', which is cutting-grown and produces no vertical stems. Adapted to cool coastal areas as well as hot inland regions. Yellow flowers bloom in late winter. Plant in winter or early spring, not in hot weather. Space at least 6 to 8 feet apart. Rapid growth crowds out less aggressive plants and overgrows curbs and walks. A legume.

Pruning & Maintenance

Continual pruning may be needed, especially if near other plants and traffic areas or if plants were planted too close together. 'Desert Carpet' grows to less than 1 foot high so it requires little pruning. Drip irrigation ideal.

Acacia rigens
Needle Bush Wattle

Native to Australia
Evergreen
10 feet high, equal spread
Full sun
Hardy to 20F
Low water use

Use as background screen or natural hedge. Foliage is needlelike; branches display interesting angularity that enhances the unusual shrub form. Moderate growth rate. Long yellow flowers bloom in spring, producing heavy coverage for a solid color show. Plant in well-draining soil.

Pruning & Maintenance

Minimum pruning required. With age, remove interior dead wood. Hedge shearing destroys plant's ability to flower. Self-fertilizing.

Acacia salicina
Willow Wattle

Native to Australia
Evergreen
25 to 30 feet high, 15 to 20 feet wide
Full sun
Hardy to 22F
Low to moderate water use

A dark-foliaged tree with semiweeping growth more upright than spreading. Winds create gentle flowing patterns with refined draping branches. A good alternative to the deciduous weeping willow. Cream-colored flowers in late spring. Water deeply but reduce by 50 percent in winter. Prefers deep, well-drained soil to develop substantial supportive roots that create stable growth. Adapted to grow in coastal and desert areas.

Pruning & Maintenance
Plant control is important. Trees need appropriate staking and ties to support heavy growth on main trunk the first two to three years after planting. Minimal pruning can begin after spring flowering. Prune up lower branches to provide space for shrub undergrowth or to mow turf. Dense interior growth develops readily, so thin out interior dead twigs and excess crossing branches to allow spring winds to flow through. Cut back strong vertical stems by one-third in second or third growing season to create fuller form. Avoid heavy pruning that can induce sucker growth. Cut back excess arching branches over several months in spring after flowering as growth surge completes its cycle. Trees are legumes; avoid fertilizing.

Acacia saligna
Golden Wreath Wattle

Native to Australia
Evergreen
20 feet high, 15 to 20 feet wide
Full sun
Hardy to 22F
Moderate water use

Vigorous, rapid-growing *A. saligna* has a denser canopy effect than

A. salicina. Green foliage drapes gracefully, with large, aggressive vertical stems and side growth. Small, light yellow flowers bloom in the spring. Encourage deep rooting to support lush growth. Avoid locating smaller plants near tree base; draping branches can affect their growth unless main trunk side branches are lifted for treelike effect. Use as a background or near water features.

Pruning & Maintenance
Heavy pruning of one main trunk or large side branches induces unwanted sucker growth; stretch out over several months. Topping can destroy natural form. Use 2-inch lodgepole stakes or galvanized pipe stakes during first two to three years as trees develop. Use flexible tree ties and check stakes about once each month to avoid girdling.

Acacia schaffneri
Twisted Acacia

Native to Texas and northeastern Mexico
Semi-evergreen
15 to 20 feet high, 15 to 25 feet wide
Full sun
Hardy to 20F
Moderate water use, low water use when established

Tree has feathery foliage on angular branches and bears yellow flowers in the spring. Appearance is striking against a light-colored wall. Short thorns are visible when leaves go dormant in the fall. Four-inch seed pods are conspicuous when they become woody and dark brown with age. Cut pods off with a pole pruner for a cleaner look.

Pruning & Maintenance
Train early for vertical growth and for an open, spreading canopy. Remove criss-crossing branches. Prune up lower branches to 6 to 8 feet to permit walking under or working near tree and for underplanting to develop. Self-fertilizing. Adapts well to any soil with good drainage. Water deeply in youth to develop strong root system.

Acacia salicina
Willow Wattle

Doing some gardening home-work will help prevent most plant problems from occur-ring. Well-adapted, properly planted plants are naturally more healthy, which makes them resistant to pests and diseases. Research the plants adapted to grow in your area, and become familiar with their cultural requirements. Before buying and planting your landscape, it also helps if you determine what kind of gar-dener you are, or plan to be. How much time do you want to spend pruning, watering and weeding? For some it's a pleasure; for others it's drudgery. Design and plant a garden that suits you.

Acacia smallii
Sweet Acacia

(Acacia farnesiana, A. minuta)
**Native to Texas and tropical
    southeastern Mexico**
Semi-evergreen
15 to 25 feet high, equal spread
Full sun
Hardy to 10F to 15F
**Moderate water use in youth, low water
    use when established**

Used extensively on golf courses, along highways and in commercial and residential settings. Canopy growth of fernlike foliage is often supported by excessive stems. Small, fragrant, orange-yellow puffballs often begin flowering in December in low elevations and continue into late winter. Can be grown as a standard. Develops excessive suckers with summer heat and extensive pruning. Adapts to almost any soil. Avoid planting near pools or landscaped areas because of thorns.

Pruning & Maintenance
Important to begin interior thinning and pruning up of overhead branch-es after winter-through-spring flow-ering. Continue into summer's aggressive growing season. For best appearance and growth, especially near pavement, thin to three trunks to induce more verticality. Remove suckers as they appear on trunks. Consider safety and appearance in locating and controlling trees. Thorny branches are dangerous; flower and seed drop messy. Wear leather gloves when pruning. A self-fertilizing legume. During winter, reduce amount of water supplied by half.

Acacia stenophylla
Shoestring Acacia

Native to Australia
Evergreen
30 feet high, 20 feet wide
Full sun to partial shade
Hardy to 18F
Low water use

Unique, rapid-growing, versatile and hardy in Southwest gardens. Narrow 16-inch leaves hang from horizontal to drooping stems that protrude from vertical branches. A clean tree with minimal leaf drop. Creamy puffball flowers bloom in fall instead of winter or spring as other *Acacia* species. Soft shade patterns create ideal exposure for partial-shade plants. Good around pools. Ideal in small areas or narrow planters.

Pruning & Maintenance
Trees are low maintenance and require minimal pruning with age. Encourage natural weeping effect with strong vertical stems and sil-houette growth. Provide sturdy stakes and ties the first few years then remove them after main trunk can support heavier growth. After several seasons, prune up lower branches to 6 to 8 feet to encourage height, allow branches to drape, and permit shrub underplanting. Topping creates heavy sucker growth that develops into dense, rounded crown. Avoid overwatering, especially in winter. Adapts to most soils. Self-fer-tilizing; additional fertilizer forces excessive growth.

Acacia willardiana
Palo Blanco

Native to western Sonora, Mexico
Deciduous
10 to 15 feet high, 6 to 15 feet wide
Full sun
Hardy to 20F to 25F
Low water use

This is a tree of simple beauty, with weeping, graceful branches that sup-port a sparse crop of leaflets. Cream-colored flowers bloom in the spring. Excellent in small courtyards or nar-row planters.

Pruning & Maintenance
Support young trees with stakes and ties and protect from heavy winds. Moderate growth rate. Whitish, papery bark peels off naturally. Little or no pruning required, simply remove dead branches as needed. Avoid overwatering.

Agastache cana
Bubble Gum Plant, Mosquito Plant

Native to western Texas and eastern
    New Mexico at 5,000 to 6,000 feet
Evergreen
2 to 3 feet high, equal spread
Shade
Hardy to 20F
Moderate water use

Both foliage and flower spikes smell like bubble gum. The leaves are also said to repel mosquitoes. Spikes of bright pink flowers attract humming-birds and hawk moths midsummer to fall.

Pruning & Maintenance
Compact growth is well controlled. Thin lightly before early spring growth. Does well in shady oasis locations. In lower elevations, after-noon shade and moderate supple-mental moisture important.

AGAVE SPECIES
AGAVES

On a 1965 visit to the Desert Botanic Garden in Phoenix, I was introduced to their extensive *Agave* collection. Today, some 100 *Agave* species are available to gardeners throughout the Southwest. The variation in size from small to very large provides a wide range of choices. In the following I've discussed a range of sizes and tex-tures adapted to home garden use. Large species, such have *Agave ameri-cana*, have not been included for the simple fact they grow much too large for most home gardens, and can become hazards if located near foot-traffic areas.

Once you have seen an *Agave* pro-duce its tall flowerhead, it will bewitch you. *Agaves* have the strange habit of dying after flowering, yet baby rosettes are often produced for a new start. Flowering can occur within 5 to 50 years, depending on the species.

Pruning & Maintenance
Plants must have good drainage and low water applied at widely spaced intervals. If using drip or spray emit-ters, place heads on the uphill side of plants. Locate 12 to 18 inches away from base to prevent root rot. Grow in filtered shade or as noted. When dead leaves occur at base of rosette, remove by pulling off or cutting off with a sharp knife.

Agave colorata
Mescal Ceniza

Native to Sonora, Mexico
Evergreen
2 feet high, equal spread
Full sun
Hardy to 15F
Low water use

This medium-sized agave forms low clumps to 2 feet tall by 2 feet across. Its gray-green leaves are short and broad, and are edged with large, dark brown teeth. Flowers are yel-low. Slow to moderate growth rate, depending on how much water it receives.

Agave felgeri

Native to Sonora, Mexico
Evergreen
2 feet high, 2 to 3 feet wide
Full sun
Hardy to 17F
Low water use

Native to a small region in Sonora, Mexico, this is one tough plant. It survives on low rainfall and tolerates full sun without any problems. It has stiff, narrow, green leaves with wickedly sharp spines on the tips. It will form clumps to 2 feet high, spreading 2 to 3 feet wide.

Agave geminiflora
Twin-Flowered Agave

Native to Mexico
Evergreen
2 feet high, 3 feet wide
Full sun to full shade
Hardy to 25F
Low water use

The versatile agave tolerates a wide range of exposures, from full sun to full shade. Forming a 3-foot, symmet-rical rosette of narrow, dark-green leaves, this plant has become a

Reduced Pruning by Growth Control

Home gardener Dan Jewett in Southern California's Coachella Valley uses a simple method of growth control to reduce pruning and maintenance. Plants in his established landscape receive normal watering via drip irrigation during the summer months. Water is turned off in early fall resulting in slower growth. Plants require less pruning and care. They are allowed to grow naturally but receive a once-a-year "clean-up." Spent flowers are deadheaded, and trees and shrubs are thinned to control. Plants are not pruned heavily at any time. Jewett's approach is in direct con-trast with surrounding landscapes that receive abundant surface irriga-tion, with hedges and trees sheared and trained in symmetrical patterns. These formal landscapes require almost weekly care to maintain an acceptable appearance.

favorite selection. The smooth leaves have terminal spines, and usually have fine white fibers along the margins, although this trait is subject to genetic variation. Compared to most other agaves, this species has a rapid growth rate, providing a nice-sized specimen in a short amount of time. Flowers in early summer are green at base flushed with red or purple. Spikes can reach 15 to 18 feet high. Some frost damage can occur in the mid-20sF. Gardeners in cold climates often grow plants in pots so they can be moved to a warmer, protected location when temperatures drop in winter.

Agave murpheyi

Native to Arizona
Evergreen
3 feet high, equal spread
Full sun
Hardy to 10F
Low to moderate water use

Gardeners in colder climates will appreciate this plant's ability to tolerate temperatures down to at least 10F. This Arizona native has narrow, gray-green leaves and reaches 3 feet high and as wide. Plant in full sun.

Agave parryi var. huachuchensis
Huachuca Agave

Native to northern Mexico and
    southeastern Arizona
Evergreen
4 feet high, equal spread
Full sun to filtered shade
Hardy to 0F
Low to moderate water use

Native to the grasslands and oak woodlands of southeastern Arizona and northern Mexico, this subspecies of *Agave parryi* is more widely grown. Plants in containers show heat stress more often than other varieties. On the other hand, we know that it is cold hardy. This medium-sized plant will form a tight rosette of wide blue-gray leaves. It has a moderate growth rate, and plantings multiply to eventually form clumps via offsets to grow to 8 feet across. In hot climates, some light shade will be welcome.

Agave parryi var. truncata

Native to Durango-Zacatecas
    border region in Mexico
Evergreen
3 feet high and 2 feet wide
Full sun to filtered shade
Hardy to 15F
Moderate water use

Generally, this variety of *Agave parryi* has more rounded leaf tips than other species, although you can see quite a bit of variation in the seedlings. Found naturally only along the Durango-Zacatecas border in Mexico, where it grows in grasslands at elevations of around 7,500 feet.

Agave victoriae-reginae
Queen Victoria Agave

Native to the Chihuahuan Desert of
    Mexico from 4,000 to 5,000 feet
Evergreen
1 foot high, 1 to 1-1/2 feet wide
Full sun
Hardy to 10F
Low water use

This petite agave is one of the best choices for containers or small planting areas. Its short, stout leaves are deep green with white markings, forming tight rosettes to 18 inches across. Queen Victoria agave is very slow growing and long-lived, taking several years to reach flowering size.

Ailanthus altissima
Tree of Heaven

Native to China
Deciduous
40 to 60 feet high
Full sun
Hardy to 0F
Low water use, no water once
    established

A tough tree for tough conditions, but one with faults. Strong, rapid, vertical, multitrunk growth to 40 to 60 feet. Subtropical leaves 1 to 3 feet long are resistant to smog. Can be grown in all parts of the United States except extreme north. Accepts most any soil. Trees produce suckers, reseed and male flowers emit a sweetish to fetid odor. Foliage most colorful in late fall and winter.

Albizia julibrissin
Silk Tree

A specimen seen growing in the city of Lancaster, California was over 30 feet tall with vigorous, multitrunk growth. It has thrived for more than 25 years on minimum water.

Pruning & Maintenance
Reseeds easily—remove seedlings as they occur. Remove vertical sucker growth from spreading roots. Thin out excessive vertical trunks at bases of mature trees.

Albizia julibrissin
Silk Tree

Native to China
Deciduous
20 to 35 feet high, 25 to 80 feet wide
Full sun
Hardy to 0F to 15F
Low to moderate water use

A graceful, cold-hardy legume, striking when viewed at a distance. Offers filtered shade. Distinctive, 5- to 8-inch-wide compound leaves alternate on stems, producing a dark green, refined, fernlike effect. Pink flowers bloom in summer. Grow either as a multistem or single trunk. Allow ample space for spreading growth.

Pruning & Maintenance
To form a single-trunk tree, prune when young. To train in umbrella shape, allow lower branches to grow until trunk develops girth to support top growth, then remove low side branches. Select new plants at nursery that are well-established in 15-gallon containers or 24-inch boxes. Plant when trees are dormant during winter. Bare-root trees slow to get started. Flower and seed pods create litter. Remove pods by trimming or knocking them off. Deep irrigate as tree ages. Cut back no more than 20 percent of foliage during dormant season.

Aloe barbadensis
Aloe Vera

Native to Africa
Evergreen
2 feet high, 3 feet wide in clumps
Partial afternoon shade
Hardy to 25F
Low to moderate water use

A favorite succulent touted for its medicinal qualities. Yellow to orange spring flowers supported on 12- to 14-inch, succulent spikes bloom on 3-foot stalks. Structure and form relate well with native plant combinations. Requires good drainage. Thrives in filtered shade of high-canopy trees. An ideal container plant.

Pruning & Maintenance
With age, pups develop around perimeter of mother plant. These can be cut and removed for replanting elsewhere. When clump becomes too large, divide and distribute to friends or plant in containers. Use a sharp knife to separate plants. Air-dry in shade a few days before replanting. After flowering, pull out or cut off old flower stalks.

Aloysia triphylla
Lemon Verbena

Native to Argentina and Chile
Evergreen (with cold protection)
3 to 6 feet high, equal spread
Full sun to afternoon shade
Hardy to 32F
Low to moderate water use

Pleasing and versatile, lemon verbena attracts bees and butterflies, and the leaves are a delightful addition to iced tea and when dried for potpourri. Locate in frost-free areas where lemony leaf and white flower fragrance can be enjoyed. Where temperatures drop below 32F, grow as a container plant to be moved inside in winter.

Pruning & Maintenance
Natural legginess requires tall stems be pruned in late spring and summer or as the seasons move along. If growth looks ragged after late frosts, reduce height by one-third to stimulate new growth. Plant in well-draining soil.

Planting or Transplanting Cacti
When transplanting cacti, it is important to position them so plants face the same direction as they did before they were planted. South and southwest sides of plants have been exposed to more direct sunlight and have become toughened and resistant to sunburn. The north and east sides of the plant are more tender. They will likely sunburn and scar or even rot if exposed to intense sunshine. Before transplanting, mark the north side of each plant with chalk or ribbon and replant with that side again facing north.

Ambrosia dumosa
White Bursage

Native to regions of Nevada, California and Arizona
Evergreen
2 feet high, 3 feet wide
Full sun
Hardy to 10F to 15F
Low water use

From north of Las Vegas to the western Mojave Desert and southwestern Arizona, white bursage is abundant on slopes and mesas 500 to 2,500 feet in elevation. Windblown pollen from sage can be a problem in small garden areas; avoid grouping too many plants in the garden. For best effect, space plants at least 6 to 8 feet apart.

Pruning & Maintenance
Plants seldom need pruning when used in natural landscape designs. Good soil drainage is important.

Anisacanthus species
Desert Honeysuckle

Native to the Chihuahuan Desert of Texas, Arizona, New Mexico, and Mexico
Deciduous
3 to 5 feet high, equal spread
Full sun, south or east exposure in hot, low elevation gardens
Hardy to 10F
Low water use

All species described here have tubular flowers loaded with nectar to attract hummingbirds and butterflies. Orange and red flower clusters of *A. quadrifidus* var. *brevilobus* 'Mountain Flame' and *A. q.* var. *wrightii* 'Mexican Flame' develop greatest show of color in spring and summer until frost. *A. thurberi* is native to Arizona and New Mexico. Its tubular orange and yellow flowers bloom spring and summer. Space plants 4 to 6 feet apart.

Pruning & Maintenance
If plants become too straggly by summer, prune stems back about one-third or less. Do primary pruning after plants go into winter dormancy by cutting back to 6 to 12 inches above ground. Plants regrow rapidly with warm spring weather. *A. thurberi* develops its own form without much pruning.

Anisodontea hypomandarum
South African Mallow

Native to South Africa
Evergreen
3 feet high, 2 feet wide
Full sun, morning sun or filtered shade in hot-summer regions
Hardy to 25 to 28F
Low water use

Flowering season is long—spring through summer and into fall. Orange, 3/4-inch flowers cover the plant. Foliage is soft gray-green. Does well in containers in well-draining soil with moderate water.

Pruning & Maintenance
To develop fuller growth and new wood, gently thin and trim in late winter. Apply light applications of liquid (not granular) fertilizer at least 6 inches away from plant trunk.

Antigonon leptopus
Queen's Wreath

Native to Mexico
Deciduous
6 to 12 feet high, 10 to 20 feet wide
Full sun
Hardy to 32F
Moderate water use

A Southwest favorite for quick cover on walls, fences and trellises. Warm weather brings on abundant pink, red or white clusters (depending on selection planted). The captivating color and 4-inch, heart-shaped leaves serve the garden well in summer. Ideal for hot west and south walls and to screen the sun on overhead trellises. Vines cover readily without training. Once established, plant and root growth continues in greater abundance with each spring renewal. With frost, vines freeze and plant goes dormant.

Pruning & Maintenance
After a heavy frost, cut the branches at ground level and gather the frozen dead growth for disposal.

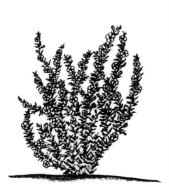

Anisodontea hypomandarum
South African Mallow

Aquilegia chrysantha
Golden-Spurred Columbine

Native to Arizona, New Mexico and
    Texas
Perennial
Flower stems to 2 feet high, basal
    growth 2 to 3 feet wide
Full sun, filtered afternoon shade in
    hot-summer regions
Hardy to 10F
Moderate water use along coast,
    high water use in hot-summer
    regions

Longer-lived than most columbines,
A. chrysantha also blooms longer—
spring into early summer. Yellow
flowers branch off each stem above
fernlike foliage at plant base.

Pruning & Maintenance
After flowering is complete, cut back
flower stems to basal clump to
encourage secondary growth and
bloom. Prune lightly to control any
time. Plant in well-draining, slightly
acid soil.

Arbutus unedo
Strawberry Tree

Native to southern Europe and Ireland
Evergreen
8 to 10 feet high, equal spread
Morning sun or partial afternoon shade
Hardy to 5F
Moderate water use

The deep green foliage is supported
by red stems. White flower clusters
bloom in the fall. Red strawberrylike
fruit follow, which are enjoyed by
birds. A compact form, 'Compacta',
grows 4 to 6 feet high and works well
in small garden areas. Modest
growth is easy to control and blend
with other plants. Use in clusters or
as a single plant. Multitrunked plants
develop best fullness.

Pruning & Maintenance
Growth is compact. Avoid shearing.
Use hand pruner to thin or to remove
interior dead wood as needed in winter. Looks attractive all year.

Asclepias subulata
Desert Milkweed

Native to southeastern California and
    southwestern Arizona from sea level
    to 2,500 feet
Evergreen
3 to 4 feet high, 3 feet wide
Full sun
Hardy to 20F
Low to moderate water use

An unusual, leafless vertical-growing
plant. White, star-shaped flower clusters attract several species of butterflies. Leafless, gray-green foliage produces a heavy, grasslike, yet controlled effect that is especially effective
when placed at bases of large boulders. Attention-getting near dry creek
beds. Cream-colored flower buds.
When seed pods open, they release
numerous fluffy seeds, adding special
interest.

Pruning & Maintenance
With adequate water, plants can be
attractive for a number of years. Lack
of moisture causes stems to deterio-
rate. After several seasons, cut stems
back to ground level in late winter to
encourage fresh regrowth. Recovery
is rapid. Winter water needs are minimal. Good soil drainage important.

Asclepias tuberosa
Butterfly Weed

Native to southwest U. S.
Perennial
3 feet high, 2 to 3 feet wide
Full or partial sun
Hardy to low 20sF
Low to moderate water use

Heavy, grasslike growth creates a
lush vertical effect. Orange flowers
attract hummingbirds and butterflies
in summer. Plant butterfly weed
along side large boulders. Effective
alone, but companion plants such as
Verbena rigida around its base create a
lasting, colorful combination.

Pruning & Maintenance
Cut back to ground level once a
year after stems go dormant with
cold weather. Avoid pruning when
weather is hot.

Asclepias subulata
Desert Milkweed

Asparagus species
Asparagus fern

Native to South Africa
Evergreen
12 to 18 inches high, 3 to 5 feet wide
Full sun or shade
Hardy to 28F
Low to moderate water use

The graceful, fernlike, light green foliage of *Asparagus densiflora* 'Sprengeri' spreads to 5 feet wide on flat ground or drapes 3 to 4 feet long over containers. White summer flowers develop into red berries by fall. Attractive around boulders and at edges of streams and ponds.

'Myers' sends up graceful, 2-foot-long stems that are densely clothed with needlelike, deep green leaves, creating a fluffy effect. A few degrees less hardy than 'Sprengeri'. An attractive container plant.

Pruning & Maintenance
Renew growth every year or two by cutting stems back to 6 inches. This is best done in early spring. Plants regrow quickly with warm weather. If damaged by frost, leaves turn dark yellow to brown. Remove damaged stems after cold weather has passed. Fertilize after cold weather to induce plant to produce rich green leaf color. For 'Myers', prune to remove occasional dead stems at base of plant. Grows in almost any soil but provide good drainage in containers.

Atriplex canescens
Four-Wing Saltbush

Native to California, Nevada, Arizona, New Mexico, West Texas, Utah and Colorado
Evergreen
3 to 6 feet high, 4 to 8 feet wide
Full sun
Hardy to 0F
Low water use when first seeded or planted from container, little or none when established

A minimum-maintenance plant with dense gray foliage. This shrub is used as a fire-retardant and for erosion control in drought conditions. Grows at elevations from sea level to 7,000 feet.

Pruning & Maintenance
Plants develop density once they are established. Cut back anytime to control growth around other plants or trees, otherwise allow natural, bushy growth to develop. Tolerates alkaline soil. Space 8 to 10 feet apart. Place in a staggered pattern for more interest.

Atriplex lentiformis
Quail Brush, White Thistle

Native to alkaline areas of Mojave and Colorado Deserts, San Joaquin Valley and Salinas Valley in California
Evergreen
6 to 10 feet high, 8 to 10 feet wide
Full sun
Hardy to 0F to 15F
Low water use

A handsome, bushy shrub with attractive, dense, gray-green foliage and yellow flower balls. Excellent for tall screening, background, slope stabilization and when naturalized for wildlife habitat. Birds are attracted to the great volume of flowers and seeds. Form improves if given additional water in summer.

Pruning & Maintenance
Grows readily by seeding or can be planted from containers. Thrives where nothing else can grow. Allow ample space for each plant to develop; thin seedlings to 6 feet apart. Little pruning is required unless growth interferes with other plants or traffic areas. To keep plants shapely in close-up garden locations, prune to remove old seed. Avoid summer pruning. Do not place drip irrigation heads on top of rootball or root rot may develop.

Aucuba japonica
Japanese aucuba

Native to Japan and mainland Asia
Evergreen
8 to 10 feet high and 6 to 8 feet wide
Light shade to deep shade., does not tolerate sun
Hardy 8F to 20F
Low to moderate water use

A shady exposure is necessary to grow this plant successfully. Variegated forms develop brown spots if exposed to any amount of sunlight. The gold-splashed leaves, common to a number of selections, provide colorful interest in typically dull shaded areas of the garden. With age, plant develops fullness.

Pruning & Maintenance

Make cuts at nodes when plant becomes irregular or too overpowering in size. Growth rate can be moderate in youth, but full size attained in just two or three seasons. Tolerant of most soils and smog resistant.

Baccharis 'Centennial'

Native to southwest U.S.
Evergreen
2 to 2-1/2 feet high, 3 to 6 feet wide
Full sun, will accept filtered shade
Hardy to 10F
Low to moderate water use

A hybrid of *Baccharis sarothroides*, a desert native, and *B. pilularis*, a coastal native. This reliable ground cover is a desert favorite, prized for its year-round good looks. Growth tends to slow down in summer, but plants do well under both dry and moist conditions if soil drainage is adequate. Deep roots can help prevent erosion on slopes. Plant 4 to 6 feet apart and at least 5 feet away from walks or curbs. When *B. pilularis* is seed-grown, white, fluffy seeds cover female plants in the late fall. Plant 'Centennial', which is cutting-grown, to avoid seeds and reseeding. It also has a more consistent, low, mounding growth.

Pruning & Maintenance

Plants grow so rapidly in the second and third growing season that mounding growth can build up. To avoid, reduce water applied in the winter and spring by 30 percent after plants are established. Trim to reduce height in winter or early spring only. High heat and sun in summer can burn interior growth. Pruning will become a long-term commitment if plants are located too close to walks, curbs or other plants.

Baileya multiradiata
Desert Marigold

Native to deserts of southwest U.S.
Perennial
6 to 8 inches high (basal growth)
Full sun
Hardy to 20F
Low to moderate water use

Stems 6 to 12 inches long on gray-leaved basal growth produce bright yellow, daisylike flowers over a long growing season. Great companion to *Larrea tridentata*, creosote bush; *Encelia farinosa*, brittle bush; *Leucophyllum* species, Texas ranger; and *Ruellia peninsularis*, blue ruellia.

Pruning & Maintenance

In winter, to stimulate new growth for next season's bloom, trim back spent flower stems and previous year's basal growth to 3 to 6 inches. Deadhead old flower stems during the flowering season. Avoid overwatering at any time. Low water use in loam or clay soil. Accepts light, sandy or alluvial soils. Reseeds freely. Volunteers increase the number of plants (and flowers) in the garden each season. Responds to summer rains or irrigation with a flush of flowers.

Bauhinia blakeana
Hong Kong Orchid Tree

Native to southern China
Evergreen
18 to 24 feet high, 12 to 18 feet wide
Full sun
Hardy to 28F
Low to moderate water use

The general appearance of Hong Kong orchid tree, with its large, 5- to 6-inch-wide, orchidlike flowers, produce a more subtropical effect than *B. variegata* (description following). When the leaves have partially shed in late fall and spring, the flower clusters create a show of color darker than that of *B. variegata*.

Pruning & Maintenance

When grown on a patio or courtyard, trees require some light thinning after flowering to control irregular growth.

Baileya multiradiata
Desert Marigold

Remove dead twigs and dead seed pods after flowering. If cold damage occurs, wait until early summer to cut back dead wood due to delayed growth. Protect from heavy winds. Staking typically necessary in youth. A self-fertilizing legume.

Bauhinia lunarioides
White Orchid Tree, Anacacho

Bauhinia lunarioides
White Orchid Tree

(*Bauhinea congesta*)
**Native to south central Texas and
    northeast Mexico**
Deciduous
15 feet high, 12 to 15 feet wide
Full sun, accepts some shade
Hardy to 15F to 18F
Low water use

In the wild, this tree grows in Texas on limestone slopes at 500 to 2,000 feet. Small, butterfly-shaped green leaves develop in the spring. Showy white to pink flower clusters add spring fragrance and color. In Tucson, Arizona, flowers have been seen to bloom in fall as well. Ideal for small gardens and patios. Can be used as an informal hedge or pruned to develop a treelike form by pruning up lower branches. Adapted to a range of climates, from arid to humid.

Pruning & Maintenance
Slow growth keeps plants within limits. Prune only to remove dead twigs and branches after spring flowering has ceased. As with many native legumes, fertilization is not needed. Provide with well-draining soil. Hardiness varies with location. Following recent severe freezes, Las Vegas plants were completely hardy to 15F. In Tucson, plants have been damaged at 17F.

Bauhinia variegata
Orchid Tree

Native to the southern Himalaya region
Semi-evergreen
20 to 35 feet high, equal spread
Full sun
Hardy to 25F
Low water use

Pink to rose, orchidlike flowers create a subtropical effect in spring. *B. varie-gata* can reach 20 to 35 feet high with equal spread—even more in the warmest regions. Moderate growth rate. Broad-lobed leaves. Trees develop well-rounded form and create dense shade with numerous stems. A large tree that is best observed at a distance.

Pruning & Maintenance
Most trees require little pruning due to development of many smaller stems. Trees produce most desirable effect when branches are left to grow from the ground level and up. Prune after spring flowering. Remove unsightly seed pods if desired with long-handled pole pruner. As trees age, remove interior dead wood anytime to improve appearance.

Beaucarnea recurvata
Ponytail Palm, Elephant Foot Tree

Native to Texas and Mexico
Evergreen
15 to 20 feet high, 8 to 10 feet wide
Full sun to partial shade
Hardy to 18F to 20F
Low water use

A favorite accent plant grown for its unusual form. The swollen trunk at base with tufts of graceful leaves attracts attention. With great age, plants can reach 15 to 20 feet. Leaves often measure up to 3 feet in length. Plants remain dwarfish if grown in containers. The swollen base often develops *pups*—young plants—that add more interest. Can be grown indoors with minimal care. Well-suited to tropical or arid themes.

Pruning & Maintenance
A low-maintenance plant, excellent in containers or in the garden with other succulents. Cut out occasional dead leaves. If moving indoor plants outside, locate in partial shade to protect from sunburn. Seems to adapt to almost any well-drained soil.

Berlandiera lyrata
Chocolate Flower

Native to Kansas and Arkansas to Texas,
    Arizona and northern Mexico
Perennial
1 to 1-1/2 feet high with equal spread
Full sun to partial shade
Hardy to 10F
Low water use

From spring into summer, butterflies enjoy the yellow, chocolate-scented flower sprays with bright red veins on undersides. Leaves are green above and whitish underneath. A good companion plant is *Salvia farinacea*, blue salvia.

Pruning & Maintenance
Deadhead spent flowers as you notice them to stimulate new growth and strengthen stems. After flower season has ended, cut leafy rosette back to 6 to 12 inches. Provide with well-draining soil.

Bougainvillea species
Bougainvillea

Native to South Africa
Evergreen
4 to 10 feet high, 6 feet wide or more
Full sun important
Hardy to 28F to 30F
Low to moderate water use

Bougainvilleas thrive on a low-water-use irrigation program, making them great companion plants with dry-climate natives. Surprisingly, bougainvilleas flower more brightly and profusely with less water. Protecting plants from frost prolongs flowering wood in the winter. Plant along warm south or west wall or in containers so plants can be shifted to a warm location if cold threatens.

'La Jolla' is an evergreen shrub form with dark green branches and leaves and rich red flower bracts. Leaf and flower drop is generally heavy, so locate away from pool areas. Or use other shrubs in foreground to catch debris.

'Rainbow Gold' produces a rich color combination of yellow and red.

Vigorous growth blends well with native plants.

'Temple Fire' is bronze-red with shrublike growth to 4 feet high and 6 feet wide. Flowers have a stacked pattern appearance.

Pruning & Maintenance
Plan on at least two or three pruning sessions a year to keep the fast-growing, arching branches under control. Growth is rapid during the summer heat. Harden off plants to cold by not fertilizing in fall prior to the winter season. If frost damage occurs, remove affected branches as new buds break out in the spring.

Brachychiton populneus
Bottle Tree

Native to Australia
Evergreen
35 to 50 feet high, 20 to 35 feet wide
Full sun
Hardy to 18F to 20F
Low to moderate water use

These trees are grown throughout arid, low- and middle-elevation regions for their strong, vertical form. Base of trunk is heavy, with a fast taper to top of tree. Leaf change occurs in late June and early July. New leaf growth pops out quickly in spring, shimmering with any breeze. White flower clusters make a show in early summer shortly after brown seed clusters begin to develop. They often act as weights to create a drooping effect.

Pruning & Maintenance
If trees develop unnatural, narrow, vertical growth for several years and lack normal side branches, it's probably best to remove tree and start over with new plant. Occasional side branch dieback sometimes occurs; remove as needed. Avoid damaging the enlarged central trunk—deep vertical fissures can develop from minor injuries. *Do not use tree spurs to climb trees.* Seed pods can contribute to litter. In Arizona, trees can be susceptible to Texas root rot. Water deeply to encourage deep rooting.

Brachychiton populneus
Bottle Tree

Buddleia davidii
Summer Lilac, Butterfly Bush

Native to China
Deciduous to semi-evergreen
8 feet high, 4 to 6 feet wide
Full sun or light shade
Hardy to 0F
Low to moderate water use

This cold-climate plant is adapted to grow in hot-summer regions. In mid-summer, dense, spiky, fragrant flowers attract butterflies. Flower colors range from white to lilac, blue, purple or pink. They are attractive as cut flowers. Spring growth is vigorous. Dark green leaves are long and narrow with smooth, feltlike, white undersides. Locate plants behind lower-growing plants with similar water requirements.

Pruning & Maintenance
If plants freeze, cut back to ground level. Otherwise, prune naturally after initial flowering in summer to maintain out-of-control growth. Avoid shearing. Good soil drainage important.

Buddleia marrubifolia
Woolly Butterfly Bush

Native to northern Mexico and Big Bend
    region in Texas at 2,000 to 3,000 feet
Evergreen
3 to 5 feet high, equal spread
Full sun to partial shade
Hardy to 15F
Low to moderate water use

Silver-green leaves provide a soft background for the 1/2-inch, aromatic, orange flowers that bloom from early spring into summer.

Pruning & Maintenance
A well-controlled plant. Flowers will be fewer if plants are sheared. Thin only or remove dead twigs after extreme cold. Protect young plants from rabbits. Requires some shade in low deserts; accepts full sun at higher elevations. Plant in well-draining soil.

Caesalpinia cacalaco
Cascalote

Native to Mexico
Evergreen
12 to 15 feet high, equal spread
Full sun
Hardy to 20F
High water use

Lush foliage carries yellow-red flowers at branch ends. Flowers come in winter so plants need a warm winter location such as a south-facing wall with a wide overhang. Thorny—avoid placement near foot traffic. But new growth on older plants is typically thornless. Provide room for the plant to grow freely.

Pruning & Maintenance
Prune after flowering has completed its cycle in winter. Wear gloves to prune. Cut back long center branches to control and to create more flowering wood the first few years. With maturity thin inside growth to provide more exposure to sun. A tropical native that needs abundant water.

Caesalpinia gilliesii
Desert Bird of Paradise

Native to Argentina
Semideciduous
5 to 6 feet high (8 to 10 feet if
    unpruned), equal spread
Full sun
Hardy to 5F to 10F
Moderate water use

Sparse, feathery foliage and an ungainly growth habit discourage use of this plant for close-up viewing. If used as background behind smaller, fuller plants, the yellow flowers with red stamens can be showy. Provides color late spring to fall.

Pruning & Maintenance
During dormancy and just before spring, cut back branches and vertical growth at least 50 percent to stimulate bushiness and new growth. If plants become straggly during early summer, appropriate pruning increases flowering wood. Grows in almost any soil. Not as many flowers as C. *pulcherrima*, but hardier to cold.

A legume capable of fixing atmospheric nitrogen, so supplemental fertilizing is not necessary.

Caesalpinia mexicana
Mexican Poinciana

Native to Mexico
Evergreen
8 to 10 feet high, 8 to 12 feet wide
Full sun
Hardy to 20F
Low to moderate water use

A large, fine-textured, mounding shrub or small tree. Plants respond to summer heat with lemon yellow flowers in clusters along branches. Flowers are most showy in midspring and fall but bloom off and on most of the year.

Pruning & Maintenance
If your goal is to develop a small tree, begin training the vigorous growth when plants are young. If grown as a large shrub, prune long, lanky branches to create more flowering wood and control size. Heavy pruning—leaving branches 4 to 6 feet above ground after spring flowers cease—cleans up irregular growth and encourages fresh regrowth in spring. Plants prefer well-draining soil. Reduce water in fall to harden off plants prior to cold weather.

Caesalpinia pulcherrima
Red Bird of Paradise

Native to West Indies
Deciduous
8 to 10 feet high, equal spread
Full sun
Hardy to 28F to 30F
Moderate to high water use

From late spring to fall the spectacular, brilliant red and yellow flowers of this plant can dominate a garden scene. Fernlike leaves provide a luxuriant effect from spring until the arrival of winter. Plants go dormant in winter. Due to their deciduous nature, use them as a background with *Cassia* or similar evergreen in the foreground. A favorite in low-elevation deserts and other hot areas.

Pruning & Maintenance
Growth can so exuberant you may need to control plants in midsummer. Major pruning should be done in late winter or early spring after danger of frost has passed. At that time cut plant stems to 6 to 12 inches above ground for complete renewal. Surge of new growth will be vigorous when temperatures warm. Seed pods can be messy. Susceptible to Texas root rot. Accepts most any well-draining soil. When planting, space at 10-foot centers to allow for wide spread. A self-fertilizing legume.

Calliandra californica
Baja Fairy Duster

Native to Baja California
Evergreen
4 to 6 feet high, 4 to 5 feet wide
Full sun
Hardy to 20F to 25F
Low to moderate water use

The refined, dark green foliage of Baja fairy duster can be dominant when combined with other native or subtropical plants. In large, open planting areas plants can be left unpruned for a dramatic effect. Space 8 to 10 feet on centers. Once established, rounded plants grow vigorously. In spring, summer and fall, red puffballs with stamens cover the plant. Hummingbirds are attracted to the flowers.

Pruning & Maintenance
As plants mature in small garden areas, prune naturally with an eye to relative proportions of other plants. Light natural pruning encourages a full skirt from the ground level up. Prune in late spring for rapid recovery. Avoid pruning in hot weather—95F or above. Severe pruning inhibits flowering. Reduce by no more than 20 percent at one time. Small seed pods do not interfere with growth; they gradually drop off and are hidden in the luxuriant foliage. If growth becomes excessive, decrease the water rate. Good soil drainage is important. A self-fertilizing legume.

Legume Demonstration Garden at Boyce Thompson Southwestern Arboretum

The Boyce Thompson Southwestern Arboretum in Superior, Arizona, features a garden devoted to plants in the legume family. It includes leguminous plants native to arid regions around the world.

The plants in the garden demonstrate the potential of legumes as food crops, ornamental plants, sources of nitrogen and cover crops for soil stabilization and improvement. For information on visiting the garden, see the listing of public gardens on page 157.

Calliandra eriophylla
Pink Fairy Duster

Native to California east into Texas
Deciduous
3 to 4 feet high, equal spread
Full sun
Hardy to 10F
Low water use

Growth of this species is compact compared to *C. californica.* Foliage is refined and graceful. The dainty pink flowers are less showy than those of *C. californica.* Flowering season begins in spring, ceases during summer, then comes on again in fall.

Pruning & Maintenance
Minimum care needed. Control natural form by thinning inside thick growth. Avoid shearing. The two-step naturalistic pruning method works well. (See page 19.) Can be cut back to 2 feet high to create a ground cover effect. Space 6 feet apart. Prune only in late spring after flowering for quick recovery. Slow growth rate but regular garden moisture increases rate of growth. Thrives in a variety of soils, even tolerates rocky soil. A self-fertilizing legume.

Calliandra haematocephala
Pink Powder Puff

Native to Bolivia
Evergreen
10 to 12 feet high, equal spread
Full sun; sunny south wall ideal
Hardy to 32F
Moderate to high water use

Large, 2- to 3-inch, pink puffballs of silky stamens provide a dramatic floral display from October into March. Rapid growth. Can be trained as an espalier. Foliage freezes at 32F. Protect from cold with a wide overhang on a south, east or west exposure. Lush, tropical, dark green foliage, with a hint of glossy copper in the juvenile stage, is a distinct contrast to other *Calliandra* species.

Pruning & Maintenance
Rapid growth on established plants requires selective control monthly with hand pruners. Growth can be rampant under the best conditions. To slow growth rate, avoid fertilization or excess moisture in early fall well before cold weather. If frost damage occurs, wait for warming trend, then make cuts below frost damage. Plant in well-draining soil. A legume.

Calliandra tweedii
Trinidad Flame Bush

Native to Trinidad
Evergreen
6 to 8 feet high, 5 to 8 feet wide
Full sun
Hardy to 32F
Moderate water use

The fernlike foliage of this plant relates well to *C. californica* and *C. eriophylla* but it is much less hardy. Growth is rapid after warm spring weather arrives. Graceful plant structure shows off bright crimson flower clusters that produce color from February into fall.

Pruning & Maintenance
To help protect from frost, plant under a wide overhang with a southern exposure. Dense intertwining growth needs thinning to encourage more fresh wood and create more definite branch patterns. Avoid shearing. Do not fertilize or prune in late fall. This encourages tender growth susceptible to frost damage.

Callistemon citrinus
Lemon Bottlebrush

(Callistemon lanceolatus)
Native to Australia
Evergreen
Shrub: 10 to 12 feet high, 10 feet wide
Tree: 15 to 20 feet high, to 15 feet wide
Full sun
Hardy to 20F
Low water use

Adapted to grow along the coast, in inland valleys and in low-elevation deserts, *C. citrinus* accepts poor soils, wind, smog and heat. Deep red flower spikes create a spectacular show in the spring and summer and sporadically at other times. Tree form needs support in youth and deep

Callistemon citrinus
Lemon Bottlebrush

water on a regular basis to develop sturdy roots.

Pruning & Maintenance
For tree form, train main stems early by staking to support heavy canopy growth. Trim crossing interior branches and remove dead wood each year at any time for better appearance. Avoid shearing. Treat for iron chlorosis in late summer if leaves begin to yellow.

Calylophus hartwegii

Native to Arizona, Mexico, New Mexico
    and Texas above 4,500 feet
Deciduous
1 to 2 feet high, 3 to 4 feet wide
**Full sun, afternoon shade in
    hot-summer regions**
Hardy to 15F to 20F
Low to moderate water use

Vibrant, lemon yellow, crinkled flowers combine well with purple verbena and *Salvia greggii*. A low-maintenance, non-traffic ground cover excellent for small areas in shrub borders. Effective around the base of blue-flowering *Leucophyllum* species such as *L. zygophyllum* or under *Cercidium floridum*, blue palo verde. Blooms spring through fall. 'Sierra Sundrop' is a commonly available cultivar.

Pruning & Maintenance
Cut plants back in early spring before new growth develops or in early winter as plants go dormant. Reduce amount of water applied in heavy clay soils or caliche soils. Avoid cultivating around established plants or root damage may occur. Plant 2 to 4 feet apart. Grows in almost any soil.

Carissa grandiflora 'Tuttlei'
Prostrate Natal Plum

(*Carissa macrocarpa*)
Native to South Africa
Evergreen
2 to 3 feet high, 3 to 4 feet wide
Full sun
Hardy to 28F
Moderate water use

One of many species with evergreen, flowing, glossy, dark green foliage.

Bears fragrant, white, star-shaped flowers in early summer. A valued foreground plant popular as a ground cover on slopes, as a border and among boulders.

Pruning & Maintenance
Prune to remove damaged wood after frost. Avoid shearing. If brown-edged leaves look messy; remove with hand pruners. Warm spring weather brings on recovery. Remove erect vertical stems that often develop after new surges of growth. Reduce water in late fall to harden off plants before cold weather.

CASSIA SPECIES
CASSIAS

Cassia species are widely distributed throughout Southern California and in the low- and mid-elevation regions of the Southwest. Plants are hardy to 15F to 25F. All grow at a moderate rate into natural, well-rounded forms reaching 4 to 8 feet high with an equal spread. Yellow flowers are produced in late winter and spring; some species flower in summer and into fall. Flowers are followed by profuse numbers of seed pods.

Many species are native to Australia, including *Cassia artemisioides* (*Senna*), feathery cassia; *C. nemophila* (*Senna*), thread-leaf cassia; *C. sturtii* (*Senna*), stuart's cassia; and *C. phyllodinea* (Senna). *C. goldmanii* is native to Baja California. *C. wislizenii* (*Senna wislizenii*) is a summer-flowering species native to the Southwest.

Plants are low to moderate water users and do best in well-draining soil. It's important to locate plants where they'll receive full sun. The ideal pruning period is after flowering in late winter or early spring. As members of the legume family, plants are able to fix nitrogen from the air.

Use the two-step naturalistic method of pruning as shown on page 19 if you need to control size of plants in small gardens. Otherwise, plants look best without pruning if you have the garden space to accommodate their size.

Cassia phyllodinea
Desert Cassia

Leaves of *Cassia* come in a variety of shapes and textures. From top: *C. phyllodinea*, *C. nemophila*, *C. artemisioides* and *C. sturtii*.

Cassia artemisioides
Feathery Cassia

(Senna artemisioides x artemisioides)
Native to Australia
Evergreen
6 to 8 feet high, equal spread
Full sun
Hardy to 18F
Low water use

Large plant form makes a fine background for tall perennials or dwarf *Dalea* species. The gray-green, feathery leaves blend perfectly with the yellow flowers that appear late winter and spring.

Pruning & Maintenance
Prune to keep plants in proportion in cool weather following flowering. Pruning will also remove some of the brown seed pods, which can also be knocked or shook off. (See photo, page 58.) Prune back up to 50 percent of growth into a natural form after plants have been growing for two or three years. This increases basal growth, which produces an overall fuller effect. Plants can become woody at the bases if strong vertical growth is allowed. Remove criss-crossing interior branches in a staggered pattern to open up centers of plants so sunlight can aid renewal of flowering wood. If plants have ample space, allow them to grow naturally without any control. Plants are susceptible to Texas root rot.

Cassia goldmanii
Goldman's Cassia

Native to Baja California
Deciduous
4 to 5 feet high, equal spread
Full sun
Hardy to 15F to 18F
Low water use

One of several yellow summer-flowering *Cassias*. A fascinating foliage pattern is produced with the onset of new bronzy leaves that eventually turn to dark green. Slow growth rate keeps the plant in proportion in most home landscapes. Blend plants with evergreen *Cassias* or Texas rangers to extend flowering season.

Pruning & Maintenance
Prune after summer flowering or while deciduous in winter. Prune naturally to keep plant form intact. As with all *Cassias* and other shrubs, do not shear into globes or squares. Fertilizing not required; it only induces legumes to develop excessive growth. Ideal location is in well-draining soil in full sun. Space plants 5 feet apart.

Cassia nemophila
Bushy Senna, Green Cassia

(Senna artemisioides x filifolia)
Native to Australia
Evergreen
4 to 8 feet high, equal spread
Full sun
Hardy to 15F
Low water use

This *Cassia* has a refreshing, refined appearance. Yellow flowers that come in late winter and spring are followed by brown seed pods.

Pruning & Maintenance
With drip irrigation, typical height and spread can increase 25 to 50 percent. Space 8 feet apart in well-drained soil. More hardy to cold than *C. artemisioides*. Susceptible to root rot. Begin training plants during the first and second growing season using the pruning method described on page 19. This helps encourage full growth, especially at the basal level. Space 8 to 10 feet apart to allow for the plant's natural spread, which will also yield the most spectacular floral results. Remove brown seed pods with a light natural pruning or knock them off after seeds set to improve appearance. A legume; not necessary to fertilize.

Cassia phyllodinea
Desert Cassia, Silvery Cassia

(Senna artemisioides sub. petiolaris)
Native to Australia
Evergreen
6 feet high, equal spread
Full sun
Hardy to 22F
Low to moderate water use

Gray-green, sicklelike leaves shimmer in the wind, creating a fuller effect than *C. nemophila.* In late winter to spring, yellow flowers literally cover the plant.

Pruning & Maintenance
Because growth is more compact, there is less need for heavy shearing or pruning. Prune when flowering is complete in late winter or early spring while weather is cool. This also reduces brown seed pods. Basal growth develops more fully as plants age and with appropriate pruning. Well-draining soil important. Susceptible to Texas root rot. Space plants 8 feet apart. A legume.

Cassia wislizenii
Shrubby Senna

Native to southeastern Arizona, southern New Mexico, and western Texas at 3,000 to 5,000 feet
Deciduous
6 feet high, 8 feet wide
Full sun
Hardy to 10F
Low to moderate water use

This is a tough plant that tolerates salinity, alkalinity, some flooding and even neglect. Bright yellow flower clusters bloom June to September against a background of dark, gray-green, 1-inch leaves. Early growth is slow, but after a season or two plants develop with more vigor. Plants are slow to leaf out in spring. Deciduous *C. goldmanii* is a valued companion plant. It is also a summer bloomer with more compact growth and colorful leaves.

Pruning & Maintenance
Although normal growth requires little pruning, you may want to direct growth at base of plant to enhance more fullness in this area. Wood is hard, making it tough to prune. Use the method recommended for *C. phyllodinea.* Prune only during winter dormancy period. Accepts most soils, including limestone. Easy to transplant. A legume, so fertilization not needed.

Ceanothus impressus
Santa Barbara Lilac

Native to coastal region of Santa Barbara
Evergreen
6 to 8 feet high, 12 to 15 feet wide
Full sun
Hardy to 30F
Low water use

Most *Ceanothus* species grow best on slopes that have good drainage and receive minimum summer watering. *C. impressus* develops dense, tall growth. In the spring, flower clusters of dark blue create a rich background for other plants.

Pruning & Maintenance
A plant that basically is best if left alone. With time, dead wood may build up inside the plant. Even so, keep pruning to a minimum. It often disrupts the plant's growth cycle. Avoid using drip irrigation or bubblers; watering with a hose is preferred. Rocky, well-draining soils ideal.

Cedrus deodara
Deodar cedar

Native to the Himalayas
Evergreen
60 to 80 feet high, 30 to 40 wide
Full sun
Hardy to 5F
Moderate water use

Deodar cedar has proven to be the most adaptable *Cedrus* species for the arid West. Trees can grow 60 to 80 feet high with plants spreading 30 to 40 feet wide at the base. Plants are evergreen (conifers) with a hardiness to 5F. Full sun important.

Pruning & Maintenance

For smaller gardens, select 'Descanso Dwarf', which grows 20 to 25 feet high in 12 to 15 years. You can also prune for size reduction by cutting side branches back by 50 percent to keep plants in proportion. In hot, arid regions prune at least 6 to 8 weeks before late spring and summer temperatures come on.

Celtis reticulata

Celtis pallida
Desert Hackberry, Granjeno

Native to south central Arizona, western Texas, southern New Mexico and Baja California at 1,500 to 4,000 feet
Evergreen (except with extreme cold)
8 feet high, 10 feet wide
Full sun
Hardy to 20F
Low water use

Spiny, intertwining branches make this an ideal security plant. Its dense green foliage also is useful as a hedge or tall screen that looks attractive without pruning. Provides good erosion control. Small green and yellow flowers bloom in late spring, followed by red to orange berries in the fall. In winter, birds are attracted to the shelter plants provide as well as the berries. Leaves drop at 20F.

Pruning & Maintenance
Little pruning required except to control rank vertical or side growth. If excessive moisture is applied this is more common. Moderate moisture helps control pruning. Wear heavy gloves when you prune.

Celtis reticulata
Western Hackberry

Native to Arizona, New Mexico and Texas along streams and valleys at 2,000 to 6,000 feet
Deciduous
10 to 40 feet high, equal spread
Full sun
Hardy to 10F
Moderate water use

This handsome, cold-hardy tree forms a canopy of graceful branches covered with thick green leaves that cast dense summer shade. The gnarled, undulating branches and unusual corky bark provide landscape interest. Trees perform best when planted in deep soil in middle or high elevation.

Pruning & Maintenance
Prune up lower branches if planting shade-loving plants underneath or to provide space for walking. Remove dead or crossing branches during winter.

Cephalanthus occidentalis
Buttonbush

Native to Texas and other areas from Canada to Mexico
Deciduous
20 feet high, 10 to 15 feet wide
Full sun
Hardy to 10F
High water use

A sunny location encourages a long period of flowers, from June to September. Globe-shaped flowers are white or pale pink, 1 to 2 inches across. Can grow to become 20-foot-high tree size with constant moisture, such as locations found alongside a lake or stream.

Pruning & Maintenance
Controlling growth takes some dedication, because the plant can become quite twisting as it attempts to grow into a tree form. Plant near a pond, home-made stream bed or where water naturally collects. Unlike most plants included in this book, prefers poor drainage, sand or loam. Reduce garden moisture in winter.

Ceratoides lanata
Burro Fat, Winter Fat

(*Eurotsia lanata*)
Native to eastern Washington to Saskatchewan, southwestern California, western Texas and Baja California at 2,500 to 7,000 feet
Evergreen
2 to 3 feet high, 3 feet wide
Full sun, afternoon shade in hot-summer regions
Hardy to 0F
Low water use

The silvery leaves of burro fat are composed of fruity spikes that glisten in afternoon light and are sure to catch your eye. It can be an interesting backdrop for annuals and perennials as it flowers from May to October. Useful in flower borders and for erosion control. In an eastern Oregon garden, burro fat made the perennial grouping come alive with its glittering foliage. Male and female flowers separate in long, narrow, hairy terminal clusters.

Pruning & Maintenance
To stimulate new growth, prune all stems and foliage near to ground level once a year in late winter. Grows in any type of soil, including alkaline soil.

CERCIDIUM SPECIES PALO VERDES

Palo verde trees are legumes, so the bark on trunks and branches of younger plants can perform 40 percent of the trees' photosynthesis in the absence of foliage growth. Palo verdes produce prodigious quantities of yellow flowers that cover the tree from March through May, depending on elevation. Each species has distinctive characteristics of size, structure and growth rate that make them easy to identify. However, species interbreed to produce a wide variety of forms. Once trees are established, they are considerably drought tolerant. Low to moderate deep watering is recommended in garden situations. All species prefer well-draining soil.

Palo verde trees are relatively clean and the small leaves either blow away or decompose. But they are still too messy to be planted near swimming pools. Avoid heavy pruning. Remove dead wood and crossing branches. Severe pruning creates regrowth problems and tree form becomes unbalanced. Mistletoe hampers growth and can sometimes kill trees. Remove infestations when you notice them.

Cercidium floridum
Blue Palo Verde, Lluvia de Oro, Shower of Gold

Native to the Sonoran Desert in
   Arizona, California, Baja California
   and northern Mexico
Semi-evergreen
35 feet high, 30 feet wide
Full sun
Hardy to 24F
Low water use, moderate in summer

Blue palo verde might well be the most colorful of all desert trees. The strong, multitrunk form with spreading canopy provides filtered shade. If water-stressed, leaves can be absent most of the year. Luxuriant golden yellow flowers in March and April compensate for bareness. Bark on youthful trees is bluish green; with age, bark on main trunk becomes darker. Locate away from pool areas.

Pruning & Maintenance
Trees prefer well-draining soil and depend on deep moisture. Tolerate alkalinity. Allow natural, angular growth. Interior growth can become dense. Remove dead or small crossing branches during winter. Avoid heavy pruning, which interrupts pattern of growth. Wear gloves when pruning. Remove mistletoe when it occurs.

Cercidium hybrid 'Desert Museum'

Discovered in 1984 at the Arizona-
   Sonora Desert Museum, Tucson,
   Arizona
Semi-evergreen
20 feet high, 30 feet wide
Full sun
Hardy to 15F
Low water use when established

This hybrid palo verde combines the best qualities of *Parkinsonia aculeata*, *C. floridum* and *C. microphyllum*. Trees are thornless, have few seed pods and produce very little litter. Trees grow rapidly and can reach 20 feet high in five years or less. Yellow flowers are larger than flowers of any of the three parents. Blooms develop mid-March to May. More follow in June and August. Growth pattern is sturdy and upright, requiring little pruning or staking. If watered in excess, foliage outgrows the root system, making young trees vulnerable to wind loss or damage. Adapted to warmer areas of low and middle elevations.

Pruning & Maintenance
Normal growth pattern is ascending branches in an orderly form. Remove only dead or crossing branches that occur with age. Fertilizer usually is not required.

Cercidium microphyllum
Little Leaf Palo Verde, Foothill Palo Verde

Native to Arizona and Baja California at 500 to 4,000 feet
Semideciduous
10 to 20 feet high, equal spread
Full sun
Hardy to 15F
Low water use

Bark, stems and leaves are yellow-green. In cold or drought, leaflets drop. Greenish yellow flowers appear April through May. Slow growing, but growth rate accelerates with added moisture. Twiggy growth and low canopy provide shelter for wildlife. Ideal as a background for screening.

Pruning & Maintenance
Can take on a craggy look, but judicious thinning shows off trunk structure, excellent as a small patio tree with character.

Cercidium praecox
Sonoran Palo Verde

Native to the Sonoran Desert in Mexico and South America
Semideciduous
15 to 30 feet high, equal spread
Full sun
Hardy to 20F
Low to moderate water use

This tree has captured the interest of tree purveyors for its distinctive, sculptured growth habit, green trunks and long, wispy branches. Branches are typically more thorny than on other species. Grows slowly into a disciplined, 15- to 30-foot canopy. Even as trees age the bark on trunks and branches remains green. Adds color excitement, with vivid yellow flower clusters along angular branches in April and May. The tree provides a strong sense of place. Its clean, organized appearance is distinct from that of other *Cercidium* species. Growth is rapid in youth. Leaf growth is more extensive compared to other two species.

Pruning & Maintenance
Allow trees time to develop natural "angular." form. Interior growth can become dense. Remove small, dead or crossing branches during winter. Avoid heavy pruning, because large cuts seldom heal well. Wear leather gloves when pruning due to sharp thorns. Remove mistletoe whenever it occurs. Does not typically require fertilization.

Cercis canadensis var. mexicana
Mexican Redbud

Native to Texas and Mexico
Deciduous
12 to 20 feet high, 15 feet wide
Shade to full sun
Hardy to 10F
Moderate water use

Most western redbud species grow as small trees. Redbuds are famous for rose-pink flowers in spring and yellow foliage in fall. Growth is rather open and horizontal. This species has small, wavy green leaves that turn clear yellow in the fall. In hottest regions, may require some afternoon shade. In higher elevations, locate in full sun. A graceful addition to any garden.

Pruning & Maintenance
Prune while dormant. Remove crossing and dead branches. With multi-trunk growth, thin out a few vertical stems if they become excessive. Well-draining soil essential. Accepts sand, loam, clay and limestone soils. A legume.

Cercocarpus montanus
Mountain Mahogany

Native to foothills and mountains below 6,000 feet in southwest U.S.
Evergreen
5 to 20 feet high, 10 to 15 feet wide
Full sun
Hardy to 10F
Low water use

Leathery leaves 1 to 2 inches long and have serrated edges. Leaves are white on undersides. A useful natural hedge that can also be trained into a tree. Extremely hardy and drought-tolerant once established. Adapted to cold-winter areas.

Pruning & Maintenance

Allow plant to develop without restraint so that natural branch structure is easily seen. Plants shape themselves quite well. Pruning generally involves removing dead wood. Prefers well-draining soil. Accepts dry conditions once established.

Chamaerops humilis
Mediterranean Fan Palm

Native to the Mediterranean
Evergreen
8 to 12 feet high, 6 to 10 feet wide
Full sun
Hardy to 6F
Low to moderate water use

The dwarfish size and slow to moderate growth of this palm make it ideal for small gardens or for container culture. An accent plant that accepts most soil types and tolerates climates from coast to desert. The fan-shaped leaves have a distinctive gray-green color and form. Blends well with other dry-climate plants and natives that have compatible moisture requirements.

Pruning & Maintenance

A low-maintenance plant. Remove lower leaves at palm base as they turn brown. Most develop pups as they mature. These can be kept or removed and replanted. If left alone, plants develop multiple-stem growth. If you remove pups, make cuts close to main trunk.

Chilopsis linearis
Desert Willow

Native to the Chihuahuan, Mojave and
   Sonoran deserts
Deciduous
15 to 18 feet high, equal spread
Full sun
Hardy to 0F to 5F
Low to moderate water use

One of the most colorful summer-flowering trees for the home garden. 'Lucretia Hamilton' has showy, dark purple flowers. 'Burgundy' and 'Rio Salado' are other selections grown for their flower color. Growth is

dwarfish. Bloom period is long, from spring through summer and into fall. Summer appearance is graceful and willowy. As flowers go to seed and leaves drop, long seed clusters become evident. Use as a specimen or group with other arid plants.

Pruning & Maintenance

Prune in winter when branches are bare and structure is visible. Branch and trunk structure of the natural multitrunk form is graceful. Some thinning of excess vertical stems is worth the effort. Avoid heavy cuts or suckering will occur. For a clean, neat look during winter through spring, remove seed pods with a pole pruner. Plant in well-draining soil.

Chitalpa tashkentensis
Chitalpa

Native to Russia
Deciduous
20 to 25 feet high, 20 feet wide
Full sun
Hardy to -10F
Moderate to high water use

This plant is a hybrid of *Chilopsis linearis* and *Catalpa bignonioides*. The large clusters of lavender-pink, trumpet-shaped flowers come from the catalpa tree. Tolerance for the tough desert climate comes from desert willow. Grows rapidly with single or multiple trunks. Strong vertical growth provides some canopy shade. Presents a litter problem in early winter. Use in a mini-oasis or transition area of the garden. Does best with well-draining soil.

Pruning & Maintenance

Clean out dead branches or rid tree of seed pods during January or February, while tree is dormant. If trunks develop sucker growth due to heavy pruning, remove excess during dormant period. Avoid topping at any time. Allow tree to develop to express its natural beauty, but tip-prune ends of branches if growth becomes excessive.

Chilopsis linearis
Desert Willow

Chorisia speciosa
Silk Floss Tree

Native to Brazil's rain forest
Semideciduous
30 to 60 feet high, 25 to 35 feet wide
Full sun
Hardy to 26F to 28F
Moderate to high water use

Abundant pink and wine red blooms create a spectacular show of color in fall and early winter. Leaves drop before flowers bloom. In hot-summer regions, it's helpful to plant new trees in beds amid 8- to 10-foot shrubs to protect green trunks from sunburn. Otherwise, whitewash the spine-studded trunk up to 6 to 8 feet during the first and second years. To avoid cold damage, locate in warmest microclimates. (See page 11.) Establishing takes a year or two.

Pruning & Maintenance
Trees have a habit of sending out branches in strange directions. Tip prune new growth to promote fullness. Avoid topping. Do not damage tender bark with ladder. Do not use climbing spurs to climb tree because bark on trunk is easily damaged. Cut off sharp spines if necessary to six feet above ground in foot-traffic areas. Good soil drainage a must.

Chrysactinia mexicana
Damianita

Native to western Texas and northeastern Mexico at 2,000 to 7,000 feet
Evergreen
2 feet high, equal spread
Full sun
Hardy to 15F
Low water use

A quality plant with a long bloom period. Plants bear a strong resemblance to *Ericameria laricifolia,* turpentine bush, which provides yellow color from September to November. Damianita bears similar daisylike flowers from April to September, providing a great way to extend the garden color season. Compact, needle-like growth also strongly resembles that of turpentine bush. Foliage has a pleasant fragrance that is difficult to describe.

Pruning & Maintenance
After a long flowering season, gentle pruning of spent flowers produces a fresh appearance. Avoid overwatering. Grows well in caliche as well as sandy soils, but good drainage is important. Fall planting ideal.

Chrysanthemum leucanthemum
Oxeye Daisy

(*Leucanthemum vulgare*)
Native to Europe
Perennial
2 to 3 feet high, equal spread
Full sun to partial shade
Hardy to 10F
Low water use

Oxeye daisy has naturalized in many areas of the United States. White flowers with yellow centers bloom summer into fall. Performs well above 2,000 feet; provide partial shade in lower desert areas. Blends well with other wildflowers. Good in perennial beds and boulder beds.

Pruning & Maintenance
For a neat appearance, deadhead flowers as they occur on long stems. In winter dormancy, clean up basal growth and cut back old flower stems. Plant in well-draining soil.

Chrysothamnus nauseosus
Rabbit Bush, Chamise

Native to western U.S. from Canada to Mexico at 2,000 to 8,000 feet
Evergreen
4 feet high, equal spread
Full sun, summer shade in hot-summer regions
Hardy to -20F
Low water use

A well-rounded evergreen shrub. From September into November, when few plants are in bloom, yellow flowers cover entire plant. In hot-summer regions, plants tend to go dormant and need some shade during warmest periods.

Pruning & Maintenance
After flowering, late fall and winter, growth becomes straggly. Cut back

Chorisia speciosa
Silk Floss Tree

Chrysothamnus nauseosus
Rabbit Bush

well-established plants to 12 inches above ground in late fall (after bloom) for a refreshing surge of new growth in spring. Accepts most soils. Protect young plants from rabbits.

Citrus sinensis
Citrus

Native to many regions in the world
5 to 25 feet high, 30 feet wide
Full sun
Hardiness varies according to
    citrus type: 20F to 30F
Moderate to high water use

Citrus trees are available in a range of plant sizes, shapes and textures, not to mention the many kinds of fruit produced. Plant selection and location in the landscape are important to growing citrus successfully. It's especially important to learn the low winter temperature in your area to determine if citrus can survive the winter cold.

Pruning & Maintenance
As citrus trees mature, their attractive globular shape develops naturally. Young trees in the first three to four years often develop strong vertical shoots that create off-balanced forms. Cut back to maintain the shape of the tree. Sucker growth may develop below the graft union and where heavy cuts have been made on large branches. Remove in both cases. Selectively remove dead branches when they occur in the tree's interior and remove crossing branches. This type of pruning keeps center of tree more open.

Most pruning should be done in spring. Avoid pruning during extreme summer heat, or branches and fruit may suffer from sunburn.

Trees allowed to grow with full skirts to ground level have fewer problems with sunburn, and roots are also protected from extremes of hot sun.

Cleome isomeris
Bladder Pod

(*Isomeris arborea*)
Native to central California interior
    valleys, western edge of Mojave
    Desert into Riverside County

Evergreen
3 to 4 feet high, equal spread
Full sun, accepts some shade
Hardy to 15F to 20F
Low water use, especially during
    summer dormancy

From January through May, the well-rounded plants are covered with bright yellow, snapdragon-like flowers borne in clusters at the tips of branches. The inflated capsules, the "bladder pods," create interesting clusters that enclose and shelter the seeds. Flowers are good sources of nectar for hummingbirds and bees. Great companion as a light green-foliaged backdrop to *Salvia greggii*, red salvia; *Encelia farinosa*, brittle-bush; and *Justicia* species.

Pruning & Maintenance
Little pruning (if any) required in low-water situations. More pruning required if plants are supplied with regular moisture. Pods not a problem and drop off readily. Shape by tipping long stems. Well-draining soil important.

Comarostaphylis diversifolia
Summer Holly

Native to coastal Baja and Southern
    California
Evergreen
6 to 8 feet high and wide as shrub; 16 to
    18 feet high as small tree
Full sun at coast, afternoon shade inland
Hardy to 25F to 28F
Low water use during summer; moder-
    ate rest of year

The appearance of summer holly is like a madroñe, with its white flowers in spring and red berries in the fall. Leaves are dark green above, gray and textured beneath. A controlled tree for the small garden or courtyard. Rounded form maintains its size well. Adapted to coastal region and inland valleys.

Pruning & Maintenance
Seldom requires heavy pruning. Prune selectively, removing interior deadwood or stray vertical branches should they occur, during winter. Avoid overwatering, especially during summer.

Young citrus trees are more susceptible to cold damage. Wrap the trunks with carpet scraps, newspaper or other insulating material for additional protection when frost threatens.

Planting A Boxed Tree

When planting a boxed tree, don't remove the box before placing the tree in the planting hole. Place tree, box and all, in the hole. Make sure bottom of hole is level and firm for base of box.

Do not remove the bottom of the box before planting. It provides a solid base that helps keep the rootball from settling, shifting or breaking. The bottom gradually decomposes and won't inhibit rooting or water penetration. Add soil to the hole halfway up the sides of the box before removing the sides. This will help support the rootball and prevent it from cracking. Continue to add soil, gently firming around rootball until soil level of the ground is the same as it was in the box.

Condalia globosa
Bitter Condalia, Security Plant

Native to sandy washes along the Colorado River east and west of Yuma, Arizona, and in California
Deciduous
8 feet high, 8 to 10 feet wide
Full sun
Hardy to 15F to 20F
Low water use

Dense intertwining branches are full of sharp spines. Ideal for hedging and for a wildlife shelter. Best used in outlying areas of the garden. Growth at head height offers effective security with no pruning needed for long periods. Small, white to green flowers that are fragrant bloom March and again in October and November.

Pruning & Maintenance
Space plantings at 8 to 10 feet on centers. Grows best in sandy soil or in other soils with good drainage. Wear leather gloves and goggles as protection from the sharp spines.

Cordia boissieri
Anacahuita, Mexican Olive

Native to Rio Grande Valley in Texas and northeast Mexico
Evergreen
10 to 16 feet high, 12 feet wide
Full sun or partial shade
Hardy to 20F to 22F
Low to moderate water use

Numerous, 2-inch, white flowers in clusters bloom spring into summer and again in October and November. They are striking accents against the large, lush, green leathery leaves. Fruit drop occurs quickly after flowering. Grow as a small tree, ideally with an underplanting to conceal leaf debris. Multiple-stem plants produce a wider canopy.

Cordia parvifolia, littleleaf cordia, is a similar but smaller version with smaller leaves and small white flowers. Plants grow 4 to 6 feet high with a similar spread. Growth is more open and airy.

Pruning & Maintenance
Little if any pruning required unless a stray branch or two juts out beyond the tree form. The thicker the foliage growth the greater the show of flowers. With age, remove the small dead interior twigs and branches. Avoid shearing or flower loss will occur. Trees in hot-summer areas develop well in full sun even with intense heat. Plants tolerate wind if protected by a high wall or evergreen windbreak.

Coreopsis lanceolata
Lanceleaf Coreopsis

Native to meadows east of the Mississippi River and in southern U.S.
Perennial
1 to 1-1/2 feet high, 2 feet wide
Full sun
Hardy to 10F
Moderate water use

From spring into early summer, bears a profusion of brilliant yellow, daisy-like flowers with yellow centers. Lush green growth is abundant at the base of plants. Adapted to grow in all western gardens. Plants self-sow profusely.

Pruning & Maintenance
Deadhead spent flowers in early summer as spring bloom completes its cycle. Cut plants to 6 inches above ground in the fall. Plants regrow with another round of flowers in the spring. Grows well in a wide range of soils.

Cortaderia selloana pumila
Dwarf Pampas Grass

Native to Argentina
Perennial
4 to 5 feet high with 5- to 6-foot plumes
Full sun
Hardy to 10F
Low water use

This selection is three times more dwarf than parent *C. cortaderia selloana*, giant pampas grass. Ideal for small gardens as an eye-catching accent. Plant withstands wind. Powerful root system ideal for erosion control.

Pruning & Maintenance
Cut plumes off near base of plant after bloom cycle is complete. Plants can become straggly by early winter. Cut back to 18 inches every two to three years in late winter. Growth renews quickly in the spring.

Coursetia glandulosa
Coursetia, Baby Blue Bonnet

**Native to Baja California and
    southern Arizona**
Deciduous
8 feet high, 12 feet wide
Full sun
Hardy to 18F to 20F
Low water use

Large, fine-textured shrub best adapted to naturalistic landscapes. Excellent combined with evergreen *Cordia parvifolia*, littleleaf cordia. Clusters of charming, pea-shaped white, yellow and pink flowers bloom in March and April; 1- to 2-inch twisted pods develop soon after.

Pruning & Maintenance
Most-effective form is typical multi-stemmed growth. Remove dead twigs or branches in interior areas when plants are in winter dormancy. If pods persist remove with pole pruners or hand shears. Prefers well-draining soil.

Cowania mexicana var. stansburiana
Cliffrose, Quinine Bush

**Native to regions in Nevada, Arizona,
    New Mexico, Mexico and Mojave
    Desert in California at 3,000 to
    8,000 feet**
Evergreen
6 feet high, equal spread
Full sun
Hardy to 15F to 20F
Low water use

Numerous branches with deeply toothed 1/2-inch, silver-gray leaves create density. Cream-colored blooms look like miniature, five-petaled rose flowers April into June. Small fruit cover the plant with a feathery effect soon after. A great food plant and haven for birds and small animals. Valued in combination with other Southwest native plants to create a natural effect. Indians used the shredded bark and foliage for baskets and cradle boards, clothing and medicine.

Pruning & Maintenance
Use light, natural pruning to control somewhat straggly growth for improved appearance in close-up garden situations. After plants are established reduce winter watering by 50 percent. Well-draining soil important.

Cuphea llavea
Bat-Faced Cuphea

Native to Mexico
Perennial
1-1/2 feet high, 2 to 3 feet wide
Full sun, afternoon shade in hot areas
Hardy to 15F to 20F
Moderate to high water use

A small shrub with vigorous, arching branches. Blooms from early spring to early fall. Flowers are a rare combination of red and purple and have the unusual appearance of a bat face. The flowers are persistent and striking combined with the plant's crisp, dark green leaves. Growth is more open and flowering is less prolific in shade.

Pruning & Maintenance
Space plants 4 feet apart. To increase flowering wood and control spread, trim back long branches during growing season. Cease pruning in early fall. Harden off plants in October by reducing water by half and do not fertilize. If frost-damaged, cut back to ground in spring and plants will regenerate. Prune naturally for size as needed after spring growth develops. Provide regular water. Do not allow plants to dry out during any season or they will die. Well-draining soil required.

Cupressus arizonica
Arizona cypress

Native to Arizona
Evergreen conifer
30 to 40 feet high, 25 to 30 feet wide
Full sun
Cold hardy to 0F to 5F
Low water use

Plants provide dense, evergreen growth and thrive in heat. Several selected forms are available. 'Gareei' has silvery green foliage. 'Pyramidalis' is compact and symmetrical. 'Blue Pyramid' has blue-gray foliage with pyramidal form. All are ideal for use as windbreaks.

Pruning & Maintenance
Space new plantings at 8 to 10 feet on centers. Trees develop solid growth pattern from base to top, requiring pruning of side branches only when they interfere with other plants. Thrives in almost any well-draining soil.

Dalbergia sissoo
Rosewood

Native to Sissoo, India
Deciduous
50 to 80 feet high, equal spread
Full sun
Hardy to 20F to 25F
Moderate to high water use

The large size and fast growth of rosewood provide luxurious welcome shade—if you have the space to accommodate it. Appearance is similar to that of *Ulmus pumila*, Chinese elm. The leaves even look similar at a distance.

Pruning & Maintenance
Train young trees to encourage verticality. Thin interior as needed to allow wind to flow through. Young trees typically require staking. With age, remove broken branches as they occur. Prune up lower branches to accommodate understory plants or turf. Roots are vigorous so irrigate plants deeply. Root guards may be required if trees are planted near pavement or curbs. See page 18.

DALEA SPECIES
DALEAS

The versatility of *Dalea* species offers a wide range of blooming periods and foliage textures. They are excellent partners in combination with plants having similar cultural needs. New species are being tested for introduction to the nursery trade. The species currently available are proving to be reliable under a wide variety of conditions. *Dalea* species are now grown as ground covers, dwarfish, 2- to 4-foot shrubs and large shrubs to 5 feet high. The recent introduction of *Daleas* from the Chihuahuan Desert of Texas, New Mexico, Arizona and Mexico has given us useful plants with soft foliage effects and purple to reddish violet, pea-shaped flowers. They provide seasonal color and accept summer heat.

Plants are hardy to 5F. Well-draining soils are preferred. All are low to moderate users of water. Because they are legumes, *Daleas* need little fertilizer.

Dalea bicolor var. bicolor

Native to Mexico
Deciduous
6 to 8 feet high, 5 to 6 feet wide
Full sun
Hardy to 5F to 10F
Low to moderate use

'Monterrey Blue' was selected from a large group of seedlings for its outstanding blue flower color and its fall bloom period. Combine with tall-growing *Leucophyllum* and *Cassia* species. Because it is relatively cold hardy, it can grow at elevations up to 3,000 feet.

D. bicolor var. *argyraea*, silver dalea, has striking silvery leaves. Flowers are purple and yellow. Drought tolerant.

Pruning & Maintenance
Plants grow rapidly. Cut back by one-third during the winter dormant period for vigorous growth in spring. Rabbits don't appear to like it. Well-draining soil is important.

Dalea dorycnioides

Native to Mexico
Evergreen
4 to 6 feet high, equal spread
Full sun
Hardy to 10F
Low to moderate water use

The selection 'Cerro Azul' has a growth pattern that is naturally round. Showy spikes of purple-blue flowers bloom for a long period from fall into winter and spring. Its size and flowering habit make a welcome complement when planted with the yellow-flowering *Cassias* and bright red flowers of *Justicia californica*.

Pruning & Maintenance
While this plant was being test-grown, it was found to perform better when cut back severely each year to encourage denser growth and increased flower production. After spring flowers have ceased, cut plants back by 50 percent. Follow this program the first three to four years after planting. Tolerates most soil types, even clay. Not bothered by rabbits.

Dalea frutescens
Black Dalea

Native to Trans-Pecos region in Texas
Semi-evergreen
3 feet high, 5 feet wide
Full sun
Hardy to 0F
Low water

Excellent foreground for tall *Cassia* species, *Leucophyllum* species and *Dodonaea viscosa*. Yellow-green leaves make an attractive background for its clusters of pink-purple flowers late summer and fall. Partial leaf drop occurs in cold or drought conditions. 'Sierra Negra' is a superior selection.

Pruning & Maintenance
If desired keep plants dwarf by pruning with a natural, flowing look. Prune in early spring before the surge of regrowth. Plant in well-draining soil. Self-fertilizing legume.

Dalea greggii
Prostrate Trailing Indigo Bush

Native to Texas and Mexico
Semi-evergreen
1-1/2 feet high, 6 to 8 feet wide
Full sun to partial shade
Hardy to 15F to 20F
Low water use

This rapid-spreading ground cover with the refined gray foliage is a proven performer in many situations. It controls erosion on steep slopes or creates a low, mounding, billowing appearance. Small purple flowers bloom during spring and fall.

Pruning & Maintenance
For new plantings, space at 4 to 6 feet on centers and at least 6 feet from curbs, walks or other plants. Plant in soil with good drainage. A gallon-size plant can cover 6 to 10 square feet in one season. After a few years, plants begin to develop a mounding habit and lose their flat look. Shear into old wood to 6 inches above ground level in early spring to create fresh growth and a more groomed appearance. New growth will develop as temperatures warm. Recovery is rapid. Old wood can build up within three years so it's often best to cut back plant to renew before it reaches a woody stage. Prune to control as needed or plants grow like a slow-moving lava flow to smother nearby accent plants or dwarfish plants. A self-fertilizing legume.

Dalea lutea
Yellow Bush Dalea

Native to northeastern Mexico
Evergreen to semi-evergreen
4 to 5 feet high and as wide
Full sun to partial shade
Hardy to 17F to 20F
Low to moderate water use

Bright yellow flowers are attractive against the lush, deep green foliage. They come on in late fall when little else is in bloom. 'Sierra Moonrise' is the most-common cultivar.

Wide-spreading Ground Covers
When locating wide-spreading ground covers such as *Dalea greggii*, place well away from curbs and walks. This not only reduces time spent cutting plantings back on a regular basis, but plants remain much more attractive when they are not sheared or trimmed to fit a space.

Pruning & Maintenance

After flowering has ceased, prune back by 50 to 60 percent to maintain a flowing, natural form. This encourages more profuse spring growth. When used with other plants provide ample room for the 6- to 8-foot spread. Rabbits will eat this species if their normal food sources are not available. Well-draining soil is preferred.

Dalea pulchra
Indigo Bush, Pea Bush, Bush Dalea

Native to northern Sonora, Mexico, and southern Arizona at 3,000 to 5,000 feet
Evergreen
3 to 5 feet high, 6 feet wide
Full sun
Hardy to 0F to 5F
Low to moderate water use

Purple flowers bloom from late fall into spring, eye-catching against the refined, silvery-gray foliage. The plant's 4- to 5-foot flowing form gives it a smoky appearance when backlit by the sun. Combine with *D. frutescens, Justicia californica,* and *D. greggii* for effective, large-area plantings.

Pruning & Maintenance

Little pruning required. After two to three years, lightly trim to a natural mounding form after the spring bloom is complete. This creates fresh growth for the coming season. Prune also to control plant height in relationship to companion plantings. Good soil drainage is important. Space new plantings at 6 feet on centers. A legume, so fertilization not necessary.

Dalea versicolor var. sessilis
Weeping Dalea

Native to southwest New Mexico, southern Arizona and Mexico
Evergreen
3 feet high, equal spread
Full sun to filtered afternoon sun
Hardy to 10F
Low water use

This plant is similar in its spreading growth habit to *Dalea greggii,* but mounds grow a little higher. The purple flowers of 'Mountain Delight' provide color in fall and winter.

Pruning & Maintenance

Avoid pruning in spring, summer or fall or flowering cycles are disturbed. Prune lightly in winter after flowering to maintain natural form only if growth is excessive. Rapid growth occurs more frequently with overwatering. A self-fertilizing legume.

Dasylirion wheeleri
Desert Spoon, Sotol

Native to southwest U.S. at 3,000 to 5,000 feet
Evergreen
5 to 8 feet high, 5 feet wide
Full sun
Hardy to 0F to 10F
Low to moderate water use

Plants grow 3 to 5 feet high in youth. Eventually they develop a trunk with plants reaching 6 to 8 feet high. After many years 12-foot flower spikes appear in late fall, although the age when this will occur is unpredictable. Mature plants may bloom every year or every other year. Narrow, gray-green leaves have sharp prongs along the edges. The base of each leaf is spoon-shaped at the point of attachment.

Pruning & Maintenance

As leaves turn brown at base of trunk, pull them off. Wear leather gloves and long-sleeved shirt when working on plants due to the sharp thorns. Cut tall flower stalk after flowering is complete. Tolerates intense sun, aridity, alkalinity, salinity and heat; prefers well-draining soil, especially gravelly or rocky soils.

Dicliptera suberecta
Velvet Honeysuckle

Native to Uruguay
Evergreen
3 feet high, equal spread
Full sun to partial shade
Hardy to 25F
Moderate water use

Dwarfish plant bears tropical, lush, velvety, gray-green leaves and showy orange flowers. They bloom in the spring, summer and fall. Effective in combination with lantana shrubs or ground cover.

Pruning & Maintenance
Lush foliage will spread and become entwined with less-vigorous plants. Thin to control. Harden off plants in the fall by slowly reducing water. Accepts most any well draining soil.

Dietes iridioides
Fortnight Lily

(Dietes vegeta)
Native to South Africa
Evergreen
3 to 4 feet high, 2 to 3 feet wide
Full sun, partial shade in
**   hot-summer regions**
Hardy to 15F to 20F
Moderate water use

Branched vertical stems are topped with white, irislike flowers that bloom spring through fall. Used around boulders or in clusters among perennials as accents.

Pruning & Maintenance
As plant ages, cut out dead leaves at base or dig out and divide for replanting in the fall. Flower stalks live for years and should be removed only after they die out. Well adapted to many soils. Accepts coastal conditions and tolerates heat and wind.

Dodonaea viscosa
Hop Bush

Native to Arizona, Australia, Mexico
**   and South America**
Evergreen
10 to 12 feet high, 6 to 8 feet wide
Full sun
Hardy to 10F
Low water use

If you ever come across this plant growing in its native habitat, you'll notice it presents a rich, bright green contrast to the soft gray or gray-green color hues of nearby native plants. Papery pink fruit add to the surprise. Nursery-grown plants adapt well. Planted in a garden, plants respond to regular water. Can be developed into a small tree or grown as a hedge. Effective in planters or even containers. 'Purpurea', purple hop bush, has bronzy purple leaves and is less hardy: to 20F.

Pruning & Maintenance
Plant reacts well to pruning almost any time but can be grown without pruning in a natural hedge form. Plants develop dense growth. It will take several years to develop size and crown for a small tree form. Whiteflies can infest plants in crowded gardens. Not a long-lived plant in heavy soils. Avoid overwatering.

Dyssodia acerosa
Shrubby Dogweed

Native to southern Nevada, Utah,
**   Arizona, New Mexico and western**
**   Texas at 1,900 to 6,000 feet**
Evergreen
6 inches high, 12 inches wide
Full sun, light afternoon shade in
**   hot-summer regions**
Hardy to 5F
Low water use

A plant with bright yellow flowers that bloom for a long period, April into October. Use in rock gardens and wildflower areas, for erosion control or as a border plant along sidewalks or on patios. Wide range of adaptability.

Pruning & Maintenance
None required except to remove aging plants that appear ragged. Deadhead old flowers in close-up garden areas for a neat look. Plants sometimes reseed.

Dodonaea viscosa
Hop Bush

Dyssodia pentachaeta
Golden Dyssodia

Native to Arizona, southern Texas, New
  Mexico, western Texas and northern
  Mexico
Perennial
6 inches high, 12 inches wide
Full sun
Hardy to 10F
Low water use

Bright yellow, 1/2-inch blooms cover
small, needlelike leaves April
through October. Fine-textured
foliage and vibrant flowers provide
colorful erosion control on slopes or
use as a border planting in flower
beds.

Pruning & Maintenance
Minimal control needed; lightly shear
in early spring to clean up any dormant growth. Plants perform well in
almost any soil.

Echium fastuosum
Pride of Madeira

Native to Island of Madeira
Evergreen
3 to 6 feet high, 4 to 6 feet wide
Full sun, afternoon shade in hot-sum-
  mer regions
Hardy to 30F to 32F
Low to moderate water use

Lush, vigorous, gray-green, hairy
branches support 6- to 12-inch,
flower spikes of purplish blue in the
spring. Informal growth blends well
in dry boulder stream areas or with
Fremontodendron californicum in the
background. Prefers a coastal influence but can accept interior climates
if planted in a relatively frost-free
location.

Pruning & Maintenance
In coastal regions, after plants are
established, hold off on summer
watering. In inland valley gardens,
irrigate weekly. Deadhead flower
spikes after flowering to increase
plant bushiness and to improve
appearance.

Elaeagnus angustifolia
Russian Olive

Native to Russia
Deciduous
15 to 20 feet high, equal spread
Full sun
Hardy to -20F to -40F
Low water use

Russian olive is a hardy performer in
high-elevation gardens. It has naturalized in areas within Arizona to the
extent that it is beginning to crowd
out native plants. It accepts tough
conditions of cold, heat, aridity and
poor soil.
Trees have long branches that typically have an angular growth habit.
Silvery leaves are 2 inches long and
contrast nicely with the dark-hued
bark. In July and August fragrant
green and yellow flowers develop,
followed by small, olivelike fruit. Use
as windbreak or dense hedge.

Pruning & Maintenance
With well-controlled pruning,
Russian olive can be trained into a
handsome tree. Growth is vigorous.
Thin small twiggy growth and suckers from plant interior when plants
are dormant in winter. Watch out for
thorns when pruning. A self-fertilizing legume.

Encelia farinosa
Brittle Bush, Incienso

Native to southern and western Arizona,
  southern Nevada, southwestern Utah,
  Baja California and southern
  California below 3,000 feet
Perennial
3 to 4 feet high, equal spread
Full sun
Hardy to 15F
Low water use

Gray foliage and long-stemmed,
daisylike flowers provide masses of
spring color throughout the
Southwest. Excessive irrigation produces succulent growth, which often
invites aphids to visit.
Encelia californica, California encelia, is
similar with a brown-centered yellow
flower. It is native to coastal areas but
is adapted to grow elsewhere. With

Echium fastuosum
Pride of Madeira

high heat and without regular moisture, both species go semidormant.

Pruning & Maintenance
After flowering ends in the late spring, trim tall flower stems down to leaves. If plants become too vigorous, thin out at least one third before heat arrives. If damaged by frost, remove affected branches in early spring. Harden off plants in early fall to reduce succulent growth before the onset of cold weather. Provide with well-draining soil.

Eremophila decipiens
Poverty Bush

Native to Australia
Perennial
2 feet high, 3 feet wide
Full sun to filtered shade
Hardy to 20F
Low to moderate water use

Bright red, 2- to 3-inch flowers lie flat at the ends of slender green stems and leaves February into May.

Pruning & Maintenance
Tip-prune plants in the fall after summer heat to stimulate new flowering wood. With age, thin if necessary. Good soil drainage important.

Eremophila maculata
Pink Emu Bush

Native to Australia
Evergreen
8 to 10 feet high, equal spread
Full sun
Hardy to 25F
Low to moderate water use

'Pink Beauty' is a recent and useful introduction, often grown as a hedge or screen. Bright green foliage shows off pink flowers in spring. Rationing water applied can help control size and growth rate.

Pruning & Maintenance
Rapid growth increases the need to prune lightly throughout the year, except in winter. Harden off plants before winter. Prune lightly to encourage dense growth habit.

Ericameria laricifolia
Turpentine Bush

Native to southern California, Arizona, New Mexico, western Texas and the Chihuahuan Desert in Mexico at 3,000 feet
Perennial
2 to 3 feet high, equal spread
Full sun
Hardy to 10F to 15F
Low water use

Against strongly aromatic, bright green refined foliage, yellow flowers cover the tips of plants from September to November.

Pruning & Maintenance
When plants become ragged or lanky with age, cut back to near ground level in early spring for denser growth. To improve appearance, remove small branches that die out. If interior stem growth turns brown, strip branches with a glove. Good soil drainage is important. Fall planting ideal.

Eriogonum fasciculatum
California Buckwheat

Native to Arizona, California and Nevada
Evergreen
1 to 2 feet high, equal spread
Full sun
Hardy to 0F
Low water use

This is a valuable revegetation plant in arid climates, from coast to desert. In open, hillside areas plant from containers at 6- to 8-foot centers to allow for natural spread. Gray foliage blends well with desert plants. White to pink flowers that bloom in summer turn dark brown in fall. They provide mottled color against the gray leaves. Use in small-scale gardens.

Pruning & Maintenance
Avoid overhead watering in summer, which encourages downy mildew. Irrigate with hose or drip irrigation. Plants often become leggy and open. New growth developing at the ends of branches makes pruning difficult; best to let plants grow on their own. Prefers loose, well-draining soil.

Irrigating Plants The First Year
Watering new plantings, especially during the first months of summer, is critical. The goal is to keep soil moist but not wet. This usually means staggered applications of slow and deep watering for one day with two or three days off, depending on how rapidly soil drains. This allows necessary oxygen to reach the root zone, and encourages root growth.

Eucalyptus species
Eucalyptus

Erythrina caffra
Kaffirboom Coral Tree

Native to South Africa
Deciduous (for a short time)
25 to 40 feet high, 40 to 60 feet wide
Full sun
Hardy to 25F to 30F
Low to moderate water use

Coral trees produce spectacular flowers in colors that range from orange-red and yellow to greenish white. Trees grow rapidly and need plenty of space. Provide with 30 to 40 feet of room in the garden for height and spread. Flowers in the form of orange-red tubular blooms are produced in spring. Leaves develop after flowers have completed their cycle.

Pruning & Maintenance
Prune to control growth after flowering has ceased. Growth can become quite succulent. Plants are legumes, so there is no need to fertilize.

Erythrina coralloides
Naked Coral Tree

Native to Mexico
Deciduous
30 feet high, 30 to 40 feet wide
Full sun
Hardy to 30F to 32F
Low to moderate water use

The branch structure of naked coral tree provides plenty of interest, but the real display occurs when flowers bloom at the tips of twisted, black-thorned branches in March to May.

Pruning & Maintenance
Prune to remove dead branches in winter—January at the latest. Wear heavy gloves because the thorns are wickedly sharp. Plant is a legume so no fertilizer needed.

EUCALYPTUS SPECIES
EUCALYPTUS

Native to Australia
Evergreen
15 to 60 feet high, 15 to 25 feet wide
  (see individual species)
Full sun
Hardy to 5F to 30F
Low water use

Eucalyptus has been prominent throughout the West since the seeds were imported from Australia more than a century ago. First used as windbreaks to protect orchards, the trees continue this role in many areas.

Over the years, many species have been grown and selected for use in home gardens. Some were grown for their interesting growth habits, or cold hardiness or flowers. Some of the most common include *Eucalyptus ficifolia*, red-flowering gum; *E. microtheca*, coolibah; *E. sideroxylon* 'Rosea', pink ironbark; *E. spathulata*, narrow-leaved gimlet; and *E. torquata*, coral gum. Each has distinct characteristics of beauty, texture, form and hardiness in many climates.

Selecting *Eucalyptus* for a home landscape requires some thought, because many species grow quite large—up to 60 feet or higher. Generally, smaller species such as *E. spathulata* or *E. nicholii* work best in a home landscape. Be especially careful when selecting trees (of any kind) if power lines are part of your landscape.

Pruning & Maintenance
The rapid growth of tall-growing species such as *E. sideroxylon* 'Rosea' calls for early tipping to develop multiple-trunk growth and strong vertical trunks. Avoid heavy pruning; trim gradually instead. For smaller species such as *E. torquata*, prune to direct irregular growth. Encourage deep rooting with drips or bubblers. After trees are established, reduce watering by half.

Eucalyptus ficifolia
Red-Flowering Gum

A round-headed form that's a favorite on the coast from San Diego to San Francisco. Grows 25 to 40 feet high and 25 feet wide. Leaves are large. Summer flowers are most commonly red, but pink and orange are also seen. Remove heavy seed pods during the tree's early development so they won't weigh down branches. Hardy to 25F to 30F.

Eucalyptus microtheca
Coolibah

A favorite in arid regions for its vigor and cold hardiness—5F to 10F. Holds up well in wind. Round form, gray-green foliage. Grows 30 to 40 feet high and 25 feet wide. If grown in heavy soils such as clay or caliche, mature size is 20 to 30 feet high. Seeds are small with minimum litter.

Eucalyptus nicholii
Nichol's Willow-Leafed Peppermint

Fine-textured, grayish, weeping foliage flows with the wind and smells like peppermint. Great small-garden eucalyptus, growing 30 to 40 feet high and 20 feet wide. Hardy to 12F to 15F. Provide with low water because abundant water can promote chlorosis.

Eucalyptus sideroxylon 'Rosea'
Pink Ironbark

Grows 20 to 60 feet high and 15 to 20 feet wide in arid regions. Appears in various forms from strong vertical to weeping. Slender leaves and pink flowers create pendulous clusters in fall and winter. Well-draining soil preferred. Hardy to 20F to 25F.

Eucalyptus spathulata
Narrow-Leafed Gimlet

Handsome, dense form grows 15 to 20 feet high and 15 feet wide. Narrow, fine-textured leaves, cream to gold flowers in summer. Attractive reddish brown bark. Makes a nice screen. Hardy to 15F to 20F.

Eucalyptus torquata
Coral Gum

Comparable to *E. spathulata* in mature size. Useful for cut flowers. Vertical growth is well suited to narrow locations. Irregular growth often requires that branches and trunk be staked and pruned to direct development. Flowers and seed pods often weigh down branches. Hardy to 17F to 22F.

Euphorbia biglandulosa
Narrow-Leafed Spurge, Gopher Plant

(E. rigida)
Native to the Mediterranean
Perennial
3 to 4 feet high, 4 to 5 feet wide
Full sun
Hardy to 0F
Low water use

Clusters of chartreuse flower bracts are dramatic against pointed, blue-green leaves that cover each stem. Delightful companion and accent to perennials and effective among boulders. A special plant in large containers. Tolerates heat.

Pruning & Maintenance
Remove old flower stems after blooming period has ended. Plant in well-draining soil.

Fallugia paradoxa
Apache Plume

Native to mountain regions at 3,500 to
8,000 feet in southeastern California,
southern Nevada, Utah, New Mexico,
Arizona and western Texas
Semideciduous
4 to 6 feet high, equal spread
Full sun, afternoon shade in
hot-summer regions
Hardy to 0F
Low water use

Five-petaled, white flowers bloom May to September, then form pink clusters of 2-inch, feathery seed tails. Natural height and spread to 4 to 6 feet can be increased with additional water. Foliage is 1 inch long and 1 inch wide, white or red underneath.

Fallugia paradoxa
Apache Plume

Produces vigorous underground stems ideal for erosion control. Nice addition to cold-climate ornamental shrub groupings.

Pruning & Maintenance
A low-maintenance plant that needs no pruning. Grows densely on its own. If plants become ragged, thin during the winter. Drainage important; well-draining gritty, alluvial soil ideal. Rabbits don't seem to care for it.

Feijoa sellowiana
Pineapple Guava

Native to South America
Evergreen
10 to 15 feet high, 8 to 10 feet wide
Full sun, enjoys heat
Hardy 15F to 20F
Low to moderate water use

Form and gray-green leaves blend well with arid plants. Good structure for screening or natural hedging. Flowers with red stamens are colorful in late spring; petals are edible. Green fruit to 3 inches long have tropical flavor and fragrance. Fruit ripen in fall and drop to the ground.

Pruning & Maintenance
Severe pruning is not required. Shearing the plant reduces flower and fruit production. Prune only to control size in winter after all fruit drops. A long-lived plant.

Ficus carica
Edible fig

Native to the Mediterranean region
Deciduous
15 to 30 feet high and as wide
Full sun
Hardy to 20F to 25F
Low water use

Due to potential fruit drop and debris, locate away from walks, driveways and patios. Provide with ample room to spread. The bold, gray-green foliage creates a luxuriant background.

Pruning & Maintenance
When planting, select well established container plants. Bare-root plants often start very slowly. California pocket gopher likes to eat fig roots. Protect by planting new plants in wire cages. To develop better fruit set on 'Brown Turkey', cut back individual stems to side buds on current year's growth. This creates new fresh growth. 'Mission' doesn't need heavy pruning. Prune to control size as needed during the winter season when trees are dormant to make it easier to harvest fruit. Frost damage can be controlled somewhat if water use is reduced in fall months.

Fouquieria splendens
Ocotillo

Native to the Sonoran and Chihuahuan
   Deserts of southern California,
   Arizona, Texas, New Mexico and
   Mexico
Semi-evergreen
12 feet high, 3 to 6 feet wide
Full sun
Hardy to 5F
Low water use

The strong vertical canes tipped with red-orange flowers make ocotillo an eye-catching plant. It plays an important role in landscaping in combination with other native plants such as *Opuntia* and *Agave* species. Use ocotillo with *Encelia* or *Justicia* species—their flowering periods often coincide. Or plant in boulder-strewn rock gardens on slopes so canes are backlit by the sun. With thorny spines on its canes, ocotillo is mistakenly called a cactus. It is actually a shrub. Its small, bright green leaves come and go, often with rainfall or humidity. Some individual plants go long periods without leaves, while others, often better established plants, produce heavy leaf growth.

Pruning & Maintenance
A minimum-maintenance plant. Roots produce no root hairs, so they take a long time to establish after bare-root planting. If any roots are broken or frayed at transplanting, make clean cuts to remove damaged portion. Dust roots with sulfur prior to planting to prevent root rot. Do not

mulch or fertilize plants, which also can damage roots. Provide with well-draining soil and avoid garden locations where plants receive excess moisture. If watering with drip irrigation place emitters at least 2 feet from base of plant.

Ocotillo flat-headed larvae attack plants by burrowing into the canes. Adults are most active in summer. They seek out stressed plants to lay their eggs. *Planting* is extremely stressful for ocotillos, which puts them at risk. Best to plant in fall when temperatures are cooler and borers are not active.

Fraxinus greggii
Gregg Ash, Littleleaf Ash

Native to New Mexico, southern
    Arizona and western Texas at 1,200 to
    6,000 feet
Semi-evergreen
15 feet high, 10 to 12 feet wide
Full sun, afternoon shade in
    hot-summer regions
Hardy to 20F, possibly lower
Low to moderate water use

Valuable for courtyard or patio, can be grown as a large shrub for screening or as multistemmed small tree. Leaves are smaller than most ashes, dark green and smooth textured.

Pruning & Maintenance
Generally requires little pruning if grown as a large shrub. To encourage multistem growth or single-trunk tree, remove lower side branches after plants are established. Prefers well-draining soil.

Fraxinus uhdei 'Majestic Beauty'
Majestic Beauty Ash

Native to Mexico
Evergreen
25 to 60 feet high, equal spread
Full sun
Hardy to 28F
High water use

An evergreen selected form of Shamel ash, 'Majestic Beauty' has become a favorite for creating heavy canopy shade. Once established, growth is rapid to 25 to 35 feet in 10 years. With age, can reach 40 to 60 feet high. A handsome, long-lived tree. Glossy, dark green leaflets are unlike the dull light green foliage of parent shamel ash. Hot, dry winds may cause tip burn. Cold temperatures can cause some leaf drop.

Pruning & Maintenance
Its tendency to produce shallow roots often causes problems. Providing with deep soil and watering deeply helps reduce surface rooting. Use drip or bubbler irrigation. Avoid planting near paved walks or curbs. Regular programmed irrigation in summer helps ensure continued good appearance. Guiding form of young trees creates a more balanced tree as it gains age. Ascending lateral branches develop well on their own after lower branches are removed to accommodate foot traffic beneath. Minimum pruning required if moisture is adequate during the first 10 years. Remove dead and crossing branches. Trunks gain size rapidly so remove stakes and ties early in youth to prevent girdling.

Fraxinus velutina
Arizona Ash

Native to Arizona, California, New
    Mexico and Texas
Deciduous
50 feet high, 35 feet wide
Full sun
Hardy to 10F
Low to moderate water use

This is a common tree along drainage areas in the Mojave and Sonoran Deserts. It is pyramidal in youth, then becomes open-headed and graceful with age as it reaches its potential 50-foot height. Compound gray-green leaves turn vivid yellow in the fall. An excellent tree for a small garden.

Pruning & Maintenance
Prune branches to allow heavy winds to sift through. Prune cautiously. Tree produces its own balanced structure with little pruning. As tree ages, prune up lower branches to allow for foot traffic beneath. Do this during dormant winter period. Appreciates fertile soil but tolerates most soils. Does best in regions with a definite winter cold season. Water deeply.

Fraxinus species
Ash

Nature's Air Conditioners

A University of Arizona study suggests that properly placed trees in a home landscape can reduce cooling costs by 25 to 30 percent, sometimes more. If you have the garden space, plant three or more wide-spreading trees on the south and west exposures of your home. The objective is to shade the roof and walls from the hot summer sun. For a summer-shade, winter-sun combination, select *deciduous* trees. They drop their leaves in winter, allowing the sun to warm your home, reducing heating costs.

Fraxinus velutina 'Rio Grande'
Fan-Tex Ash

Native to Texas
Deciduous
20 to 50 feet high, 20 to 30 feet wide
Full sun
Hardy to 10F
Low to moderate water use

A durable, long-term tree. It is deciduous so is excellent for summer shade and winter sun. The well-known 'Modesto' ash is susceptible to ash whitefly and ash decline. Fan-tex ash is more vigorous and grows at a faster rate, is highly resistant to cold and drought, and less subject to chlorosis. Leaves of fan-tex are large and leathery, and resist being burned by the sun or the wind. As a color bonus, the dark green leaves turn golden yellow in fall.

Pruning & Maintenance
Provide deep moisture to promote development of deep roots. If planting near sidewalks or in parking lot dividers, install root guards. Require minimum of 8 to 10 square feet of planting area. Little pruning is required. Ascending branches develop naturally into well-spaced structure. Prune in winter, removing dead interior branches or crossed branches as needed. Space at least 20 to 25 feet apart for shade coverage.

Fremontodendron californicum
Fremontia

Native to San Diego County (Otah Mt.),
    south into Baja California
Evergreen
10 to 20 feet high, 8 to 10 feet wide
Full sun
Hardy to 20F to 25F
Low water use

Fremontia is considered one of the 10 best shrubs native to the United States. Plant in combination with other California natives that have similar cultural requirements. Flower color is deep, orange-yellow, 3 to 5 inches wide and 1 to 3 inches long. Peak bloom is in April. Plants may be available at native plant nurseries. Best grown along coast or in inland valleys on slopes.

Pruning & Maintenance
This is a plant that doesn't want to be disturbed. Plants need coarse, well-draining soil to succeed. Avoid summer watering after plants are established. Stake plants in youth. Keep moisture from plant trunk to avoid fungus problem.

Gardenia jasminoides
Cape Jasmine

Native to China
Evergreen
4 feet high, 3 to 4 feet wide
Filtered sun in hot regions, full sun
    near coast
Hardy to 20F to 22F
High water use

Gardenias such as 'Mystery' and 'Radicans' are a bit of a challenge to grow in arid climates. However, 'Veitchii' has performed well in well-draining soil or in soil that has a high pH, improved with lots of organic matter. Where plants are located is important. Direct sun burns up the white, fragrant flowers in late spring and summer. Locate in east or north exposure in filtered shade. Planting among other plants to increase humidity helps see gardenias through long, hot summer periods.

Pruning & Maintenance
Minimum pruning required, except to remove dead flowers. Avoid keeping soil area excessively moist. Do not cultivate around roots. Acidic fertilizer applied monthly helps keep plants healthy. Not low water use, but the fragrant flowers make it worth the effort. Plant crowns of roots higher than existing grades. Add a layer of organic mulch over roots, but not around crown. (Mulch against the crown can cause root rot.)

Gazania rigens
Gazania

Native to South Africa
Perennial
1 foot high, equal spread
Full sun, partial shade in hot summer
    areas
Hardy to 15F
Low to moderate water use

'Sun Gold' is productive in arid regions. Colorful yellow flowers have distinct black "eyes." Flowers bloom spring and fall. Plants are dormant for three to four months during summer heat.

Pruning & Maintenance
As plantings age, remove weak plants. Monitor irrigation schedule and be ready to reduce watering in fall as temperatures cool. Avoid overhead irrigation, and do not allow soil to remain too moist or plantings will experience problems with fungus diseases. Water with drip irrigation or flood root zone. Shear off old flowers as you see them to maintain appearance. Plant from flats or containers in fall and early spring. Plants reseed readily. To extend planting areas, transplant new plants to open areas in early spring.

Geijera parviflora
Australian Willow, Wilga

Native to Australia
Evergreen
20 to 35 feet high, 18 to 20 feet wide
Full sun
Hardy to 18F
Moderate water use

A graceful, finely-textured tree with small white flower clusters in spring. Main branches sweep up and out, small branches hang down. Long, narrow, drooping, medium-green leaves provide willow effect. Australian willow has the grace of a willow and the toughness of a *Eucalyptus* without heavy debris. Ideal small-garden tree. Considered water-efficient, but with ample moisture growth is more aggressive. Roots grow deep and are noninvasive. Growth rate is moderate with a long life span. Takes heat and wind. Trees are pest-free. Full sun and well-drained soil important.

Pruning & Maintenance
Pruning requirements are minimal. Some leaf drop occurs in summer caused by heat stress. Increase moisture during to summer to prevent.

Gelsemium sempervirens
Carolina Jessamine

Native to southeastern U.S.
Evergreen
10 to 20 feet high, 10 feet wide
Full sun
Hardy to 15F
Moderate water use

A favorite yellow-flowering vine that combines well with low-water-use plants. Fragrant tubular flowers appear in late winter and early spring. Vining growth is substantial to 20 feet, so supply strong support structure. Can also be used as a slope cover. Note: All plant parts are poisonous.

Pruning & Maintenance
After three to six years the stems and vining branches become too woody. To create new growth and fresh, flowering wood, cut back severely to just above ground level after vine ceases flowering in the spring. It regrows quickly.

Grevillea robusta
Silk Oak

Native to New South Wales and Queensland
Evergreen
40 to 60 feet high, 20 to 30 feet wide
Full sun
Hardy to 20F to 25F (young trees), mature trees hardy to 15F to 20F
Low to moderate water use

Strong vertical and pyramidal form in youth. Develops wide canopy with age. The fernlike foliage becomes rather dense three or four seasons after planting. Prior to leaf change in the spring, old leaves drop off is complete so leaf debris accumulates all at once. Flat-topped clusters of yellow-orange flowers appear on old wood after leaf drop and create more debris.

Pruning & Maintenance
Remove dead branches as they appear. Cut back stray side branches if they break out of vertical pattern. Watch for signs of iron chlorosis in mid- to late summer—common if

Geijera parviflora
Australian Willow

trees are planted in lawns. Provide deep irrigation during growing season. Reduce water during winter. Root guards required if planted near paving or curbs.

Hemerocallis
Daylily

Native to central Europe, China and Japan
Perennial (can be evergreen in mild-winter areas)
1 to 2 feet high, equal spread
Full sun
Hardy to 18F
Low to moderate water use

A prolific producer of flowers, with hundreds of colors and combinations available. Plant form consists of stemless clump of narrow straplike leaves. Flowers appear in clusters at the ends of branches. Colors may be yellow, orange, pink and shades of white. Numerous landscape uses: in rock gardens, perennial borders, in masses or in well-spaced clumps to provide accent and color.

Pruning & Maintenance
Be careful when cultivating around plants so as not to disturb shallow roots. As flower stems turn brown, remove by pulling or cutting off at leaf cluster level. Spider mites can infest browning leaves. Divide clumps of mature plants for renewal or to harvest rhizomes to place in other garden areas. Plant rhizomes about 1 inch below soil level in fall or early spring, or plant from containers. Space plants 2 to 3 feet apart. Does best in fertile, well-prepared soil that has good drainage.

Hesperaloe funifera
Coahuilan Hesperaloe

Native to the Chihuahuan Desert in Mexico south of Texas
Evergreen
6 feet high, equal spread
Full sun
Hardy to 15F
Low water use, moderate in summer

The green, 4-foot-long, sharp-tipped leaves produce a strong vertical accent. This plant grabs your attention, and is even more eye-catching when the tall, 12-foot-high flower spike develops, with its clusters of small, bell-shaped white flowers. Oval capsules on the spikes follow flowers.

Pruning & Maintenance
Little pruning is required. Leaf debris is minimal. Plant away from foot-traffic areas to avoid potential injury from sharp leaf tips. After flowering, cut stalks at the plant base.

Hesperaloe parviflora
Red Yucca

Native to the southwest U.S.
Evergreen
3 feet high, 3 to 4 feet wide
Full sun
Hardy to 0F
Low water use

In the arid garden, red yucca is a star performer from spring into fall. Coral red flowers on top of spikes to 6 feet high attract hummingbirds. Even when not in bloom, the 2- to 3-foot-high clumps of narrow, blue-green leaves are attractive in rock gardens, containers and planters. New flower spikes often develop in late summer and early fall on well-established plants.
A light yellow-flowering selection has recently become available. It has the same growth characteristics and cultural requirements as red yucca.

Pruning & Maintenance
A minimum-maintenance plant that is content to grow in almost any soil. Remove dead leaves at base of plant as they occur. Pull out or cut dead flower spikes after they turn brown or set seeds. When planting, space clumps at least 6 feet apart to allow for spread. Plants are easy to divide as clumps spread. Pull apart, make clean cuts with a sharp knife to separate. Allow roots of transplants to dry for a short time in a shaded area before replanting. This allows the cuts to "seal." Reduce amount of water applied during cool periods of the year.

Hesperaloe parviflora
Red Yucca

Heteromeles arbutifolia
Toyon, California Holly

Native to California at elevations from
    sea level to 3,500 feet
Evergreen
6 to 20 feet high with equal spread
Full sun
Hardy to 15F to 20F
Low to moderate water use

A handsome, tall shrub with serrated
leaves. Flat-topped clusters of small
white flowers develop in June and
July. Clusters of hollylike berries follow and remain on plant from
November to February. Most effective
as a background shrub or specimen.
A coastal and inland valley favorite
due to its winter color display.

Pruning & Maintenance
Can be trained as a small tree. Be
patient and allow trunk to develop 3
to 6 inches in diameter so it can support heavy berry crop in winter.

Hibiscus moscheutos
Rose Mallow

Native to the mideastern U.S.,
    Michigan to Florida
Deciduous
6 to 8 feet high, 4 to 5 feet wide
Full sun
Hardy to 15F
Moderate water use

Rose mallow is an exuberant plant.
Dormant in winter, it begins flowering at the onset of hot weather. The
8- to 12-inch flowers, among the
largest of *Hibiscus* species, come in
rose, pink, red or white. Oval leaves
are grayish on undersides. Plant at
the rear of perennial beds where
height provides a rich dark green
background. Named varieties are
often grown in containers, or you can
start plants from seed. In the Mojave
Desert, rose mallow plants or
seedlings and flowers were found to
develop better if given shelter from a
windbreak hedge, fence or wall.
Provide deep, moderate water. Avoid
overwatering during winter.

Pruning & Maintenance
During the growing season it may be
necessary to tip-prune vertical
growth to control size and create

more flowering wood. Once plants
become dormant in winter, cut back
to near ground level. Apply a light
application of fertilizer during late
spring and summer.

Hibiscus syriacus
Rose of Sharon

Native to eastern Asia
Deciduous
6 to 10 feet high, 4 to 5 feet wide
Full sun
Hardy to 15F
Low to moderate water use

A favorite *Hibiscus* species with flowers that have a distinct tropical
appearance. As the shrublike plants
age it's possible to create a tree form
with more open growth. Compact
growth provides strong base for prolific flowers in summer. Flowers are
single, 2 to 3 inches in diameter, and
come in blue, purple, pink with a red
center and white. (You may have to
special order new selections.) Use as
a background for low-growing perennials or shrubs 2 to 4 feet high.
Leaves are coarse with three lobes.
Can be grown in colder areas of low
and middle elevations.

Pruning & Maintenance
Minor selective pruning can help
direct vertical growth. In winter cut
back past season's growth to several
buds. Do not prune in squares or
globes. Allow natural form to develop. Reduce watering by 50 percent in
winter. Requires well-draining soil.
Some protection from severe winds
helps flower production. Resistant to
oak root fungus.

Hymenoxys acaulis
Angelita Daisy

Native to north central Arizona, New
    Mexico, Colorado, Nevada and south-
    ern California at 4,000 to 7,000 feet
Evergreen perennial
12 inches high, equal spread
Full sun
Cold hardy
Low to moderate water use

With a growth habit similar to that of
Baileya multiradiata, desert marigold,
angelita daisy has been grown in

Europe as an ornamental. This plant seems to be able to tolerate heavy soils, something desert marigold cannot. Its yellow, daisylike flowers bloom from March to November. If the winter is mild, it can keep right on blooming. Will naturalize in the landscape. The Hopi Indians reportedly make a stimulating drink from this plant and for pain relief.

Pruning & Maintenance
Deadhead spent blossoms after flowering. Plant in well-draining soil.

Hyptis emoryi
Desert Lavender

Native to southern Arizona, Sonoran
   Desert in southern California and
   Baja California
Deciduous
5 to 10 feet high, 8 feet wide
Full sun
Hardy to 20F
Low water use

Desert lavender is an excellent background plant in home garden situations. Foliage is gray with fragrant, violet-blue flowers. Flowering begins in the spring and recurs sporadically at other times during the growing season. Temperatures at 20F and below can cause leaf drop. Plants naturalize up to elevations of 2,000 feet. Space at 6 to 8 feet apart. Low water use after plants are established.

Pruning & Maintenance
If frozen to ground, cut back for regrowth. Little pruning is required, because plants maintain a well-shaped form. If vertical growth becomes too vigorous, cut back to 1 to 1-1/2 feet to encourage fullness. Plant in well-draining soil.

Ilex species
Chinese Holly

Native to China
Evergreen
3 to 6 feet high, 3 to 4 feet wide
Full sun, partial shade in hot-summer
   regions
Hardy to cold
Low to moderate water use

In the arid West, several *Ilex* species perform well with little maintenance.

Ilex cornuta 'Rotunda' grows 3 to 4 feet high and spreads 4 to 5 feet wide. It has a dense, mounded form and is adapted to grow in full sun to partial shade.

I. vomitoria 'Stokes', dwarf yaupon holly, is a compact form, growing 2 to 3 feet high and spreading 3 to 4 feet wide. The rich green leaves are dense and twiggy. White flowers appear May to June.

Pruning & Maintenance
Low maintenance with little or no pruning required to shape plants. In hot-summer regions leaves may burn if exposed to reflected sun and heat.

Jacaranda mimosifolia
Jacaranda

Native to Brazil
Deciduous
40 feet high or more, 30 to 40 feet wide
Full sun
Hardy to 20F
Moderate water use

There is something special about a jacaranda in a home garden, as long as you can give it the space it needs to grow to its potential. Flowers are a spectacular lavender-blue and bloom in midspring while the branches are bare, before the spring flush of growth. Fallen flower petals create a colorful carpet on the ground that is attractive. Circular, woody seed pods follow the flowers. Temperatures at 20F can freeze small branches. If much colder, the main trunk may be killed back to base. In regions where these cold temperatures occur, most trees develop multiple trunks as a result of cold damage.

Pruning & Maintenance
Severe pruning to control growth is often required, because trees will grow to 40 feet or more and 30 to 40 feet in diameter. Pruning induces numerous sucker stems that can destroy the shape of the tree. Prune in winter to thin and remove undesirable growth. Allow ample room for spread. Best growth occurs when trees are planted in deep, loose, well-draining soil.

Jacaranda mimosifolia
Jacaranda

Juniperus species
Juniper

Native to Northern Hemisphere
Evergreen (coniferous)
2 to 4 feet high, 4 to 5 feet wide
Full sun to partial shade
Hardy to 0F
Low to moderate water use

Junipers that cover the ground shade the soil better than more open growers. For many gardens *J. sabina* 'Arcadia' is a wise choice. It develops lacy, rich green foliage and has a controlled, low-growing form. *J. sabina* 'Tamariscifolia' has a dense, dark, blue-green form. Spread can reach over 8 feet.

Pruning & Maintenance
Grassy weeds such as Bermudagrass create problems by invading planting areas. Little or no pruning except to cut back vertical growth if it occurs. All species are low-maintenance, requiring deep irrigation and good soil drainage.

Justicia californica
Chuperosa

Native to upper Sonoran Desert
Evergreen
4 feet high, 4 to 6 feet wide
Full sun
Hardy to 25F
Low water use

The tubular, 1-inch, red flower clusters command attention during spring and other intermittent bloom periods throughout the year. Well behaved in garden settings. Plants are often leafless. Space plants at 6 to 8 feet apart in well-draining soil.

Pruning & Maintenance
Harden off plant tissues by reducing water in October. Wait until cold weather passes before pruning any frost-damaged stems. If pruning to shape or control plants, hold off until flowering is completed in the spring. However, plants generally look best when left alone. With age some interior pruning stimulates production of new flowering wood. Do not prune hardwood excessively at any time.

Justicia spicigera
Mexican Honeysuckle

Native to Mexico and south to Colombia
Semideciduous
4 feet high, 3 to 4 feet wide
Full sun, afternoon shade in
**   hot-summer regions**
Hardy to 24F
Low water use

Loved by hummingbirds, the orange flowers of Mexican honeysuckle bloom in clusters late spring into fall. Smooth, velvety, gray-green leaves produce a subtropical effect. In hot-summer regions, plants appreciate some shade, such as that supplied by high-canopy trees. Avoid planting locations in reflected sun and heat.

Pruning & Maintenance
If plants are left alone, they usually develop quite nicely. Allow branches to grow all the way to ground level in order to shelter root area.

Koelreuteria bipinnata
Chinese Flame Tree

Native to southwestern China
Deciduous
15 to 40 feet high, equal spread
Full sun
Hardy to 0F
Moderate water use

This is a well-adapted small shade tree for a home garden. Growth is lush with an open-branching form that provides dense to medium shade. Bears clusters of small yellow flowers in summer. Buff to brown capsules create a show in early fall. Roots are noninvasive.

Pruning & Maintenance
Prune during winter dormancy. To create a tree form, remove lower branches on main trunk. Main branch structure will likely be irregular in maturity if it is not directed the first two to three years after planting. Avoid making several heavy cuts at once. If they are necessary it's best to stretch them out over several seasons. Accepts heat, cold, wind and alkaline soil.

Justicia californica
Chuperosa

Lagerstroemia indica
Crape Myrtle

Native to China
Deciduous
Shrub forms to 8 feet high and as wide
Tree forms 20 feet high, 15 feet wide
Full sun
Hardy to 20F
Low to moderate water use

A summer-flowering plant in interior valleys such as San Joaquin and San Fernando valleys and in desert regions in the Southwest where hardy. Crapelike flower clusters cover the plants of various species in pink, purple, even red or white. Flowering can begin in early May. Leaves turn bright colors in fall. Shrub or tree forms combine well with arid plants.

Pruning & Maintenance
Stake trees if required, then remove stakes within two years. Prune during winter months, especially tree forms. Cut back old flowering wood at least 12 to 18 inches. Removing small flowering branches and spent flowers on shrub forms improves flowering the following summer season. Avoid spraying foliage with water at any time, which can encourage mildew. Select mildew-resistant varieties to reduce that problem and apply mildew spray on foliage prior to summer blooms. Drip irrigation is an excellent way to water.

Plants develop slowly, so plant in the fall or winter so they'll be established before summer. Good soil drainage is important. Water deeply at widely spaced periods.

Lantana species
Lantana

Native to tropical North and South
    America
Evergreen
1-1/2 to 6 feet high, 3 to 6 feet wide
Full sun
Hardy to 28F
Moderate water use

These tropical natives are in harmony combined with dry-climate plants of the Southwest. The shorter the frost period the more extensively lantana covers the soil during warm months.

In colder areas lantanas are often used as annuals, planted in early spring. The low shrub form is used in foundation planters and can even be trained as a low hedge. Foliage is prickly and pungent. Be careful when locating plants near foot-traffic areas.

These hybrids grow to 2 to 4 feet with equal spread: 'Christine', cerise pink to yellow flowers; 'Dwarf Pink', 'Dwarf White' and 'Dwarf Yellow'.

Trailing selections include the vigorous *L. montevidensis*, also known as *L. sellowiana*. It is used in cross-breeding, and plants are more hardy—20F to 30F. Flowers are a rich purple. A vigorous new hybrid, 'New Gold', introduced by Texas A&M University, is a rich gold color that grows 1-1/2 feet high and 2 to 2-1/2 feet wide. It flowers from spring through fall. Plants will freeze back but recover well even when temperatures drop to 10F. Flowering is heavier on 'New Gold' because it does not produce seeds.

Pruning & Maintenance
Harden off plants before cold weather begins. Cease fertilizing and begin to reduce applications of water. If plants are frost-damaged, wait for regrowth the following spring before removing damaged stems and branches. Overfeeding and excess moisture can reduce flowering and encourage more foliage, which of course requires more pruning. Prune lateral and vertical growth during growing season to help keep plants in proportion. When growth builds up excessively, cut back in early spring to achieve rapid recovery. Lantanas are aggressive and have a tendency to crowd out nearby plants.

Larrea tridentata
Creosote

Native to southwest desert regions in
    U.S. from sea level to 5,000 feet
Evergreen
4 to 8 feet high, equal spread
Full sun
Hardy to cold
Low water use

Creosote bush doesn't receive the attention it deserves. It should be

Lagerstroemia indica
Crape Myrtle

used more frequently in home gardens and other landscape projects. The twisted ascending and spreading trunks and branches create a unique background for other colorful plants such as *Aloes*, *Daleas* and *Baccharis*. Plants may be straggly under dry conditions but growth is dense with irrigation. The small, dark green leaves have a varnished look with gum secretion. They produce a distinctive, refreshing scent after a rain. Small, star-shaped yellow flowers bloom spring and late summer.

Pruning & Maintenance
Plants seldom require much pruning because they develop their own form naturally. If a hedge or screening pattern is desired, plants fill in readily with side pruning. Space plants at 12 to 15 feet on centers in garden groupings. Accepts almost any soil.

Lavandula
Lavender

Native to Mediterranean region
Evergreen
1 to 4 feet high, equal spread
Full sun
Hardy to 15F
Low to moderate water use

The flowers and aromatic foliage of lavender provide year-round interest. Its texture and form blend well with *Salvia*, *Verbena*, *Rosmarinus*, *Santolina* and *Leucophyllum* species. In addition, all having moderate water requirements.

Lavandula angustifolia, English lavender, grows in a compact form to 3 to 4 feet high and wide. Deep lavender flowers appear on 1- to 2-foot, fragrant spikes from July through August. 'Munstead' is more dwarfish, to 1 feet high and as wide. It bears lavender-blue blooms in late May, June and July. Hardy to 0F.

L. dentata, French lavender, has narrow, toothed, gray-green leaves. Flowers are short with lavender-purple flower spikes. Plants grow to 3 feet high.

Pruning & Maintenance
Apply low to moderate water, depending on soil type. (See pages 25 and 26.) More water will be required in fast-draining sandy soils; less with clay soils. As flowers complete their bloom cycles, deadhead stems. Renew growth after each flowering season. Cut branches back individually. Avoid shearing so as to retain the natural form. Each species prefers well-draining soil.

Leucaena retusa
Golden Ball Lead Tree

Native to southwestern Texas, southern
    New Mexico and northeastern
    Mexico
Deciduous
12 to 20 feet high, equal spread
Full sun
Hardy to 10F
Low water use

Golden ball lead tree provides a tropical effect with its lacy foliage. The golden yellow, ball-shaped flowers that bloom in summer after rains are spectacular. Partial shade beneath tree is well suited for an underplanting of perennials or small shrubs. Can be trained into a small multitrunk tree but limbs are weak and subject to storm damage.

Pruning & Maintenance
To develop attractive, multitrunk form and reveal the gracefulness of basal trunks, thin out lower branches. Thin inside canopy branches gradually (a little each season) to avoid creating excessive growth surges. Seed pods create debris in fall and winter. Growth can be rapid or excessive. Reduce water to control. Protect from winds. A legume that manufactures its own nitrogen, so fertilizer is not required.

Downsize That Lawn
Nothing is better for a play surface than a grass lawn. But if you do have a lawn, it's not necessary that it dominate the entire front or back yard. There are many attractive and practical ways to contour, zone and plant your property with a blend of trees, shrubs, ground covers and perennials. Thoughtful plant combinations offer much more interest than just green grass. But do avoid covering large areas with gravel or stone. They increase reflective heat, collect debris and with time usually become infested with weeds.

LEUCOPHYLLUM SPECIES TEXAS RANGERS

Native to the Chihuahuan Desert
Evergreen
3 to 8 feet high, equal spread,
    depending on species
Full sun
Hardy to 10F
Low water use

Leucophyllum species play an increasingly important role as workhorse shrubs throughout the arid West. New selections continue to be produced. Introductions have come from Texas A&M University through the work of horticulturist Benny Simpson, and from Phoenix, Arizona, nurseryman Ron Gass. The many selections provide a wide range of flower and foliage colors, textures and sizes. Plants are adapted to grow in many climate zones, from the hot low desert, to interior valleys in California, to colder, higher elevation regions such as Las Vegas, Nevada. High humidity in the middle of summer encourages flowering, although normal bloom period is during fall.

Pruning & Maintenance

Plants generally perform well without pruning if given enough space to grow to their natural height and spread. Thinning is occasionally required to renew flowering wood and to control growth of older plants in small gardens. Shearing creates stubby growth. Prune in a naturalistic form by tipping strong vertical growth on taller-growing forms. Plants produce minimum amount of litter. Full sun and well-draining soil are important for growth and health.

Leucophyllum candidum

The selection 'Silver Cloud' has deep violet flowers that bloom in summer and fall set against tiny silvery leaves. It grows to 4 feet high and as wide. Trademarked by Texas A&M.

'Thunder Cloud', released by Texas A&M after 'Silver Cloud', almost identical to 'Silver Cloud', blooms more frequently and profusely than 'Silver Cloud'. *L. candidum* is suscepti-ble to overwatering and moist soil; plant in well-draining soil.

Leucophyllum frutescens
Texas Ranger, Texas Sage, Cenizo

This is the "original" Texas ranger. It has gray leaves with flowers that are usually light purple. (See photos, page 54.) Like other *Leucophyllum* species, it blooms during the warm summer months when the humidity is high, hence its other common name, *barometer bush*. It also blooms in the fall. *L. frutescens* can grow 6 to 8 feet high and as wide with a rangy, open growth habit. All *Leucophyllum* species discussed here are hardy to at least 10F and thrive during hot summers. In a 40-year-old Palm Springs California, garden, plants have been pruned as bonsai. The effect is attractive, and plants have aged well.

'Compacta' is smaller with a tight, dense growth habit. Grows to 5 feet high and as wide. It has gray leaves and pink flowers. Generally does not require pruning to maintain an attractive, natural form.

'Green Cloud' is a selection introduced by Texas A&M. This plant has bright green leaves and deep pink flowers. Its lush foliage has made this clone very popular, but most people don't plan for its large size—6 to 8 feet high and wide, sometimes larger. This is the most deciduous of the Texas rangers with cold temperatures, dropping some leaves as temperatures fall.

'Rain Cloud' is a hybrid of *L. frutescens* and *L. minus*. It has an unusual vertical growth habit, growing to 6 feet high and 3 to 4 feet wide. Leaves are silver-gray. Flowers are violet-blue.

'White Cloud' looks like *L. frutescens* but its flowers are white. Selected and trademarked by Texas A&M University. Grows 6 to 8 feet high and as wide.

Leucophyllum laevigatum
Chihuahuan Rain Sage

This plant has an open, angular growth habit that blends well with native plants. It is often used by landscape architects in naturalized settings. It does not look as attractive in a container at the nursery compared to other *Leucophyllum* species so it may be passed by. It has tiny, dark green leaves and lavender flowers. Mature size is 4 feet high and 4 to 5 feet wide. Prune in spring to reduce leggy growth and to keep plants in control.

Leucophyllum langmaniae
Canyon Rain Sage

Selection 'Rio Bravo' has a compact growth habit similar to that of *L. frutescens* 'Compacta'. It has become popular due to its bright green leaves, and dense, rounded form. Plants eventually grow to 5 feet high and wide. Flowers are lavender. Like *L. candidum*, it is sensitive to too much moisture around its roots so be sure to plant in well-draining soil. Moderately drought tolerant. Prune to control height in spring to early summer. Hardy to 10F.

Leucophyllum pruinosum
Fragrant Rain Sage

'Sierra Bouquet' is an improved selection. It is grown for the incredible fragrance of its flowers; they smell like grape bubble gum. The shrub has silver foliage and purple flowers. Its growth habit is fairly rangy, reaching up to 6 feet high and as wide, so locate accordingly. Occasional pruning helps keep plant dense. Useful as a background shrub for smaller plants in the garden. Use in masses to get the most benefit out of the great fragrance. Hardy to 10F.

Leucophyllum revolutum
Curl Leaf Rain Sage

'Sierra Magic Mix' is a selection of *L. revolutum* native to high elevations in Mexico. This means it is well suited to grow in colder climates. It is decidedly evergreen in the Phoenix area but blooms later than some of the other species. Leaves are light green; flowers are medium purple. Grows slowly to 4 feet high and 4 to 5 feet

wide. 'Houdini' is similar but flowers are violet and larger than those of 'Sierra Magic Mix'. Prune occasionally to keep plants dense. Hardy to 10F.

Leucophyllum zygophyllum
Blue Ranger, Blue Rain Sage

The selection 'Cimmaron' is a great choice for medians or tight spaces, growing to only 3 feet high and as wide. Leaves are soft gray-green and have a unique structure—they cup up. It blooms more profusely than other selections of *L. zygophyllum* and is less susceptible to overwatering. The flowers are light blue, hence the common name blue ranger. Prune only to remove deadwood on underside of plant. Drought tolerant. Hardy to 5F to 10F.

Liatris spicata
Blazing Star, Gayfeather

Native to North America
Perennial
2 to 3 feet high, 1 feet wide
Full sun, filtered shade in
    hot-summer regions
Hardy to 15F
Moderate water use

A low-maintenance plant that displays exclamation points of rose-pink, magenta or white. Basal growth of grasslike leaves supports 6- to 9-inch flower spikes in late summer to fall. Flowers open from the top downward, making them striking in cut flower arrangements. Adapted to all regions of the arid West. As winter approaches, clumps go dormant then come alive in the spring for complete recovery. Accepts heat and cold, but locate in wind-protected area.

Pruning & Maintenance
Minimum maintenance required. Deadhead flower stems as they occur. Cut back stems to their bases as they go dormant. Provide with well-draining soil. When planting, set clusters 12 to 18 inches apart.

Three Simple Ways To Reduce Time Spent Pruning

1. Select plants according to height, spread and shape so they can grow naturally in the allotted space with minimal pruning. Space plants far enough apart to avoid crowding.

2. Purchase dwarf plants-- those that reach knee- or waist-high at maturity. They naturally require less pruning and shearing.

3. Plant plants that have casual growth habits. After they are established, such plants will look attractive even when left alone. Many plants native to the Southwest fall into this category.

Ligustrum species
Privet

Native to China and Korea
Evergreen
10 to 30 feet high, 6 to 20 feet wide
Full sun to partial shade
Hardy to 15F
Low to moderate water use

Ligustrum species have long been used as hedge plants or as small trees. The plants react favorably to shearing or can be grown informally. L. lucidum, glossy privet, can reach 30 feet high and 20 feet wide. It is often used as a street tree.

L. japonicum, often called *L. texanum*, Japanese privet, is more compact, growing 10 to 12 feet high and 8 to 10 feet wide. Leaves are medium green, glossy and are spongy to the touch. Avoid growing in caliche soil. *L. ovalifolium*, California privet, is semideciduous at elevations above 2,000 feet. It is typically more evergreen at lower elevations. If grown as a hedge, be aware that it requires more trimming.

Pruning & Maintenance
L. lucidum drops heavy crops of blue-black fruit. After trees or shrubs have been shaped, maintenance remains constant during growing seasons. If plants are left unsheared, growth is more open.

Linum perenne lewisii
Blue Flax

Native to California, Alaska to northern Mexico
Perennial
2 feet high, equal spread
Full sun
Hardy to cold
Low to moderate water use

Vase-shaped plant with an airy look and narrow leaves; doesn't crowd other plants. Lively blue flowers bloom late spring into fall. Grows well in cool climates.

Pruning & Maintenance
Minimum pruning required. Cut back foliage in late fall to early winter as plants go dormant. Plant in well-draining soil. Don't overwater; overly moist soil weakens plants.

Liquidambar styraciflua
American Sweet Gum

Native to eastern U. S.
Deciduous
40 to 80 feet high, 20 to 25 feet wide
Hardy to cold
Full sun
Moderate to low water use

Tall, narrow and pyramidal in youth, sweet gum develops rigid horizontal branches as trees age. The maple-shaped leaves are green in summer, turning bright red, yellow and purple in the fall. Recent introductions include 'Burgundy', 'Palo Alto' and 'Rotundiloba'. Trees are adapted to grow along the coast, in inland valleys and at higher elevations. They are not adapted to grow in low- and middle-elevation desert regions because of the high heat.

Pruning & Maintenance
Trees develop an attractive form on their own so require minimum pruning. Avoid pruning the central leader, which would destroy the natural pyramidal shape. Sharp-pronged seedheads should be cleaned up after they drop from tree. Drought tolerant, but plant appearance and health are better with deep irrigation. Do not plant in alkaline or salty soils. Resistant to oak root fungus.

Lobelia laxiflora
Cardinal Flower

Native to New Mexico
Perennial
2 feet high, 1-1/2 feet wide
Bright shade
Hardy to cold
Moderate water use

Creeping underground roots support the erect and narrow, 2-foot-high stems. Tubular orange-red flowers bloom June to August.

Pruning & Maintenance
Deadhead stems to encourage summer flowers. After flowering ceases, cut vertical stems to control growth. Plant in moderately rich soil in bright shaded location. A thick layer of organic mulch protects roots in winter and keep them moist in summer. Plant in clusters 18 to 24 inches apart.

Ligustrum species
Privet

Lysiloma watsonii var. thornberi
Feather Tree

(Lysiloma microphylla var. thornberi)
**Native to southern Arizona and along
California-Mexico border**
Evergreen
15 feet high, equal spread
Full sun
Hardy to 25F
Low water use

The graceful and fine-textured feather tree, with its slender, arching branches, come alive with puffballs of white flowers in May and June. Flowering is followed by 6- to 8-inch seed pods late summer and fall. Growth is more sparse in heavy shade. Provides an airy, tropical effect in patios or courtyards. In frost-free regions, trees can reach 30 to 40 feet high.

Pruning & Maintenance
Most attractive trees have multiple trunks. Remove lower branches gradually as plant ages. With delicate and selective thinning, size and growth can be controlled to show off interesting trunk structure below the ferny canopy. Overzealous pruning results in heavy sucker growth. If the many seed pods are bothersome, remove with pole pruner or hand pruner. Decrease water in fall to harden off tree for the cold weather to come. Plant in well-draining soil. A self-fertilizing legume.

Mahonia aquifolium
Oregon Grape

Native to Pacific Northwest
Evergreen
5 to 6 feet high, 4 to 5 feet wide
**Full sun, partial shade in
hot-summer regions**
Hardy to 10F to 15F
Moderate to high water use

Grown for its glossy, hollylike leaves with bronze to purple hues and clusters of yellow flowers in the spring. Blends well with other glossy-foliaged plants.

M. aquifolium 'Compacta', compact Oregon grape holly, grows to 2 to 3 feet high, spreading 3 to 4 feet wide.

M. repens, creeping mahonia, grows 12 to 15 inches high and 3 to 4 feet wide. It is hardy to 10F to 20F. Leaves turn bronze color in winter.

Pruning & Maintenance
After two or three growing seasons, severely trim vertical stems. Make cuts at varying lengths for more natural appearance near ground level. Do this during winter months. Can be grown where oat root fungus persists. Plants sometimes afflicted with iron chlorosis, most often noticed in late summer. Plant in well-draining, acid soil.

Malephora luteola
Golden Ice Plant

Native to Africa
Succulent perennial
1 foot high, 2 to 3 feet wide
Full sun
Hardy to 28F
Low to moderate water use

The dense, light, gray-green leaves support 1-inch yellow flowers throughout the year. Heaviest bloom occurs late spring into early summer. A useful ground cover for small or narrow planters or on mounds or slopes to control erosion.

Pruning & Maintenance
Plant on 18- to 24-inch centers. Cut back growth if plant crowds other plants as necessary, otherwise plants are low maintenance. Succulent growth cannot handle foot traffic. Good soil drainage is necessary.

Maytenus boaria
Mayten

Native to Chile
Evergreen
30 to 50 feet high, 20 feet wide
Full sun
Hardy to 20F to 25F
Low to moderate water use

This is a suitable evergreen alternative to the deciduous weeping willow, *Salix babylonica*. Adapted to grow along the coast and in interior valleys, but not in low-elevation deserts. Side branches drape to the

Cold Temperature Tolerance

Every plant has a low-temperature tolerance. When the temperature drops below this point for a certain period of time, plant tissues are damaged. If the cold is severe or prolonged, the plant could be killed. How long cold temperatures last and how quickly they drop affect the extent of the damage. The faster the temperature drops, the more severe the injury. Cold that lasts for an hour or less may not hurt plants, but if it stays cold for several hours, severe damage is likely.

Monarda didyma
Beebalm

ground to produce a graceful effect. Effective around natural pools or among boulders. A single tree is most effective.

Pruning & Maintenance
Trees generally require staking for one or two seasons. Check ties monthly to avoid girdling. Thin out excessive interior growth, but do so gradually. Some leaf drop may occur after cold temperatures. Deep watering is important to avoid surface rooting. Plants sucker readily.

Melaleuca quinquenervia
Cajeput Tree, Swamp Tea Tree

Native to Australia
Evergreen
25 to 40 feet high, 25 feet wide
Full sun
Hardy to 28F
Low to moderate water use

The thick, light colored, spongy trunks provide close-up interest. Stiff, narrow leaves hang gracefully on pendulous branches. Slender spikes of white flowers bloom in April or May. Provides a strong vertical element in the landscape, particularly against two-story structures. Develops interesting multitrunk form.

Pruning & Maintenance
Plant 15 to 25 feet away from walls, structures and walkways. Root growth is vigorous. Install barriers if plants are near sidewalks or other paving. (See page 18.) Young trees grow rapidly, sometimes producing excessive growth. Thin as needed to control size. Prune gradually rather than making large cuts. Pruning large branches—4 to 6 inches in diameter — causes heavy sucker growth. Weight of flowers may cause branches to drop down into foot-traffic areas.

Melia azedarach
Chinaberry, Texas Umbrella Tree

Native to the Orient
Deciduous
30 to 40 feet high, equal spread
Full sun
Hardy to 25F to 30F
Low water use

Chinaberry was once a popular tree valued for dense shade, its dark green leaves and branch structure with round-headed canopy. Main trunk becomes quite large, as do interior support branches. Lavender-purple flowers bloom in May and are followed by yellow clusters of berries enjoyed by birds.

Pruning & Maintenance
Avoid heavy pruning. Thin lightly to control and shape in winter as needed. Berries drop from tree in winter and are messy. Consider locating trees on landscape perimeter. Tolerant of heat, drought and wind.

Mimulus cardinalis
Scarlet Monkey Flower

Native to Oregon, California, Nevada,
  Arizona and New Mexico
Perennial
1 to 2 feet high, 3 feet wide
Full sun, afternoon shade in
  hot-summer regions
Hardy to cold but goes dormant
Moderate to high water use

Narrow, glossy green leaves grow in pairs and are often sticky. Tubular, velvety, scarlet flowers bloom April through October.

Pruning & Maintenance
After first surge of growth and flowers are complete, prune flower stems and unruly growth to produce more flowers. Accepts heat with shade.

Monarda didyma
Beebalm, Bergamot

Native to North America
Perennial
2 to 4 feet high
Full sun, afternoon shade in
  hot-summer regions
Hardy to 0F
Moderate water use

Vibrant-colored flowers bloom during summer months. Attracts butterflies and hummingbirds. Suffers in heat. In hot climates plant in shade. *M. didyma* var. *menthifolia* is more heat and drought tolerant so is a better choice for these areas.

Plants have square-shaped stems and aromatic, toothed, opposite leaves alternating in pairs, characteristic of the mint family. Small, long, tubular flowers in shaggy, dense heads appear on top of hollow, brittle, erect stems that grow 2-1/2 to 4 feet high during the summer months. Leaves emit a distinct basil and mint scent when brushed.

Pruning & Maintenance
Start new plants from seed in the spring. Space 12 to 15 inches apart. Provide plant with a wire hoop or stakes for support after stems reach 12 inches high. As plants age, replace with new seedlings. Cut back to just above ground level after flowering period ends. Cage plants to protect them from rabbits.

Morus alba
Mulberry

Native to Europe and North America
Deciduous
25 to 30 feet high, 35 feet wide
Full sun
Hardy to 0F
Low to moderate water use

Mulberry is not considered a quality tree because of its many problems. In fact, it is banned from many counties in the West. It is, however, able to provide fast shade under adverse growing conditions. Most productive cultivated varieties include 'Fruitless', 'Kingan' and 'Stribling.' Trees are available in containers and as bare-root plants in the winter season.

Pruning & Maintenance
Mulberries suffer more from negative pruning than any other tree. The deliberate *stubbing*, also called *topping*, has potential for trouble as it contradicts all pruning guidelines. (See photo, page 52.) It not only is unattractive but weakens the structure of the tree. Over time, stubbing invites decay and pest and disease infestations. Branches *can* be thinned and tipped in youth but should not be stubbed. It tells a sad story of poor tree management as one drives down streets and counts the number of stubbed mulberry trees.

Can you restore a stubbed tree? Not completely, but you can improve its health and appearance. Begin by

stopping all stubbing. Cut off existing large stubs during winter, then select two or three new sprouts on each main branch in the spring. Tip-prune these after they become 3 to 4 feet long to strengthen them. Cuts made to remove stub heads will generally heal over in a season or two. If the tree is too old or beyond salvage, or trunk is split or sunburned, remove the tree and replant with a new adapted species. Shallow irrigation can cause surface rooting. Deep watering with bubblers or drips helps encourage deeper roots.

MUHLENBERGIA SPECIES
MUHLY GRASSES
Ornamental grasses are important garden accent elements in many regions of the United States. *Muhlenbergia* species are quality grasses that add a refreshing new look to shrub borders, flowerbeds and rock gardens.

Plant explorers, nursery growers and landscape architects in the Southwest discovered *Muhlenbergia*, with its graceful leaves and interesting seed-head patterns. Plants thrive in almost any soil, prefer sun and are low to moderate water users. All are hardy to cold. Ideal time to prune is after leaves turn brown—in late winter or slightly earlier. Regrowth is rapid. To make pruning and disposal easier, tie leaves together with twine about 12 inches above ground. Trim old growth with sharp hand shears to about 6 inches high.

The hardy *Muhlenbergia* species native to Texas, California and Mexico include the following described here.

Muhlenbergia capillaris

Native to Texas
Evergreen
4 to 5 feet high, 3 feet wide
Full sun, afternoon shade in
    hot-summer regions
Hardy to 0F
Low to moderate water use

When the fluffy, pinkish purple plumes of selection 'Regal Mist' reach 4 to 5 feet high in the fall there is a

Muhlenbergia rigens
Deer Grass

spectacular show of color and elegance. Graceful, dark green leaves form 3-foot clumps. Plants are evergreen in low-desert gardens and along the coast. Great plant among boulders in small clusters or in groups in a perennial border.

Pruning & Maintenance
To renew plants after winter and to remove spent flower spikes, cut back in late February or early March to 6 inches above ground level. Mature clumps can be divided readily in early spring. Make three or four divisions by cutting into base of plant and roots. Transplant divisions into moist soil and water thoroughly. Established plants may need supplemental water in extreme summer heat to keep foliage lush and green. If hungry enough, rabbits will eat plants.

Muhlenbergia dumosa
Bamboo Muhley

**Native to southern Arizona and northwestern Mexico
Evergreen
4 to 5 feet high, equal spread
Full sun
Hardy to 20F
Low to moderate water use**

The growth and refined texture of bamboo muhley differ considerably from other *Muhlenbergia* species. Stems resemble bamboo and growth is more open. With maturity, the effect is refined and feathery. At 20F leaves turn brown but recover in early spring.

Pruning & Maintenance
Most attractive if allowed to grow freely. After two seasons of growth, plants can be cut back for refreshing new growth surge in early spring.

Muhlenbergia emersleyi
Bull Grass

**Native to Arizona, New Mexico and Texas
Evergreen
Clumps to 3 feet high, 4 feet wide
Full sun
Hardy to 10F
Low water use**

'El Toro' is a popular selection with bright green foliage. Creamy white flower clusters grow above foliage clumps. Flowers develop by late summer and persist into fall. Space plants 6 to 8 feet or more apart; any closer they eventually become crowded.

Pruning & Maintenance
Cut grassy clumps back to 6 inches above ground in late winter before the arrival of warmer weather. This will stimulate new fresh growth in spring. Requires regular moisture during summer to look attractive.

Muhlenbergia lindheimeri
Lindheimer's Muhley

**Native to Arizona, New Mexico, Texas
Evergreen
3 to 4 feet high, 3 to 4 feet wide
Full sun
Hardy to 10F
Low to moderate water use**

'Autumn Glow' is a superior selection. Flower clusters produce a silvery show in the fall. Colorful seedheads bloom on top of stalks 4 to 6 feet high.

Pruning & Maintenance
If tall seedheads become straggly, cut them back as needed. Provide with well-draining soil.

Muhlenbergia rigens
Deer Grass

**Native to southern California, western Texas and northern Mexico
Evergreen
2 to 3 feet high, 3 to 5 feet wide
Full sun
Hardy to 10F
Low to moderate water use**

The soft, thin, 1- to 2-foot-long leaves sway gently in even the softest breeze. In low-elevation deserts, foliage remains relatively green. Elsewhere leaves turn brown with the first frost. The white flower stalks to 3 feet high bloom in summer and fall, enhancing the mounding 3-foot plants. Use for soil erosion control and in shrub borders as an accent. Groupings of three or more spaced 6 to 8 feet apart are effective in a large garden. Place in the foreground with taller shrubs or perennials.

Pruning & Maintenance
Even if a dry spell in the early summer turns foliage a straw color, cut back entire clump to 6 inches. With adequate moisture, recovery can be rapid for balance of growing season. A low-maintenance feature in the garden.

Myoporum parvifolium
Trailing Myoporum

Native to Australia
Evergreen
1 foot high, 4 to 8 feet wide
Full sun, afternoon shade in
    hot-summer regions
Hardy to 24F
Low to moderate water use

Prostrate growth spreads quickly once established, carpeting the ground. Trailing myoporum provides a lush effect in courtyards, on small patios and on slopes. Branches root as they spread, which makes this a good choice for erosion control. Flowers create an attractive white carpet in spring. Better adapted to areas east of the Colorado River in low-elevation deserts than in high summer heat of the Coachella Valley, Borrego Springs, Yuma or Imperial Valley.

'Dwarf Pink' is a miniature version of the species. Excellent in small areas and narrow planters.

Pruning & Maintenance
Long-term growth relies on planting in well-draining soil. Plant from 1-gallon containers in fall so new plantings can become established before hot weather. Space on 2- to 4-foot centers to allow for spread. If possible, water with low-volume drip-heads to keep soil moist for rooting and to keep moisture off foliage. Overhead watering can cause dieback. Reduce watering in winter. Control spreading growth or it will weave its way among shrubs and invade other planting areas. Nematodes are sometimes a problem with plantings in loam or sandy soil.

Myrtus communis 'Boetica'
Desert Myrtle, Twisted Myrtle

Native to the Mediterranean region
Evergreen
4 to 6 feet high (to 12 feet with great
    age), equal spread
Full sun
Hardy to 20F
Low water use

A sturdy, exuberant plant with great endurance in desert climates. Compact growth creates a handsome, informal, low-maintenance hedge. Stiff, leathery, dark green leaves point upward. White spring flowers have an unusual fragrance.

M. communis grows 6 to 8 feet high with an equal spread. *M. communis* 'Compacta' is a dwarfish version, growing 3 to 4 feet high and as wide. These two species grow more rapidly than desert myrtle so require more pruning maintenance.

Pruning & Maintenance
Slow growth of desert myrtle reduces amount of pruning required. Maintaining low water applications helps keep growth rate under control. Few disease or insect problems with the exception of black scale, an occasional pest. Plant in well-draining soil.

Nandina domestica
Heavenly Bamboo

Native to the Orient
Evergreen
6 to 8 feet high, 3 to 4 feet wide
Full sun, partial or afternoon shade in
    hot-summer regions
Hardy to 10F
Low to moderate water use

A popular, reliable and compatible plant useful in combination with native and introduced plants. Provides a bamboolike effect. Excellent in narrow planters and containers. Recently introduced dwarf selections add considerable variety.

Pruning & Maintenance
The tall, sturdy stems provide strong support for the refined foliage. Little pruning is required as plants develop after planting. When plants are four

The Right Pruning Tool
Use the proper tool for the size of branch you plan to remove. Hand pruning saws are ideal for limbs 1 inch or larger in diameter. Use the three-step method for pruning large branches as shown on page 17. Pruning loppers are best for limbs less than 1 inch in diameter. Hand pruning shears (bypass types are preferred) work well for small twigs and stems.

Nerium oleander
Oleander

to six years old, consider thinning out stems at different heights to induce plant to produce fresh new growth. Clumping growth enlarges with age so it's worth removing some stems at plant base. Do this any time. Tolerant of soil types other than clay and caliche. In hot-summer regions, provide with afternoon shade.

Nerium oleander
Oleander

Native to the Mediterranean region
Evergreen
4 to 6 feet high, equal spread
Full sun
Hardy to 18F to 24F
Low water use

Many selections of oleander are available, but consider these two colorful species: 'Petite Pink' grows 5 to 6 feet high and as wide. Pink flower clusters are more vivid, growth more vigorous than the species. 'Petite Salmon' is smaller at 4 to 6 feet in height and width. Flowers are salmon color. Use as part of plant combinations, in clusters or as a low hedge. Plant 4 to 6 feet apart for hedge. Place at least 6 feet apart if you want plants to grow without interfering with other plants.

Pruning & Maintenance
Prune during warm weather. This exposes interior of plant to sunlight, stimulating new flowering wood. Do not prune into globes or squares. Avoid shearing, which reduces flowering wood. Note that all plant parts are poisonous. Do not burn wood or smoke can cause irritation.

Oleander leaf scorch is a recent problem, affecting mature plantings throughout California and the Southwest. See page 46 for more information.

Nolina matapensis
Tree Beargrass

Native to Mexico at 3,000 to 6,500 feet
Evergreen perennial
8 to 10 feet high, 3 to 4 feet wide
Full sun
Hardy to 5F to 10F
Low water use

Shiny, tough green leaves grow 3 to 4 feet long. Tall flower stems are mounted with clusters 2 feet long and 1 foot wide in late spring and early summer. Tall, thin trunks develop with great age. Older plants with many stems can develop into small trees. Useful in large-scale arid landscapes. Like other *Nolina* species, it is rather cold hardy.

Pruning & Maintenance
As old flowers and stems die, cut off for a neater appearance. For best effect remove old leaves on lower stems. Gravelly or rocky soil is ideal, providing the necessary good drainage.

Nolina microcarpa
Sacahuista, Beargrass

Native to southeastern Arizona, far west Texas, and southwestern New Mexico
Perennial
3 to 6 feet high, 5 to 8 feet wide
Full sun
Hardy to cold
Low water use

Plants are at home in oak woodlands at 3,000 to 6,000 feet. They thrive in gravelly, sandy, well-draining soil. The main stem is wholly subterranean. The narrow, 3-foot leaves have margins with minute teeth. Native Americans use the leaf fibers for weaving baskets and mats. Flower stems rise 4 to 5 feet above dense rosette clumps. White flower panicles become brown seeds. Space 12 to 15 feet apart among boulder groupings for natural effect.

Pruning & Maintenance
In garden setting, cut off lower dead basal leaves. When flowering is complete, remove tall flower stems.

Oenothera missourensis
Yellow Evening Primrose

Native from Missouri to Nebraska south to Texas
Perennial
1 foot high, 2 feet wide
Full sun to partial shade
Hardy to 0F (but goes dormant in cold)
Low to moderate water use

Oenothera speciosa var.
berlandieri
Mexican Primrose

Deep green foliage is exuberant from spring to fall. From spring into early summer, 4-inch yellow flowers bloom in the evening.

Pink-flowered *O. speciosa* var. *berlandieri,* Mexican primrose, provides a color show with its bright pink flowers in spring.

O. caespitosa, white-tufted evening primrose, also blooms during spring. For these species, follow the pruning and maintenance schedules for *O. missourensis.*

Pruning & Maintenance
Plant on 2-foot centers. After flowers have ceased blooming, shear off tops for a surge of new growth. Thrives in most well-draining soils.

Olea europaea
Olive

Native to the Mediterranean
Evergreen
20 to 30 feet high, equal spread
Full sun
Hardy to 15F
Low to moderate water use

A quality tree with an informal, picturesque growth habit. Unfortunately, its high volume of pollen production has caused it to be banned in some regions. Check locally to see if olive can be grown in your area. Can be grown as a standard form or with multiple trunks. Canopy-shaped crown creates dense filtered shade. Plant fruitless types to avoid dealing with messy fruit. Availability of the fruitless selection 'Swan Hill' provides relief from having to follow spraying programs to prevent fruit set.

Pruning & Maintenance
Avoid heavy pruning. Excessive pruning, especially late spring through summer, can allow sun to damage trunks. Topping should be avoided—it only creates suckers and the need to remove excess growth. Likewise, "poodling" restricts normal growth and is an invitation to serious branch and trunk sunburn. Remove suckers at base of main trunk. Thin interior small branches gradually to keep canopy structure intact. Olives accept almost any soil, endure heat, cold and wind.

Olneya tesota
Desert Ironwood, Palo de Hierro

Native to arid, low-elevation regions in Arizona, California and Mexico
Evergreen to deciduous
15 to 30 feet high, 20 to 25 feet wide
Full sun
Hardy to 20F to 22F
Low water use

Desert ironwood and olive, described here, are similar in appearance, at least from a distance. Desert ironwood has a more open, textured look and is more vertical in growth. Trees develop slowly with multiple, gray-barked trunks. The finely divided, gray-green leaves set off the delicate, lavender, pea-shaped flowers that bloom in April or May. If you can grow citrus in your area, you can probably grow this special tree. Locate away from walks; sharp spines can be a hazard.

Pruning & Maintenance
Trees are long lived and seldom experience pruning problems because growth is relatively slow. It is also a tree that develops its own attractive form without needing much guidance. Provide with well-draining soil. A self-fertilizing legume.

Parkinsonia aculeata
Mexican Palo Verde, Jerusalem Thorn, Rataina

Native to Mexico and South America
Deciduous
15 to 30 feet high, equal spread
Full sun
Hardy to 15F
Low to moderate water use

The sparse irregular, yellow-green branches filter sunlight, revealing an intricate branching structure. The shade pattern created is open and textured, and is not too dark. The long, narrow leaves to 16 inches long are bright green. Displays of lemon-yellow flowers cover the tree in early spring. As with many arid land plants, persistent brown seed pods follow flowers. Thorns are a problem in traffic areas. *Parkinsonia* reseeds easily and can become a "weed tree" in some regions.

Olea europaea
Olive

Pennisetum setaceum
'Cupreum'
Purple Fountain Grass

Pruning & Maintenance

Remove crossing interior branches, low drooping branches and dead wood while trees are dormant in winter. Maintain the tree's natural form; avoid heavy pruning and stubbing. Leaf litter can be a problem in flowerbeds. Locate trees in natural areas or place in background of landscape where leaf debris is not noticeable. A legume that does not need fertilization. Accepts tough conditions of heat, alkalinity, wind, dust and low rainfall.

Passiflora edulis
Passion Vine

Native to Brazil
30 feet high, 20 to 30 feet wide
Full sun to partial shade
Hardy to 28F
Moderate water use

The vigor of rich leaves and abundant, unusual, white-to-lavender, 4-inch flowers create a tropical effect. Flowering occurs in spring and summer and is followed by small, edible, purple fruit that has a tropical aroma and acid flavor. Vines cling by tendrils. It's wise to provide young plants with a sturdy support for them to climb, such as a pergola, lattice fence or trellis.

Pruning & Maintenance

Thin out heavy growth in early spring. To determine when fruit is ripe, cut with a knife or pruning shears.

Pennisetum setaceum
'Cupreum'
Purple Fountain Grass

Native to Africa
Perennial grass
4 to 5 feet high, 3 to 4 feet wide
Full sun
Hardy to 18F to 20F
Low water use

The graceful, nodding, purple plumes and purplish stems provide a long season of color. Use as a garden accent in perennial borders and rock gardens. This species does not reseed like *P. setaceum*, fountain grass, which has become an invasive pest in many regions of the West.

Pruning & Maintenance

In early spring after frost, cut entire plant back to 6 inches above ground level. The goal is to remove straggly leaves and induce plant to produce new growth in spring. For fresh growth in late summer, cut back again in August. Plants tolerate wind, dust and alkaline conditions.

PENSTEMON SPECIES
PENSTEMON

Throughout the Southwest, the perennial *Penstemon* species are beginning to receive the recognition they deserve. The richness and variety of flower colors—purple, red, pink, salmon and white—blend beautifully with other arid land plants. The wide range of plant heights, 1-1/2 feet to 5 feet, contributes to their utility when blended with taller shrubs. Species flower in spring, summer or fall. Leaves at the base of the stalks range from 1 to 3 feet high. Water use is low to moderate in spring and fall, depending on soil drainage. After flowering, cut tall stems to basal growth. Hardiness ranges from 0F to 15F.

Penstemon baccharifolius

Native to central Texas
Perennial
1 to 2 feet high, equal spread
Full sun, partial shade in hot-summer regions
Hardy to 5F
Low to moderate water use

'Del Rio' is a recently selected form with a dwarfish, shrublike appearance. Red flower spikes 12 to 18 inches high bloom from June into September.

Pruning & Maintenance

Trim spent flower spikes when flowering is complete. Good soil drainage essential. Be cautious about overwatering at any time. Space at least 2 to 3 feet apart when planting.

Penstemon eatonii
Firecracker Penstemon

Native to Arizona and Colorado
Perennial
Flower stems 3 to 4 feet high, basal
    growth to 2 feet wide
Full sun, filtered shade in hot-summer
    regions
Hardy to 18F
Low to moderate water use

Flowers come in February, making
this plant among the first to bloom
each spring in low-desert gardens.
Full sun encourages strong, 3- to
4-foot vertical stems. Planted where
it receives too much shade causes
sprawling stem growth.

Pruning & Maintenance
A light mulch in summer helps keep
roots cool and reduces water need.
Grow in well-draining soils.

Penstemon parryi
Parry's Penstemon

Native to central Arizona and Sonora,
    Mexico
Perennial
Flower stems 3 to 5 feet high, basal
    growth 2 feet wide
Full sun, filtered shade in hot-summer
    regions
Hardy to 18F
Low to moderate water use

Widely adapted to grow in desert climates. Responds to moderate water
and fertilizer. Tall, strongly vertical,
3- to 5-foot stems show off flowers in
shades of pink. Looks attractive in
mounded rock gardens, around
mesquites and acacias or as a foreground among desert shrubs.

Pruning & Maintenance
Allow flowers to reseed, then cut
back to top of leaf rosette. Plants will
bloom again the following year.
Some moisture required in summer
but avoid overwatering. Good soil
drainage is necessary. Don't plant in
heavily shaded locations, or growth
will be weak.

Penstemon superbus
Superb Penstemon

Native to Arizona and Chihuahuan
    Desert in Mexico
Perennial
Flower stems 2 to 4 feet high, basal
    growth 2 feet wide
Full sun, filtered shade in hot-summer
    regions
Hardy to 5F to 10F
Moderate water use

Coral flower colors complement pas-
tel shades of spring wildflowers.
Flower spikes are upright and strong.
Individual flowers are sharply
defined and show well. Flower
spikes average 2 to 3 feet high. With
good care and possibly with some
staking they can reach 4 to 5 feet
high. Plant in clusters with other
species, but keep plant and flower
heights in mind. Place larger species
to the back of planting area.

Pruning & Maintenance
In wind-prone regions, provide
stakes to support tall stems. Avoid
overhead watering; drip irrigation is
preferred method. Moderate but not
high water during summer is essential or problems can develop with
root rot. Transplants easily in winter.

Perovskia atriplicifolia
Russian Sage

Native to Russia
Deciduous
3 to 4 feet high, equal spread
Full sun
Hardy to cold
Low water use

The delicate, lavender-blue flower
spikes bloom over a long period from
spring to fall. Many branching,
woody stems support small, toothed,
gray-green leaves coated with tiny
hairs. Effective companion with
Salvia greggii, red salvia, and many
Leucophyllum species, Texas ranger.

Pruning & Maintenance
Trim tips and spent flowering wood
gently to encourage rebloom. After
plants go dormant in winter, trim

With Pruning, Timing Is Everything
The most common time to
prune is during the winter,
when plants are dormant.
But many plants should be
pruned following their primary
flowering season. Be aware
the bloom periods of annuals
and perennials are greatly
influenced by climate,
including elevation, moisture
and temperature. Because of
these variables, flowering
periods can vary up to two
weeks or more from year to
year and from region to
region. Woody trees, shrubs,
vines and some cacti and
succulents are less influenced
by temperature and moisture
and generally have more
predetermined growth and
flowering schedules. Refer to
the Master Flowering and
Pruning Chart
on pages 67 to 74.

back growth to 12 to 18 inches above ground using two-step method as shown on page 19. Prefers lean, gritty, well-draining soil.

Phlomis fruticosa
Jerusalem Sage

Native to the Mediterranean region
Evergreen to deciduous
4 feet high, equal spread
Full sun
Hardy to 25F
Low to moderate water use

Dense, thick, furry, deeply creased gray leaves combine with dusky yellow flowers in whorls along the stems. Flowers bloom in spring and again in fall. High heat may slow bloom cycle. Combines well with *Salvia* and *Lavandula* species.

Pruning & Maintenance
Plant new, young plants, checking bottom of container at the nursery to see if they are rootbound. Also check plants for mealybugs before planting. If necessary, treat with appropriate insecticide; ask at your nursery. Cut back flowering stems after each flowering period for a repeat bloom. In late fall prune back plants by about one-half so they will respond the following season with fresh growth. Grows in almost any well-draining soil. Accepts sun, heat and drought.

Phormium tenax
New Zealand Flax

Native to New Zealand
Perennial
6 to 9 feet high, 3 to 5 feet wide
Full sun along coast; afternoon shade in
    hot-summer regions
Hardy to 10F
Moderate water use

Large forms create a bold point of interest with their subtropical structure and mass of swordlike leaves. Leaf colors range from green to bronze, dark purplish red to variegated. Dull red flowers on tall stalks grow well above the leaves. Use for dramatic outdoor flower arrangements in large containers. Dwarf selections to 18 inches high with various leaf colors are also available.

Pruning & Maintenance
Minimum-maintenance plants. As leaves die out at base of plant, remove by shearing or pulling them off close to trunk. When flower stalks mature remove at base of stem. A location in partial shade or beneath a high-canopy tree benefits plants in hot-summer climates.

Photinia species
Chinese Photinia

Native to China
Evergreen
10 to 12 feet high, 8 to 10 feet wide
Full sun
Hardy to 5F to 15F
Moderate water use

Of the two most common *Photinia* species, *P. serrulata* is better-adapted at elevations up to 2,000 feet. *P. fraseri* is used more frequently at lower elevations. Both have colorful bronzy foliage in the spring and again in late fall. White flower clusters bloom above the leaves in spring.

Pruning & Maintenance
Plants have large leaves, so shearing creates an undesirable coarse texture. Prune as described and shown on page 19 to produce a more natural appearance. Chlorosis is a common problem with alkaline soils. Treat with iron sulfate products. In low-elevation gardens plants do better with filtered or afternoon shade. Provide deep, moderate irrigation. Space new plants 6 to 8 feet apart to allow for natural, wide-spreading growth.

Pinus eldarica
Afghan Pine, Mondale Pine

Native to southwest Asia
Evergreen conifer
30 to 80 feet high, 20 to 30 feet wide
Full sun
Hardy to 0F
Low to moderate water use

Rapid, dense, pyramidal growth make this pine a good choice as a landscape specimen or for windbreaks. It has proven its adaptability to tough conditions, thriving in desert climates in severe winds, heat

Phormium tenax
New Zealand Flax

Pinus eldarica
Afghan Pine

and cold. Pyramidal growth is dense in youth, then becomes more open 10 to 12 years after planting.

Pruning & Maintenance
Little pruning is required. In fact, it's better to allow trees to develop their own form. Grows best in well-draining soils. Plant in an alternating pattern at 20 to 30 feet apart for windbreak. Leave lower branches intact to help diffuse wind flow. Water deeply to establish strong root system.

Pinus halepensis
Aleppo Pine

Native to eastern Mediterranean region
Evergreen conifer
40 to 60 feet high, 35 to 40 feet wide
Full sun
Hardy 15F to 20F
Low to moderate water use

This pine is commonly grown throughout the Southwest. It grows rapidly, eventually developing a wide irregular crown.

Pruning & Maintenance
Attention has been given to aleppo pine blight. To date there is no known tangible cause. Visual signs are bronzing, chlorosis and sometimes dieback of large branches or entire trees. These symptoms generally appear in March through May or October through November. Studies indicate irrigation practices may be at fault. Water deep and at drip line and beyond so moisture reaches entire root mass. (See illustration, page 8.) Maintain uniform water supply. Also helpful to plant in soils with good drainage and avoid planting in caliche soils.

Pistacia chinensis
Chinese Pistache

Native to China
Deciduous
40 to 60 feet high, 40 to 50 feet wide
Full sun
Hardy to 10F
Low to moderate water use

Uniform growth at a moderate rate the first five years. Dormant in winter, but the glory of red fall color creates vivid seasonal interest. A well-controlled garden tree useful for shade.

Ascending branches develop without trimming or pruning. Compound foliage comes in 12-inch leaflets. Leafs out slowly in the spring.

Pruning & Maintenance
Trees develop on their own without much pruning. Major branches rarely need to be pruned. As trees develop, prune up lower branches to form a crown high enough to walk under. Sturdy trunk growth reduces need to stake except in extremely windy areas. Provide low to moderate deep water. Accepts heat, cold, wind and drought. Grows best in deep soil that has good drainage. Shallow or difficult soils will retard growth. Susceptible to Texas root rot.

Pithecellobium flexicaule
Texas Ebony

Native to southern Texas and northeast
    Mexico
Evergreen
15 to 25 feet high, 15 to 20 feet wide
Full sun, accepts some shade
Hardy to 20F
Moderate water use

Informal, quality, slow-growing tree with striking features. Unusual thorny, dark green leaflets create a crown of intertwining branches. The silhouette is dramatic when dense clusters of yellow to white catkinlike flowers briefly cover the tree in late spring through early summer.

Pruning & Maintenance
Train tree gradually first one to four years. Do not remove lower branches. Leave them in place so they'll help strengthen main trunk. Prune up as desired after this period to suit landscape situation. Avoid planting close to traffic areas due to thorns. Wear gloves to prune. Best time to do major pruning is late winter but seldom required. If you find seed pods unsightly, cut them off with a pole pruner. Some trees develop more pods than others. A self-fertilizing legume. Provide with good soil drainage and moderate moisture. Trees grown in regions in mild, warm winters (and planted in sunny locations) often surpass the average mature size by 20 percent.

Pistacia chinensis
Chinese Pistache

Pithecellobium mexicanum
Mexican Ebony, Palo Chino

Native to Sonora, Sinaloa and southern
  Baja, Mexico
Deciduous
20 to 30 feet high, 20 to 25 feet wide
Full sun
Hardy to 10F to 15F
Low to moderate water use

Tree grows with an open canopy and
branching pattern. Growth rate is
rapid, comparable to that of Chilean
mesquite. Tree is armed with cat-
claw-like thorns. Foliage and immature bark are pale gray-green, similar
to those of *Olneya tesota*, desert ironwood tree. Cream-colored blooms
appear in March and April. Brown
seed pods 1 to 3 inches long similar
to those of *P. flexicaule*, Texas ebony,
mature by midsummer.

Pruning & Maintenance
Catclaw thorns make it difficult to
prune. Clean out dead wood or
crossing branches at least once a year
during winter dormancy. However,
plant form develops naturally rather
well without pruning. A self-fertilizing legume.

Pithecellobium pallens
Tenaza Ape's Earring

Native to Texas
Semi-evergreen
20 to 30 feet high, 15 to 25 feet wide
Full sun
Hardy to 20F
Moderate water use

A recently introduced *Pithecellobium*
from Texas with an interesting difference from *P. flexicaule*—branches are
long and straight with small thorns
on old and new growth. Thorns are
few on main trunk. Fragrant flowers
are creamy white in 2- to 6-inch clusters from May to August. Used as a
small courtyard tree in Texas gardens;
adapted to grow in most warm-sum-
mer regions.

Pruning & Maintenance
Thin canopy as needed to allow wind
to flow through branches. Remove
dead wood and long, erratic, crossing
branches. Self-fertilizing legume.

Pittosporum phillyraeoides

Native to Australia
Evergreen
20 feet high, 15 feet wide
Full sun
Hardy to 10F
Low water use

Slender, heat-tolerant tree well-suited
for small gardens. Narrow, 4-inch,
gray-green leaves on branchlets bend
over and elongate, flowing to the
ground. The yellow flowers are small
with considerable fragrance in late
winter and early spring. Later, large
yellow berries develop in a precise
manner that suggests rosary beads.
With its refined features, consider use
near a pond or simulated boulder
stream bed or in narrow sideyard
locations.

Pruning & Maintenance
New plantings generally require
staking until main trunk develops
strength. Lower side branches should
be kept for two to three years to help
develop a stronger trunk. With age
some interior branches die and need
to be removed. Encourage deep rooting by watering deeply to reduce surface suckering. Water needs are low.
Do not top trees.

Platanus wrightii
Arizona Sycamore

Native to riparian areas in southern and
  eastern mountains of Arizona and
  New Mexico at 2,000 to 6,000 feet
Deciduous
40 to 80 feet high, 80 feet wide
Full sun
Cold hardy to 0F
High water use

There is a big difference between
P. wrightii, Arizona sycamore, and
P. racemosa, California sycamore.
The Arizona native's large, maplelike
leaves are more deeply lobed. The
bell-shaped seed clusters have individual stalks branching from a common stalk. Bark is attractive, with a
thin, matted white and tan effect.
Heavy vertical trunks form a graceful
structure. Growth is vigorous, with
potential for 80 feet in height and

Platanus species
Sycamore

spread. Definitely a tree for large areas. In heavy clay or caliche soils, growth is curtailed. Voracious, high-water-use plants.

Pruning & Maintenance
Under certain conditions with poor drainage, iron chlorosis occurs. Apply iron chelate to correct. When nursery-grown trees are planted from containers, growth is typically more robust. With age, severe pruning creates sucker growth. This in turn causes increased density and more thinning. Trees tolerate heat, cold and wind. Browning leaves are a sign of distress.

Plumbago scandens
Summary Snow

Native to southern Arizona, southern Florida and tropical regions in the western hemisphere
Evergreen
4 feet high, equal spread
Full sun to partial shade
Hardy to 20F
Low to moderate water use

From spring into fall, five-petaled white flowers bloom until plants go dormant. By the second and third year after planting, plants become lush and produce more flowers. Growth is more luxuriant in full sun but plants in hot regions appreciate some shade. Combine with evergreen plants such as *Ruellia peninsularis*. Place plants 5 feet or more from walkways to avoid the problem of fruit sticking to clothing of passersby.

Pruning & Maintenance
Cut back frost-damaged foliage while plants are dormant in winter. Recovers rapidly in spring. Good soil drainage is important. Don't overwater during winter.

Populus species
Poplar, Cottonwood

Native to many regions
Deciduous
30 to 60 feet high
Full sun
Hardy to 10F to 15F, some to -40F
Moderate to high water use

These are fast-growing trees, widely used as windbreaks and screens and for shade. All are deciduous.

Although they have undesirable qualities, poplars are useful in wide, open areas. Do not plant near paved drives, walks, curbs, pools and septic tanks. Select trees that possess a vertical growth habit for windbreaks or canopy growth.

P. balsamifera can grow 30 to 60 feet high. It has been tested extensively in the Mojave Desert and is also adapted to grow in low-elevation regions.

A more vertical poplar is *P. alba* 'Pyramidalis', bolleana poplar. Fast growing. Both species need regular water to establish.

Pruning & Maintenance
After establishing, poplars quickly develop their own form, requiring little guidance. Excessive sucker growth and dead interior wood are principle problems. If pruning is required, do so during dormant season. Accepts a wide range of soils.

Portulacaria afra
Elephant Food

Native to South Africa
Evergreen
12 feet high, 8 to 12 feet wide
Full sun, afternoon shade in hot-summer regions
Hardy to 32F
Low water use

Elephant food is an old-time plant, and continues to be as much a favorite as it was 50 years ago. Grows in South Africa to a height of 12 feet with equal spread. Does best in a coastal environment. In hot inland valleys and low-elevation deserts, locate in shade and with overhead protection to avoid cold damage. Allow for spread to 12 feet. Effective in large containers.

Pruning & Maintenance
A low-maintenance plant that can be trained into almost any shape. Cuttings develop roots quickly to extend plantings or to share plants with friends. When thinning or controlling size, always cut back to a node to direct growth.

Populus species
Poplar

PROSOPIS SPECIES MESQUITES

Among the most attractive features of mesquites are the trunk and branch structure and the graceful foliage. Other advantages include hardiness, low water use, and a range of native and introduced species available for a variety of landscape uses. Root activity and top growth are aggressive during the first two to three years after transplanting. Young trees often produce horizontal or downward-arching branches that must be pruned to direct vertical growth. Provide adequate deep moisture. Deep watering helps develop extensive roots, helping to provide stability in heavy winds. But excessive moisture creates heavy top growth in spring and summer. Adequate guying or staking young trees with flexible ties is usually required in windy areas. It also helps to thin canopies prior to seasonal winds. Avoid using round root guards with mesquites. Their rapid and aggressive root growth requires a large volume of soil area. Without enough soil area for roots to spread, serious problems can occur. (See photo, page 52.) All are legumes.

Prosopis alba
Argentine Mesquite

Native to Argentina, Bolivia, Peru, Paraguay and Uruguay
Evergreen to semideciduous
30 to 35 feet high, equal spread
Full sun
Hardy to 15F
Low to moderate water use

The selection 'Colorado' is proving to grow more uniformly and without the long thorns that are typical of *P. alba*. A rapid producer of shade compared to other species. In warm, low-elevation desert areas trees are semideciduous. Growth is rapid—up to five feet per year in the first three years. Cream-colored flowers are produced during the spring months. Fernlike leaves are dark green. Trunks are dark brown. Full sun important.

Pruning & Maintenance
Judicious pruning is essential during the first three years. Rapid growth requires interior thinning to open up canopy and allow winds to flow through. Prune gradually. Do not remove more than 20 percent of foliage at one time. After two to three years, prune outside draping branches to 6 to 8 feet above ground to allow for traffic and underplantings. Pruning may be required three or four times during the heat of summer when plants grow most rapidly. Supply sturdy stakes to support young trees, because top growth often develops more quickly than root structure. Use at least three 2-inch diameter metal pipe stakes or 3-inch lodgepoles (10-foot length). Adjust ties as trunk diameter increases. Prune large branches in the winter to reduce sap flow from heavy cuts. Sucker growth develops after pruning on main stems. Provide moisture at drip line and beyond (see illustration, page 8) as top growth expands.

Prosopis chilensis
Chilean Mesquite

Native to Bolivia, Chile, Peru and northwestern Argentina
Semievergreen
30 feet high, equal spread
Full sun
Hardy to 12F
Moderate water use

Symmetrical and rapid-growing, these trees are popular in Southwest desert landscapes. They are appealing because of their foliage density, which provides shade for gardens and patios, and can screen unsightly areas. Use as a windbreak or even a barrier plant. Twigs are typically spiny but this varies with individual trees.

Pruning & Maintenance
To develop height and framework, retain lateral branches on lower trunk. This builds girth and strength and encourages a permanent structure above head height. Young trees are often shallow-rooted. With vigorous growth, they are subject to blow-down in severe winds. Stake and tie the first two to three years. Check

and adjust ties every other month to reduce possibility of trunk injury. When crown structure has developed, which takes three to four years, remove lower lateral branches on main trunk, if desired, or if space is needed for foot traffic. Heaviest pruning season begins with heat and continues until late summer, but remove no more than 20 percent at one time. Plant in deep soil.

Prosopis glandulosa var. glandulosa
Texas Honey Mesquite

Native to Mojave, Sonoran, Lower
    Colorado and Chihuahua Deserts
Deciduous
25 feet high, 35 feet wide
Full sun
Hardy to 0F
Low to moderate water use

Texas honey mesquite could be considered the best mesquite for landscape use. The fine-textured, fernlike leaves closely resemble those of *Schinus molle*, California pepper. (See illustrations, right.) They also share similar-looking trunks and wide, sprawling canopies. Both are at their best in open spaces. The 2- to 3-inch, fragrant yellow flower spikes bloom in April.

Pruning & Maintenance
It does take some pruning to train the multiple trunks of young trees to develop into the stately, picturesque trees you see in nature. Begin by selecting trees at the nursery that have multiple trunks. Deep watering helps the tree become well established. Thin interior branches in the early spring to allow wind to flow through.

Prosopis glandulosa var. velutina
Arizona Velvet Mesquite

Native to Arizona and Sonora Mexico,
    at 1,000 to 4,000 feet
Deciduous
10 to 20 feet high, 15 to 30 feet wide
Full sun
Hardy to 10F
Moderate to high water use

Dense short hairs cover practically all of young plants, even seed pods. With age, trunks become gnarled and shaggy, resulting in trees of great character. Due to slow growth in youth, plants look more like shrubs than trees.

Pruning & Maintenance
Stake young trees properly as shown on page 30. Avoid heavy pruning at any one time to prevent sucker growth. Water deeply.

Prosopis pubescens
Screwbean Mesquite

Native to flood plains, valleys and along
    streams in the Southwest to 4,000 feet
Deciduous
10 to 20 feet high, equal spread
Full sun
Hardy to 0F
Low to moderate water use

This is a tough and hardy tree, useful as a windbreak or screen. It can also be trained into a small shade tree. Grows as a large shrub or small, shaggy-barked, single or multitrunked tree. Grayish spring twigs contrast with the fine-textured, lacy green foliage. Yellowish flowers bloom from April to June. Tree is easy to identify because of its 10-inch-long bean pods that are tightly coiled in a spiral.

Pruning & Maintenance
Allow to grow naturally without pruning so branches reach to the ground, appreciated by wildlife. Or prune up branches to develop a canopy and shade for underplantings. With extra moisture in summer, growth rate increases. If pruning is excessive, suckers develop vigorously. Remove dead or crossing interior branches as they occur. Topping is known to sometimes kill trees.

Prunus caroliniana
Carolina Cherry

Native to North Carolina west to Texas
Evergreen
8 to 20 feet high, 8 to 12 feet wide
Full sun, afternoon shade in
    hot-summer regions
Hardy to 20F
Moderate water use

A comparison of leaves of *Schinus molle*, California pepper, top, and *Prosopis glandulosa* var. *glandulosa*, Texas honey mesquite, bottom.

Pyrus species
Ornamental Pear

Deep green, glossy foliage grows compactly. Plant closely at 3 to 4 feet apart for hedge or as a vertical form for natural or formal pruned effect.

Pruning & Maintenance
Avoid planting in saline or alkaline soils. Good drainage important. Ideal planting time is fall to early spring in high-temperature low elevations. Tight, compact growth reduces need to prune. Avoid shearing; brown edges on leaf tips are unsightly.

Psilostrophe species
Paperflower

Native to eastern Arizona, New Mexico, western Texas and Mexico at 4,000 to 7,000 feet
Perennial
2 feet high, equal spread
Full sun
Hardy to 15F
Low water use

P. cooperi, paperflower, has been grown for some time as a semiwoody perennial. It reaches 1 foot high and 1 foot wide. Yellow flowers cover the plant April through October.
P. tagetina produces larger yellow flowers and larger leaves. Use in combination with *Salvia farinacea* and *S. clevelandii,* which have similar moisture needs.

Pruning & Maintenance
Little maintenance required. Plants perform well on their own if allowed to grow undisturbed. Well-draining soil a must. Don't overwater.

Punica granatum
Pomegranate

Native to southern Asia and southeast Europe
Deciduous
10 to 18 feet high, 10 to 12 feet wide
Full sun
Hardy to 20F
Moderate water use, high water use for flowers and fruit

Pomegranates were important in the early mission gardens and in the development of arid landscaping. Today pomegranate hedges provide protection from winds in desert orchards. Orange-red flowers bloom in the spring, red fruit follow in summer. Useful as espalier or small multi-trunk tree. The dwarf selection 'Nana' grows to 3 feet high with similar flowers as the species, but produces inedible fruit.

Pruning & Maintenance
Avoid shearing because this reduces flowers and fruit. Prune dead or twiggy interior growth in winter months. Provide regular moisture during growing and fruiting periods. Reduce water applied in winter.

Pyracantha species
Pyracantha

Native to Taiwan (*P. koidzumii*)
Evergreen
Height and width vary with species
Full sun
Hardy to cold
Moderate water use

Pyracantha is available in a wide range of forms and berry colors. Some can be grown as espaliers on fences or walls (see photos, page 59) or used as barrier plants and hedges. 'Ruby Mound' has graceful, spreading branches that develop into a rounded form 2 to 4 feet high and 4 to 6 feet wide. White flowers bloom in spring followed by red berries in the fall and winter. *P. koidzumii* 'Santa Cruz' at 3 feet high is more prostrate and spreads to 4 feet wide. 'Victory' is vigorous and shrublike to 10 feet high and 6 to 8 feet wide. It develops red berries late and holds them longer than other selections. A great espalier plant that attracts birds.

Pruning & Maintenance
Plants will not tolerate excessive moisture. Long, sharp thorns make them a bad choice near foot-traffic patterns but good for security screening. Susceptible to scale, woolly aphids, mites and fireblight disease. Prune to control plants after flowering ends in the spring. This helps reduce incidence of fireblight that typically accompany rains. Spring is the time to prune espaliered plants and train horizontal and vertical stems. Wear gloves when pruning.

Pyrus species
Ornamental Pears

Native to Taiwan
Deciduous
18 to 30 feet high or more, 30 feet wide
Full sun, afternoon shade in
    hot-summer regions
Hardy to cold
Low to moderate water use

P. kawakamii, evergreen pear, is a small tree or large shrub to 18 to 24 feet high and as wide. It is one of the earliest plants to flower, blooming in late winter to early spring.

P. calleryana 'Bradford' typically grows to 30 feet high with horizontal branches and oval, glossy leaves. Flowers bloom in late winter in white clusters. Fall color is purple-red. Not as susceptible to fireblight as *P. kawakamii.* Many other selections with various forms and shades of fall color are also available.

Pruning & Maintenance
Little pruning required. Stake trunks as needed to support. Fireblight occurs more on *P. kawakamii* and afflicted branches should be removed carefully. Prune far enough back of afflicted branches so as not to allow shears to cut into diseased wood. Disinfect shears in bleach between each cut. Rainfall after pruning causes conditions that encourage the blight in the spring and occasionally in late summer.

Quercus agrifolia
Coast Live Oak

Native to coastal ranges and interior
    valleys of California
Evergreen
50 to 70 feet high, 40 to 60 feet wide
Full sun
Hardy to 10F
Moderate water use

This is a quality tree for California gardens. It is a tree to cherish if you have a mature specimen, or one to plant for future generations. The rugged growth pattern and sturdy branches support rich green leaves. (See photo, page 62.)

Pruning & Maintenance
Growth in youth is often twiggy. Encourage more substantial branching by pinching off the tips of small branches. Avoid heavy pruning because this contributes to sucker growth. Plant in deep soil for better root anchorage; oaks tend to develop shallow roots. Water deeply well away from main trunk to avoid conditions that encourage oak root fungus. Well-established, mature oaks are naturally adapted to winter-moist and summer-dry pattern of irrigation, so reduce water applied during summer. But if you have a mature oak, don't alter its watering schedule abruptly. Change it gradually over a period of a few months.

Quercus engelmannii
Engleman oak

Native to San Diego and L.A. counties
    in California to Baja California
Evergreen
50 to 60 feet high, equal spread
Full sun
Hardy to 0F
Low to moderate water use

As trees develop, character in form and structure becomes evident. Allow plenty of space for spreading growth. Even trees grown in hot-summer regions seem to thrive.

Pruning & Maintenance
If the soil grade around a mature oak is altered by construction activity or if irrigation schedules change dramatically, the tree may have difficulty adjusting. New young trees accept such changes easier and their growth can be rapid. To encourage development, pinch or cut out twiggy growth. This helps promote stronger vertical branching. Deep irrigation helps develop deep rooting. As plants mature, avoid heavy pruning so as not to induce suckering. Prune gradually during winter season.

Quercus species
Oak

As your landscape plants mature, the shape of your garden changes slowly as well. Trees get taller and cast more dense shade, influencing what can be grown under and around them. Evaluate the sun and shade exposures of your garden from time to time. Trees may need to be trimmed professionally, thinning out branches, to allow more sunlight to reach other garden plants once again.

Quercus fusiformis
Escarpment Live Oak

Native to Texas
Evergreen
30 to 40 feet high, 30 to 50 feet wide
Full sun
Hardy to 0F
Low water use

A Texas oak that grows slowly but is worth the wait. The native Texas oaks provide a strong structural element with their high crowns and multitrunk growth.

Pruning & Maintenance
Unlike many trees, provide support to protect tree from wind for several years. To develop multitrunk growth and high canopy, direct growth early. Remove crossing branches and dead wood. Tree trunks and horizontal branches grow naturally without requiring pruning after the first few years. Accepts sand, loam, clay, limestone and even calcareous soils as long as they are well draining.

Quercus gambelii
Gambel Oak

Native to Arizona and Mexico
Deciduous
50 feet high, equal spread
Full sun
Hardy to 0F
Low water use in heavy soils; moderate water use in sandy soils

With adequate drainage, established trees can grow two feet per year. Prefers cool winter temperatures such as those found in Albuquerque and Las Vegas. The deeply lobed, deciduous leaves put on a color show of red, orange and yellow in the fall. The rough, gray bark gives the tree a strong character.

Pruning & Maintenance
Thinning twiggy growth can help establish leader branches for more vertical growth. Prune lightly in winter season. Heavy pruning can cause suckering. Deep moisture is important. Deer like to browse young trees.

Quercus ilex
Holly Oak

Native to the Mediterranean region
Evergreen
30 to 50 feet high, equal spread
Full sun
Hardy to 24F
Low to moderate water use

Known in Europe as the Holm oak. This tree, like many oaks, grows slowly at first but with time can become quite massive. Dense branching and leaves form an oval crown while young. This eventually becomes a rounded, symmetrical form with maturity. Dramatic as a street tree or specimen tree. Leaves are dark green on top and silvery to yellow below. Leaf shape and size vary from 1 to 3 inches long and 1/2 inch to 1 inch wide. They often have toothed margins that resemble holly. Small acorns grow from inconspicuous flowers. Bark is usually smooth and dark.

Pruning & Maintenance
Tolerant of being grown in a lawn but infrequent deep irrigations (rather than frequent sprinklings) are preferred. Spring feedings with a complete fertilizer encourage healthy dark foliage and rapid growth. Prune trees when young to create a balanced scaffold. Thin as needed to reduce wind resistance. Staking may be required the first two to three years to maintain upright growth habit. Few pests plague holly oak. Aphids on new growth can be a nuisance. Best growth in soil with good drainage that is deep enough to allow for deep rooting.

Quercus lobata
Valley Oak, California White Oak

Native to interior valleys and foothills of California
Deciduous
50 to 70 feet high, equal spread
Full sun
Hardy to -10F
Moderate water use

Once established, these trees can grow as much as three to four feet per year. They tolerate heat and some soil alkalinity. A picturesque, large, heavy-branched tree, often with twisted and weeping growth. Provide ample room—this is a big tree. Avoid planting near pool or patio areas because of debris.

Pruning & Maintenance
Use care when pruning to retain the picturesque stature, keeping its natural form. If pruning is necessary, prune during winter. Do so gradually to reduce suckering. The "oak balls" that fall late in the year are lightweight and not harmful to the trees. Provide with deep, well-draining soil. Deep watering is also essential.

Quercus muehlenbergii
Chinquapin Oak

Native to southern U.S.
Deciduous
40 to 60 feet high, 20 to 40 feet wide
Full sun to partial shade, depending on elevation
Hardy to 0F
Low to moderate water use

This tree is easy to identify by its serrated, dark green leaves that turn in fall to yellow with green, purple and rust hues. Because it's deciduous, growth is more rapid than for evergreen species. Often seen growing near creeks in its native environment.

Pruning & Maintenance
Prune to remove rubbing or crisscrossing branches and dead wood as they occur. Allow tree to develop its own structure. Well-draining soil and deep water needed for good root development. Accepts alkaline soil.

Quercus texana
Texas Red Oak, Spanish Oak, Buckley Oak

(*Q. shumardii* var. *texana*)
Native to the Edwards Plateau in Texas
Deciduous
15 to 30 feet high, equal spread
Full sun to partial shade
Hardy to 15F
Moderate water use

The leaf structure is indented with wide spacing between vein ribs.

Foliage is a rich red in fall. Most trees develop into an attractive, multi-trunk form.

Pruning & Maintenance
Prune to remove crossing branches in winter. However, natural growth creates strong structure so little pruning is required. Remove dead wood as trees age. Drought-tolerant once established. Grows well in limestone soils.

Quercus virginiana
Southern Live Oak

Native to southeastern U.S.
Evergreen
40 to 50 feet high, 40 to 100 feet wide (Mature size may be smaller in desert regions)
Full sun
Hardy to 10F
Moderate water use

The selected form 'Heritage' has proven to be well adapted to hot-summer regions. It is a handsome, quality shade tree that should be used more often. Dark green leaves have smooth edges and drop in spring before new leaves develop. This tree creates large shade patterns. Grows to a substantial height and spread so give it space. Space at least 60 feet apart on centers.

Pruning & Maintenance
Thin heavy dense growth inside canopy the first five years to allow winds to flow through. But don't prune more than 10 percent at any one time. Remove stakes and ties as soon as trees are stable on their own to prevent girdling the trunk. Trees tolerate widely spaced irrigations once established. Grows well in sandy, loam or alluvial soils.

Rhaphiolepis indica
Indian Hawthorne

Native to India
Evergreen
2 to 5 feet high, equal spread
Full sun to shade
Hardy to 20F to 24F
Moderate water use

This plant is surprisingly well adapted to a range of climates, from low-elevation desert regions to the coast, and in inland valleys. Selected species flower in white, rose or pink in late spring.

Pruning & Maintenance
Do not shear plants, which destroys flowering wood. Prune only to control form and shape after flowering ceases in late spring. Overwatering can encourage fungus diseases. Plant in well-draining soil.

Rhus glabra
Smooth Sumac

Native to Texas
Deciduous
10 feet high, equal spread
Full sun
Hardy to 18F to 24F
Low water use

Grown as large shrub or small tree. The vigorous growth and underground roots are excellent for erosion control. Color interest throughout the year includes spectacular red leaves in early fall, white pyramidal flowers in spring and early summer, and scarlet, conical fruit clusters in winter. Attracts animals and birds.

Pruning & Maintenance
Looks best free of controls. For dense growth, cut back to near ground level during dormancy. Grows rapidly in almost any well-draining soil but avoid planting in alkaline soil. Accepts drought and cold once established, but may appear unkempt without supplemental water.

Rhus lancea
African Sumac

Native to Africa
Evergreen
20 to 25 feet high, 25 to 35 feet wide
Full sun
Hardy to 15F to 20F
Low water use

The rapid growth, high canopy and fine-textured, dark green leaves create dense shade. Textured, multi-branched, reddish brown trunk with rough bark forms picturesque shapes. Train as a single-trunk or multitrunk tree. Can also be grown as a large, dense hedge. Leaf, pollen and flower litter can be a problem on patios and around pools.

Pruning & Maintenance
Clean out twiggy and dead interior branches to open inside of canopy for an airy look. Prune up droopy branches to allow sunlight to reach underplantings and to keep multiple trunks visible. Avoid making many heavy cuts on large branches at one time. Gradual pruning reduces suckering and stress. In windy areas, plants grown as trees need staking and sturdy, flexible ties for support the first one to two years. Limbs are susceptible to storm damage when trees are mature. When planting new trees in narrow planters or near landscaped areas, install root guards to contain roots. Good soil drainage required. Provide deep moisture to encourage deep roots. Roots growing just below the surface can develop sucker growth. Plants reseed easily. Susceptible to Texas root rot.

Rhus microphylla
Desert Sumac, Little leaf Sumac

Native to Texas, Arizona and New Mexico
Deciduous
4 to 12 feet high, 10 to 20 feet wide
Full sun to partial shade
Hardy to 5F
Low water use

The 2- to 4-inch, white flower clusters arrive in the spring. In summer and fall, orange fruit clusters add to plant interest. In late fall, leaves change from rose to purple.

Pruning & Maintenance
Can be thinned for open growth or trained as a thick hedge by clipping outside branches. To grow as small tree, prune up lower branches.

Rhus lancea
African Sumac

Rhus ovata
Sugar Sumac

Native to coastal and inland valleys,
    low-elevation deserts, central
    Arizona and Baja California at 3,000
    to 5,000 feet
Evergreen
10 to 18 feet high, 12 feet wide
Full sun, afternoon shade in
    hot-summer regions
Hardy to 5F
Low to moderate water use

A dense, slow-growing plant that can
be used as a large screen or hedge.
Folded leathery leaves have a vanilla
fragrance. They provide a sturdy
background to the 1-inch clusters of
red buds that open into white or pink
flowers. Orange to red berries follow.

Pruning & Maintenance
This is a solid plant that seldom
needs pruning, certainly no shearing,
if conditions are normal. With age,
give minor attention to removing
dead twigs from interior. Root rot is a
problem in some areas, especially in
clay soils. Deep, well-draining soil
preferred.

Rhus virens
Evergreen Sumac

Native to western Texas and
    northern Mexico
Evergreen
8 to 12 feet high, 8 feet wide
Full sun, afternoon shade in
    hot-summer regions
Hardy to 5F
Low water use

White flowers arrive in summer in 2-
inch clusters. Close-knit growth is a
refreshing green. Leaves drop and
regrow rapidly. They remain evergreen all winter, then in a week's time
new foliage arrives in spring. Orange-
red fruit covered with sticky hairs
provide fall and winter food for small
mammals and birds. Grow as a hedge
or screen.

Pruning & Maintenance
Tight growth habit keeps plants controlled. Pruning is minimal. Grows
with full foliage to ground level.
Excessive moisture creates excess
growth. Best in well-draining soil.

Ribes aureum
Golden Currant

Native to California
Deciduous
3 to 8 feet high, equal spread
Full sun, partial shade in
    hot-summer regions
Hardy to 0F
Low to high water use

Golden currant grows as a shrub. Its
light foliage and flower character
work well in natural settings as well
as in traditional gardens. Favors
moist to dry areas throughout
California inland valley regions. In
low-elevation desert areas, provide
with some shade. Showy, yellow,
tubular flowers with spicy fragrance
bloom February to June, followed by
red, orange or black berries favored
by birds.

Pruning & Maintenance
For bushy form, prune long branches
on young plants during winter dormancy. Old stems may need to be cut
back in winter at base of plant to
encourage new growth. Provide with
well-draining soil.

Romneya coulteri
Matilija Poppy

Native to coastal California from Santa
    Barbara County south to San Diego
    County, at 1,000 to 2,000 feet
8 feet high, 8 to 10 feet wide
Full sun
Hardy to 10F
Low water use

Matilija poppy is considered one of
California's most spectacular plants.
Locate where plants can spread and
grow freely. Large white flowers 4 to
9 inches across with yellow centers
are quite dramatic. They bloom in
June and July.

Pruning & Maintenance
In late fall after flowering when
plants appear a little straggly, cut
back to near ground level for rapid
recovery. Plants are more attractive in
summer if given extra water.

Rosa banksiae
Lady Banks Rose

Native to China
Perennial
20 feet high, 20 to 25 feet wide
Full sun, some shade in hot-summer
  regions
Hardy to 10F
Low to moderate water use

A time-honored introduction from China that is timeless in the garden. *Rosa banksiae* 'Lutea' is a deciduous, thornless semiclimbing rose. It grows vigorously so needs space of 20 to 30 feet or more to spread. Can be used on slopes as a ground cover. Grow as a backdrop on overheads and fences. The light yellow flowers blend well with the numerous, yellow-flowering native plants available. 'Alba Plena' is semi-evergreen. Flowers are white and have a light fragrance, blooming in early to late spring. Some plants have a few thorns.

Pruning & Maintenance
Both species require little pruning but growth can become rampant. Leave them untouched to cover large areas, or prune errant branches for situations that require more control. Prune in late summer after flowering season is complete. Reduce amount of water applied when plants are dormant in winter.

Rosmarinus officinalis 'Prostrata'
Prostrate Rosemary

Native to the Mediterranean region
Evergreen
2 feet high, 4 to 8 feet wide
Full sun
Hardy to 10F
Low water use

This rugged, low-growing plant seems to thrive in heat, sun and poor soil. Ideal for slopes and banks, especially for erosion control on large areas. Not suited for foot traffic. The pale blue flowers that bloom in early spring attract bees.

Pruning & Maintenance
Growth increases rapidly once plants are established. Plants can be invasive, requiring control around companion plants and along the edges of curbs, walks or turf on a regular basis. To renew plants each year, cut back into hard wood about 6 to 12 inches. Do this after flowering but before heat comes on in spring. Prune ends of long, spreading branches for better coverage. In regions with high summer heat, additional moisture is necessary for good appearance. Irrigating with a drip system is ideal. Space rooted cuttings and 1-gallon-size plants 3 feet apart on centers.

Ruellia species
Wild Petunia

Native to the Sonoran Desert
Evergreen to semideciduous
1-1/2 to 4 feet high, equal spread
Full sun, tolerates some shade
Hardy to 28F
Low to high water use

Ruellia species are favored for their ability to provide color during the hottest summer weather. *R. brittoniana* has dark green leaves and deep, blue-purple, petunialike flowers that bloom with heat. Underground spreading roots transplant easily in late winter, and plants also reseed. Prior to end of winter, cut off old growth to about 6 inches above ground. Hardy to 28F.

R. brittoniana 'Katie' produces unique compact growth that remains at just 1-1/2 feet high, spreading to 2 feet wide. Plants thrive in containers. More flowers are produced when plants are in full sun. The crinkled leaves are 1/2-inch wide and 4 to 6 inches long. Hardy to 28F. Moderate water use. Plants spread by underground roots and can be invasive, so choose locations accordingly.

R. californica, wild petunia bush, has sticky leaves, unlike other *Ruellia* species. Plants grow 2 to 4 feet high with a compact habit. Locate in full sun. Seldom requires heavy pruning. Hardy to 28F.

R. peninsularis, Baja ruellia, grows 3 to 4 feet high and as wide. The petunialike flowers bloom consistently with heat.

Pruning & Maintenance

Pruning is minimal unless plants are damaged by frost. If this is the case, remove small, damaged twigs in early spring. Hardy to 22F. Reduce water applied in fall up to 50 percent to harden off plants.

Salix babylonica
Weeping Willow

Native to the Orient
Deciduous
35 feet high, equal spread
Full sun
Hardy to cold
Moderate to high water use

The airy and graceful form of willows are recognized throughout the Southwest. In the hottest regions, plants have a short life span mainly due to trunk, branch and leaf sun burn. Other trees that can simulate the willow's landscape effect are better suited to hot climates. Most are low to moderate water users with graceful forms. These include *Acacia salicina,* willow wattle; *Acacia stenophylla,* shoestring acacia; *Callistemon viminalis,* weeping bottlebrush; *Chilopsis linearis,* desert willow; and *Chitalpa tashkentensis,* chitalpa.

Pruning & Maintenance

If dieback occurs with willows, it is often caused by sunburn. Remove dead portions when trees are dormant in winter. Avoid heavy pruning. Protect trunks from sunscald. Water deeply.

SALVIA SPECIES
SALVIAS

In a recent review of nursery sources for *Salvia* species, over 40 selections were found to be available. Some are adapted to coastal climates, others to inland valleys, others to low- and middle-elevation deserts. In our descriptions we include a selection of species that thrive in these areas. Many are remarkably long-lived and are among the most colorful and responsive groups of plants. Consult your nursery for the most appropriate choices in your area.

Salvia chamaedryoides
Blue Sage

Native to southern Chihuahuan Desert
and Mexico at 7,500 to 9,800 feet
Evergreen
1-1/2 feet high, 2 feet wide
Full sun
Hardy to 15F
Low water use

Cobalt blue flower spikes bloom against silvery leaves from spring into fall. Leaves are 1 inch long and 1/2-inch wide. *Psilostrophe cooperi,* paperflower, blooms at a similar time of year.

Pruning & Maintenance

By late winter, cut back plants by at least one-third. This will stimulate the plant to regrow the coming spring. Trim selectively and naturally rather than shearing. As with the other *Salvia* selections mentioned here, well-draining soil and sunny location are essential. Avoid overwatering in summer.

Salvia clevelandii
Chaparral Sage

Native to coastal hills and valleys of San
Diego County in southern California
and to Baja California
Evergreen
4 feet high, equal spread
Full sun
Hardy to 20F
Low water use

Heavily veined, gray-green leaves provide a strong background for the showy, blue-purple clusters of flowers May into August. Leaves emit a pleasant, musky fragrance when brushed. An attractive, long-lived, dry-garden plant. Blends well with *Leucophyllum* species, *Dalea greggii* and *Encelia farinosa.* Effective massed in clusters.

Pruning & Maintenance

After whorled flower clusters have completed their bloom cycle in August or September, deadhead for a clean look and to make room for next year's growth and flower crop. (See photo, page 58.)

Plant Spacing

When planting, allow for mature height and spread to reduce the need to constantly prune or trim. Regular trimming creates unsightly stubby hard wood with a hedgelike look. It also reduces the ability of flowering plants to bloom. When possible select dwarf or compact-growing forms if garden space is at a premium.

Salvia columbarie
Chia

Native to California and New Mexico
Evergreen
10 to 12 inches high, 18 inches wide
Full sun
Hardy to 32F
Low water use

This annual is a member of the mint family. Leaves are wrinkled and square stems pass through the buttons of lavender and blue flowers. Use in herb gardens, rock gardens and perennial beds.

Pruning & Maintenance
Cut back old stems and basal growth in early winter for new growth the next season. Thrives in sandy soils. Plants go dormant with 32F temperatures.

Salvia columbarie
Chia

Salvia dorri var. dorri
Desert Sage

Native to southwestern California, southern Nevada and northwestern Arizona at 2,000 to 7,000 feet
Evergreen
2 feet high, equal spread
Full sun, partial shade in hot-summer regions
Hardy to 16F
Low water use

The silver-gray foliage and rounded, 1-inch, violet-blue flowers make a striking color combination. After flowers complete their bloom cycle, dry brown flower spikes provide an interesting contrast.

Pruning & Maintenance
For a neater appearance, hand-clip flower spikes after flowers turn dry and brown. A low-maintenance plant.

Salvia farinacea
Mealy Cup Sage, Blue Salvia

Native to Texas and southern New Mexico
Perennial
1-1/2 feet high, equal spread
Full sun
Hardy to 24F
Moderate water use

A popular color plant in the Southwest and in other areas of the U.S. The 6-inch, violet-blue spikes flower best during the hot summer, beginning in May and continuing through September. Plants require additional water when temperatures exceed 100F. Combine with *Coreopsis* species for a striking, blue-yellow combination. 'Victoria', with compact growth to 12 inches high, is a quality selection.

Pruning & Maintenance
Trim back spent spikes that sometimes become afflicted with mildew during late summer. Roots are cold hardy. Cut back to near ground level after coldest weather has passed but before warm days of spring. This cleans up leggy growth and encourages plant to create new flower spikes for the coming season.

Salvia greggii
Autumn Sage

Native to Texas and Chihuahuan Desert in Mexico
Perennial
2 to 3 feet high, 3 feet wide
Full sun, filtered shade in hot-summer regions
Hardy to 0F
Low to moderate water use depending on soil and drainage

'Sierra Linda' is a preferred selection. The mother plant in Phoenix, Arizona, is over 20 years old and still blooming. Within about six months after planting from gallon-size containers, plants become established and are covered with magenta flowers. Hummingbirds enjoy the rich nectar. Other good selections include 'Ruby Red', 'Cherry Red' and 'White'.

Pruning & Maintenance
For optimum flowers, prune in tune with the gardening seasons. As with other salvias, cut off old flower stems to the green leafy area after flowering to stimulate growth of new flowering wood. Make last cuts in late April. Avoid summer pruning, then prune plants again by late September to encourage winter color. Once a year in late winter, cut plants back by one-

half. Prune into old wood and thin out some older interior stems to create new growth. Plants are water-efficient and go into slight dormancy during summer heat. Well-draining soil preferred.

Salvia leucantha
Mexican Bush Sage

Native to eastern and central Mexico
Evergreen
3 to 4 feet high and as wide
Full sun to partial shade
Hardy to 24F
Low to moderate water use

The violet, velvety flower spikes provide brilliant color during summer and into fall. Gray-green foliage blends well with many arid plants. Flowers are long-lived in arrangements. Root growth is extremely vigorous.

Pruning & Maintenance
In late fall after flowering is complete, cut all stems and branches back to 6 to 12 inches above ground. (See photos, page 57.) Plants regrow quickly with warm spring weather. In low-elevation gardens, growth develops earlier—during late winter.

Salvia leucophylla
Purple Sage

Native to the coastal ranges of
    California from San Luis Obispo to
    Orange County
Evergreen
4 to 6 feet high, 5 to 6 feet wide
Full sun, partial shade in hot-summer
    regions
Hardy to 20F to 25F
Low water use

Lavender-pink whorls bloom early to late spring and are similar to flowers of *S. clevelandii* although lighter in color. Leaves are gray-green.

Pruning & Maintenance
Whorls of spent flowers can be deadheaded for a neater appearance if desired but look acceptable if left on plant. Good soil drainage is essential.

Schefflera elegantissima
False Aralia

(Dizygotheca elegantissima)
Native to New Caledonia and Polynesia
Evergreen
6 to 15 feet high, 5 to 7 feet wide
Filtered morning sun only in
    hot-summer regions, full sun with
    afternoon shade elsewhere
Hardy to 32F
Moderate to high water use

As the name implies, growth is vertical with elegant, 6- to 10-inch, reddish brown leaves and stems. An indoor plant as well as a great accent on protected patios along the coast. In inland valley and low-elevation arid gardens, shelter from wind.

Pruning & Maintenance
Seldom requires pruning. Provide with well-draining soil. Generally pest-free.

Schinus molle
California Pepper

Native to South America
Evergreen
25 feet high, 40 feet wide
Full sun
Hardy to 20F
Low to moderate water use

The bright green, graceful foliage of California pepper is attractive at a distance and up close. Growth is rapid and branches hang to the ground, heavy with leaves. *Prosopis glandulosa* var. *glandulosa*, Texas honey mesquite, has a similar appearance with look-alike, bright green leaves and graceful branches.

Lacy foliage hangs gracefully in clusters for unusual soft effect. Use in open garden areas where competitive roots can spread freely. White summer flowers develop into clusters of red berries in winter.

Pruning & Maintenance
Young trees—three to five years old—require minimum maintenance. The challenge occurs when trunks and branches become large. Quite often, they are damaged by windstorms. Limb breakage causes trees to become unbalanced and exposes the

Schinus molle
California Pepper

trunk to decay. Prune to thin out excessive growth early in spring prior to hot weather. Exposed branches sunburn readily. Well-draining soil required for long-lived trees. In clay or caliche soil, trees are more susceptible to Texas root rot.

Sequoiadendron giganteum
California Big Tree

Native to California
Evergreen
30 to 45 feet high, 25 to 30 feet wide (in garden setting; in nature can grow more than 300 feet high)
Full sun
Hardy to cold
Low to moderate water use

Closely related to the coast redwood, *Sequoia sempervirens,* but this tree accepts heat of interior valleys and foothill slopes. Not for the desert, however. Foliage grows tight around large trunks and is considered slow in comparison to other conifers. A feature in the landscape to be viewed at a distance. Use with other native plants.

Pruning & Maintenance
Minimum, if any, pruning. Avoid pruning because trees shape themselves naturally. Provide deep irrigation.

Simmondsia chinensis
Jojoba

Native to desert foothills in southern California and Arizona at 1,000 to 4,300 feet
Evergreen
4 to 8 feet high, equal spread
Full sun
Hardy to 15F
Low water use

A distinctive native desert shrub that's also grown commercially for its acornlike seeds. Gray-green, leathery leaves grow densely and in well-controlled form. Its mounding growth habit is well adapted to informal as well as formal designs. Use as a foundation plant, hedge or background shrub. Male and female flowers are borne on different plants, so both must be present for the female to produce seeds.

Pruning & Maintenance
Due to slow growth rate and compact habit, little or no pruning required. Prune in late spring to control plant size as needed. Plant in well-draining soil. A true low-maintenance plant.

Sophora secundiflora
Texas Mountain Laurel

Native to Texas, New Mexico and northeastern Mexico at 1,000 to 5,000 feet
Evergreen
15 to 20 feet high, 8 to 10 feet wide
Full sun
Hardy to 10F
Low water use

Other common names for this plant include mescal bean, frijolito and sophora. The dense, glossy green leaves develop on low, thornless branches or multiple stems. Relates well as shrub background with lower-growing companion plants such as *Cordia parvifolia, Dalea frutescens* and *Encelia farinosa.*

Purple flowers in 4-inch to 8-inch clusters drape like wisteria. They emit a fragrance similar to grape soda.

Pruning & Maintenance
Prune carefully. Excessive pruning can inhibit flowering because flowers are produced only on one-year-old wood. This is not a plant to be sheared or even thinned if it can be avoided. Shearing eliminates flowering growth. Natural growth of plants is dense enough for a hedgelike effect. Or prune up lower spreading branches, encouraging vertical growth to develop into small tree. Remove dead interior branches any time. Remove and dispose of seed pods. The orange seed inside is poisonous but difficult to reach. Larvae of the pyralid moth feed on leaves, young twig growth and immature seed pods. Control with applications of *Bacillus thuringiensis* (commonly called B.T.), a widely available biological control agent. Adapted to well-draining alkaline soils and high temperatures.

Tagetes lemmonii
Mt. Lemmon Marigold

Native to southeastern Arizona at
   3,000 feet
Evergreen
3 to 4 feet high, equal spread
Full sun
Hardy to 28F
Low to moderate water use

This is a shrubby, long-lived plant that is widely adapted to dry climates. Foliage produces an intensely aromatic fragrance when brushed. Golden orange, daisylike flowers add color in winter and spring. Blend with other Chihuahuan and Sonoran natives as a foreground shrub.

Pruning & Maintenance
For dense growth, more flowering wood and stronger stems, cut back after bloom in late spring. After time, growth may sprawl. Cut back by one-third to control in early summer. Provide with well-draining soil.

Tamarix aphylla
Tamarisk, Athel Tree

Native to northern Africa and eastern
   Mediterranean region
Deciduous
30 to 50 feet high, 40 feet wide
Full sun
Hardy to 0F
Low water use

In the past, tamarisk helped stabilize wasteland areas made inhospitable due to wind, drought and alkaline conditions. It has the ability to develop new growth in sandy soil areas when land is disturbed. But in your own landscape, it is important to eradicate tamarisk plants. Their roots search out moisture with a remarkable tenacity. If you inherit established tamarisk trees and you want to keep them (they do reduce sand and wind blow), it may be wise to install root barriers to keep roots from invading other areas of your garden. Leaf debris is an ongoing problem.

Pruning & Maintenance
Avoid cutting side branches or topping plants. This only creates more regrowth and leaf drop. To control invasive roots, dig trench 3 feet deep 4 to 6 feet away from trees. Install 3-foot-wide galvanized metal or plastic panels (see page 18) to contain roots.

Tecoma stans var. angustata
Yellow Bells, Yellow Trumpet Flower

Native to southeastern Arizona,
   southern New Mexico and Texas
Evergreen
5 to 10 feet high, 6 to 8 feet wide
Full sun
Hardy to 20F
Low to moderate water use

Lush, dark green leaves set off the yellow, 2-inch, trumpet-shaped flowers that bloom from April until November or first frost. Strong vertical stems support flowers in a well-distributed pattern. 'Duval' produces deep yellow flowers.

Pruning & Maintenance
Harden off growth by reducing water and no fertilizer applications after September. Low to moderate water use produces best growth and flower display. Cut back long, straggly growth as needed. Plant in well-draining soil along a south-facing wall or fence for cold protection. (See illustration, page 11.) If frost damage occurs, remove affected parts in early spring. Plant will respond with new growth as warm weather comes on.

Tecomaria capensis
Cape Honeysuckle

Native to South Africa
Evergreen
10 to 14 feet high, 10 to 20 feet wide
Full sun to partial shade
Hardy to 28F
Moderate to high water use

A vigorous, fernlike plant that thrives in heat. Its orange, trumpet-shaped flowers are at their best from late fall well into late winter. Rapid-growing, vining branches need direction in youth if they are trained on fences or walls. If used as a ground cover, pin down long branches with U-shaped pins. Can also be grown as a large shrub to 8 to 10 feet high or as a wide-spreading vine to 25 feet.

Overwatering
Watering too much and too often is a common cause of plant problems. A fine line exists between the correct amount of water and an excessive amount. Keeping plants on the dry side but irrigating deeply helps produce deep roots. This helps make plants better conditioned to accept the stress of extreme heat, drying winds and cold.

Pruning & Maintenance

Because of rapid growth rate, you soon learn to have pruning shears handy as you inspect plants to keep them in control. This is especially true from spring to early fall. To reduce the chance of frost damage, cut back amount of water applied in fall 20 to 30 percent. This also helps promote heavier flowering. Plant after frost in the spring and early summer.

Thevetia peruviana
Yellow Oleander

Native to Peru
Evergreen
6 to 8 feet high, 10 to 12 feet wide
Full sun
Hardy to 30F to 32F
Moderate water use

Clusters of yellow to apricot flowers bloom six months of the year: April through September. Leaves are deep green and 3 to 6 inches long, giving the plant a luxuriant, tropical appearance. Mostly grown as a colorful, 8- to 10-foot hedge, but over time can be trained as a tree to 20 feet high. A similar species, *T. thevetioides*, giant thevetia, has darker leaves and grows more treelike to 12 feet high and as wide. Flowers 4 inches in diameter are bright yellow and develop in clusters.

Pruning & Maintenance

Plants are frost tender and also require wind protection. Plants grow rapidly through hot weather and the lush growth usually needs some control. Prune gradually so as to maintain color into fall. Thin rather than shear. Harden off plants by reducing water by 30 percent and ceasing fertilization in October. Plant in deep soil with good drainage.

Trachycarpus fortunei
Windmill Palm

Native to China and northern Burma
Evergreen
15 feet high, 4 to 6 feet wide at crown
Full sun to partial or filtered shade
Hardy to 10F
Low to moderate water use

A dramatic palm, whether used alone or in clusters. Size makes it appropriate for small patios or courtyards. Slow-growing, bearing a compact crown, 3 feet in diameter, composed of dark green fans. Slender, fibrous stems are matted with long hair. Does well in the Mojave Desert at 2,000 to 2,500 feet and in most Sonoran Desert areas, including Phoenix and Tucson. Not adapted to hot, sunny areas in the upper Sonoran Coachella Valley. Protect from heavy winds.

Pruning & Maintenance

Remove dead fronds and seed stems as they occur. Do not "skin" heavy trunks. Best time to transplant is when weather warms in late spring. Container plants establish best. Provide moderate water during growing seasons. A low-maintenance plant.

Tulbaghia violacea
Society Garlic

Native to South Africa
Perennial
1 to 2 feet high, 1-1/2 feet wide
Full sun to light shade
Hardy to 20F to 25F
Low to moderate water use

Low-growing, blue-green clumps bear rose-lavender flowers on clusters of 1- to 2-foot stems. Flowers are most profuse in spring and summer. Basal leaf clumps grow to 12 inches high. Despite the garlic odor that emits from crushed leaves, plants find favor in many regions of the arid West. In hottest regions, light shade and moderate moisture improve blooming. Tolerates full sun and requires less water in milder climates. A selection with variegated foliage is now available. Use as a border plant in small areas or in containers.

Pruning & Maintenance

A choice, low-maintenance color plant. Cut back flower stems at basal clumps after bloom period.

Tulbaghia violacea
Society Garlic

Vauquelinia angustifolia
Slimleaf Rosewood

Native to Chihuahuan Desert in Big
    Bend region in Texas, and Mexico
Evergreen
15 feet high, 10 feet wide
Full sun, afternoon shade in
    hot-summer regions
Hardy to 10F
Low to moderate water use

The 4-inch, narrow, serrated leaves
are somewhat different from those of
V. californica, following. This plant is
a suitable alternative to oleander.
Fragrant white flower clusters bloom
from June into August.

Pruning & Maintenance
Plants are well behaved. Avoid shearing. As plants mature remove interior
dead wood as needed. Provide with
well-draining soil.

Vauquelinia californica
Arizona Rosewood

Native to southern Arizona from 2,500
    to 5,000 feet
Evergreen
6 to 14 feet high, 10 to 12 feet wide
Full sun
Hardy to 15F
Low to moderate water use

Stiff, dark green leaves are 1/2 inch
wide and 2 inches long and have
toothed edges. Flat-topped, white
flower clusters bloom during spring
and early summer. Brown fruit hang
on branches into winter.

Pruning & Maintenance
Plants seem to develop fullness without pruning—they become naturally
dense. They can be trained to become
small trees by pruning up lower
branches after three or four years of
growth.

Vauquelinia pauciflora

Native to Chihuahuan Desert
Evergreen
10 to 25 feet high, equal spread
Full sun
Hardy to 10F
Low water use

A *V. californica* look-alike but growth
is more vigorous and leaves are
smaller, creating a more dense, compact appearance. Clusters of white
flowers in spring stand out against
dark green leaves. Young plants are
slow starters but growth rate increases after plants become established.
Makes a natural tall hedge as an
alternative to oleander.

Pruning & Maintenance
Dense, close-knit growth reduces
need to prune. If light selective pruning is required, do it during winter.
Avoid shearing. For a small tree,
begin pruning lower branches gradually, after plant reaches 8 to 10 feet
high. Good soil drainage is required.
Plants have some tolerance to alkaline soils.

Verbena gooddingii
Gooding's Verbena

(*Glandularia gooddingii*)
Evergreen
1 foot high, 3 feet wide
Full sun
Hardy to 10F
Moderate water use during growth peri-
    ods; low water use in dormancy

This species is becoming a Southwest
favorite with its vigorous, spreading
growth, lush appearance, fragrant
lavender flowerheads and soft,
deeply cut, medium green, oval
leaves. Plants flower profusely in
spring and sometimes into fall,
reseeding readily in the process.

Pruning & Maintenance
Trim away frayed, tired growth when
plants are dormant during winter.
Cut back invasive growth anytime to
prevent overgrowing nearby plants.

Verbena peruviana
Peruvian Verbena

(*Verbena chamaedryfolia*)
Native to Peru
Evergreen
8 to 10 inches high, 36 inches wide
Full sun, some shade in hot-summer
    regions
Hardy to 24F
Low water use

Tool Care
After using pruning tools,
they should be thoroughly
washed then dried and
coated with a light oil. This
will prevent tools from
rusting. Store tools out of
the weather. Keep blades
sharp so all cuts you make
are clean. Dull tools make
ragged, uneven cuts, which
are slower to heal and can
invite pests and diseases.

These vigorous-growing plants have dark green, fine-textured leaves that weave together in a thick mat. Flower colors include purple, salmon, red, pink and white. Flowers are most attractive in spring and fall. Usually best to use in small areas rather than in large masses. This is because plants tend to die back under unfavorable conditions, such as too much or too little moisture, poor drainage or excessive heat.

Pruning & Maintenance
Prune to remove spent flowers. Cut back plants to reduce buildup of old wood and to encourage new flowering wood. Best time to prune is late winter, prior to the surge of new growth in spring.

Verbena rigida
Sandpaper Verbena

(Verbena venosa)
Native to Argentina
Evergreen
2 feet high, 4 feet wide
Full sun
Hardy to 15F
Low to moderate water use

Unique foliage is composed of toothed, rough-textured, 2- to 4-inch-long, dark green leaves. Tall, stiff stems support vivid purple flowers in cylindrical clusters. A low-maintenance ground cover that accepts considerable drought once established.

Pruning & Maintenance
If planting beds begin to create mounds, trim plants back to 6 inches above ground. Cut edges back along walks or curbs and reduce growth around other plants.

Verbena tenera
Moss Verbena

(Verbena tenuisecta)
Native to South America
Evergreen
6 to 12 inches high, 4 to 6 feet wide
Full sun
Hardy to 20F
Low water use

This plant is distinguished by lacy, finely cut leaves and wide-spreading growth. The far-reaching branches readily take root as they spread in all directions. Showy purple flowers provide a show of color during the heat of summer except in hot, low-elevation areas. Flowers reseed generously. Plant in open, sunny areas for most colorful effect.

Pruning & Maintenance
A light, late-spring trimming cleans up faded flowers and sets the stage for more flower production later on. Overwatering may promote excessive foliage growth that can reduce flowering.

Viguiera deltoidea
Golden Eye

Native to southwestern California and Arizona and southern Nevada at 1,000 to 3,500 feet
Evergreen
3 feet high, equal spread
Full sun
Hardy to 25F
Low water use

A compact-growing plant with gray-green leaves. Yellow, daisylike flowers 1 inch across bloom from spring into early summer. Moderate size of plants makes them useful in perennial beds as a background planting. Also effective among boulders, where it nestles naturally between stones.

Pruning & Maintenance
Pruning after each bloom cycle helps produce denser growth and more flowers.

Vitex agnus-castus
Chaste Tree

Native to southern Europe
Deciduous
20 to 25 feet high, 25 feet wide
Full sun
Hardy to 20F
Low water use

Hot weather is a must to develop the 15- to 18-inch flower clusters. In addition to the lavender flowers of the species, 'Alba' (white) and 'Rosea' (pink) are also available. All bloom in summer. Strong shrubby growth provides support for the 6-inch, fan-shaped leaves.

Pruning & Maintenance
Deadhead old flower stems after bloom has ceased. Plants require some interior thinning in winter to renew growth, but don't overdo it. Can be trained as a small multitrunked tree, but requires encouraging vertical growth when tree is young.

Washingtonia filifera
California Fan Palm

Native to mountain canyons of the Coachella Valley near Palm Springs and other regions in Sonoran Desert
Evergreen
60 to 75 feet high; 20 to 25 feet wide
Full sun to partial shade
Hardy to 18F
Moderate to high water use

The massive trunks of California fan palm can reach 3 feet in diameter, but growth is much slower than that of *W. robusta*, Mexican fan palm. Large, fan-shaped leaves, 4 to 6 feet wide, develop and grow for one year into heavy masses. They then turn into light brown petticoats, hugging the trunk, after they mature and complete their growth cycle. Roots are fibrous and grasslike with no taproot. In spring, cream-colored flowers are abundant on the long, stringy, hanging branches. By late summer, black-berry-like fruit develop. Winds and birds generally knock off fruit by the fall. These palms are ideal accents in open areas and around large structures but grow out of proportion when used in residential gardens.

Pruning & Maintenance
To maintain their natural look, locate in areas where debris will not be a problem. The long seed branches are difficult to remove unless you remove the frond skirts. Pruning work should be done with hydraulic lift equipment rather than by allowing someone to climb the stout trunks. Palms growing 8 to 20 feet high can usually be handled with sturdy ladders. At no time should climbing spurs be used due to the damage they can inflict on trunks.

This is especially true if trunks have been "skinned," when the old frond stubs, which help protect the trunk, have been removed.

Experience shows that only dead fronds and seed branches should be removed. Green, growing fronds should be left on the tree. Overly zealous pruning that causes the top of the trunk to taper produces what's called a *paintbrush effect*. This sets the stage for serious problems, with the newly exposed, tender crown tissue an invitation to the giant palm borer. (See illustration, page 47.) The pest's habit is to invade the trunk and eat extensive tunnels, eventually killing the tree. The same beetle has been known to attack commercial date palms and *Brahea armata*, blue fan palm. Exit holes in trunk surfaces indicate beetle activity.

Treatment for giant palm-borer:
Wayne Price of Price Nursery in Cathedral City, California, has used the following treatment to combat palm borer infestations. Treatment should occur in March and April, periods when beetles are busy laying their eggs. This is when they are most vulnerable.

Mix 1 cup of powdered malathion to 5 gallons of water. It is necessary to apply this solution from *above* the crown area. About the only way to do this is in a crane bucket lift. Pour the malathion solution *over the top* of fronds. This is where the beetles enter the crown.

Palms that are drought-stressed appear to be more susceptible to attack. Help avoid infestations by keeping trees healthy with regular deep irrigations.

Washingtonia robusta
Mexican Fan Palm

Native to Baja California
Evergreen
50 to 75 feet high; fronds and crown to 15 feet wide
Full sun
Hardy to 25F
High water use

The fronds of Mexican fan palm are much smaller than those of the

When pruning palm trees or when having them pruned, don't prune too severely, creating a tapering, "paintbrush" form. (See example, above right.) If too many fronds are removed, the newly exposed area is susceptible to insect attack. Wait until fronds die and turn brown before removing, so palm maintains a more natural form. (See example above left.)

California fan. Growth is also more rapid—so much so that trees quickly become too tall for most residential settings. Look most effective in clusters using plants with varying heights. Single trees produce an uninteresting "telephone-pole effect" after a period of time.

Pruning & Maintenance

Most important maintenance tip is to allow green and growing fronds to remain on the trunk for as long as possible. They help to provide healthy growth. Many maintenance people trim the fronds up to a tapering paintbrush, which can interrupt growth. (See illustration, page 153.) Remove only *dead* fronds and seed-producing branches. Ideal time to prune is in summer. Do not allow maintenance workers to use climbing spurs on this palm; they can severely damage the exterior bark, producing potential entry holes for pests and diseases. Keep palms healthy with sufficient summer water. Mature palms require up to 20 to 35 gallons of water or more per day.

Westringia fruticosa
Coast Rosemary

Native to Australia
Evergreen
3 to 6 feet high, 8 to 12 feet wide
Full sun, afternoon or filtered shade in hot-summer regions
Hardy to 20F
Low water use

Pale gray leaves resemble rosemary, but growth of coast rosemary is much more natural and mounding. Form and foliage work well with many other low-water-use plants. Star-shaped white flowers develop in small clusters in spring as well as during warm months of the year.

Pruning & Maintenance
Maintains form well on its own so requires little pruning. Give plants plenty of space to grow to their natural mature size. Accepts wind and salt spray, and sandy or alkaline soils.

Xylosma congestum
Glossy Xylosma

Xylosma congestum
Glossy Xylosma

Native to Lima, Peru
Evergreen
6 to 10 feet high, 8 to 10 feet wide
Full sun to afternoon shade
Hardy to 15F
Moderate water use

This is a versatile, medium-size shrub with glossy, light green foliage. New growth has a reddish tint. A time-honored favorite in Las Vegas, Tucson, Phoenix and the Coachella Valley. It can be used as an espalier for wall covering and also as a small tree, shrub or hedge. Side branches arch gracefully. A dwarf selection, 'Compactum', grows 4 to 6 feet high.

Pruning & Maintenance
Flexible side branches make it an ideal plant for espalier training. After framework has been developed, shear side growth. Graceful, arching growth does not lend itself to be pruned into square or round shapes.

YUCCA SPECIES
YUCCAS

Yuccas native to arid regions play important roles in gardens that emulate the natural environment. They provide a definite sense of place as accents, in containers and among boulder groupings. *Yucca brevifolia*, Joshua tree, for example, certainly makes a statement that it is a symbol of the Mojave Desert.

Yucca brevifolia
Joshua Tree

Native to the Mojave Desert
Evergreen
15 to 30 feet high, 6 to 10 feet wide
Full sun
Hardy to 10F
Low water use

As you travel through the Mojave Desert, you'll probably notice *Yucca brevifolia*, one of the best-known *Yucca* species. Some of these plants are among the oldest living creatures in the Mojave Desert. White flower clusters are produced in summer. Many side branches develop on older plants.

Pruning & Maintenance
Does not accept transplanting into low-elevation desert areas well. Better adapted to higher-elevation regions. Must have well-draining soil.

Yucca elata
Soaptree Yucca

Native to western Texas, Arizona, New Mexico and Mexico
Evergreen
6 to 20 feet high, 5 to 10 feet wide
Full sun
Hardy to 15F
Low water use

A graceful plant in youth that grows rapidly. Best as background planting. Trunks can be single or branched. Linear leaves grow to 38 inches long, 1 inch wide, with white or green margins.

Pruning & Maintenance
Needs well-draining soil.

Yucca recurvifolia
Pendulous Yucca

Native to southern U.S., Georgia to Mississippi
Evergreen
6 feet high, with equal spread
Full sun
Hardy to 10F
Low water use

Flexible leaves are tipped with spines that also bend to the touch. Graceful, appearance that is attractive in perennial beds and rock gardens. White flower clusters grow 3 to 5 feet high. Often develops offsets, which increase size and spread of planting.

Pruning & Maintenance
Yucca beetle can be a serious problem, attacking roots, causing plants to look stressed for moisture. Treat affected plants or prevent infestations with application of diazinon as a soil drench. Follow all product label directions. Remove dead basal leaves as they occur to maintain a clean, neat look. Requires well-draining soil.

Yucca rigida
Blue Yucca

Native to the Chihuahuan Desert in Mexico
Evergreen
8 feet high, 3 feet wide
Full sun
Hardy to 0F
Low water use

Composed mainly of simple stems and a few branches. Rigid, concave, blue-green leaves reach to 2 feet long. Plant well away from traffic areas due to sharp spines at ends of leaves.

Pruning & Maintenance
Remove dead leaves as they occur. Plant in well-draining soil.

Yucca rupicola
Twisted-Leaf Yucca

Native to south central Texas
Evergreen
3 feet high, 4 to 5 feet wide
Full sun
Hardy to 15F
Low water use

Graceful, twisting leaves create an unusual effect, different from other *Yucca* species. Clumps form readily, creating an appealing effect with natural, open clusters.

Pruning & Maintenance
Remove dead leaves as they occur. Provide with well-draining soil.

Yucca whipplei
Our Lord's Candle

Native to California and Baja California
Evergreen
3 feet high, with equal spread
Full sun
Hardy to 20F
Low water use

Sturdy flower spikes with creamy white flowers can reach to 10 feet high during summer months. Leaves are gray-green.

Pruning & Maintenance
Provide with well-draining soil. Remove dead leaves as they occur for groomed appearance, often desired in close-up locations. In natural settings retain natural effect by not removing

leaves. As flower stalks complete flowering, remove at base.

Zauschneria californica
California Fuchsia, Hummingbird Trumpet

Native to California, southern Arizona
    and southwest New Mexico
Perennial
1 to 2 feet high, 4 to 6 feet wide
Full sun important
Hardy to 32F
Low to moderate water use

Colorful and low-growing, with gray leaves and tubular, orange-red flowers that bloom summer into fall. Hummingbirds appreciate the long, late flowering season. To develop established, underground runners, especially around boulders or in rock gardens, provide with moderate water. If given low water, growth persists but is ragged.

Pruning & Maintenance
Goes dormant when temperatures reach 32F. After dormancy or frost, trim dead growth at ground level. Plants will regrow the following spring. Underground runners respond to warm temperatures with vigorous growth. Prefers poor soil.

Zephyranthes candida
White Rain Lily

Native to La Plata region of South
    America
Deciduous
12 inches high, equal spread
Full sun tolerable, prefers filtered shade
Cold hardy
Low water use

Narrow, glossy green leaves give plant a lush appearance. White flowers in fall are almost a surprise when they appear on thin stems. Excellent for small-space areas. Plants with pink flowers also available. Leaves are wider than the species but it does not bloom quite as profusely. Use in clusters 12 to 15 inches apart among rock groupings.

    Z. sulphurea is similar with profuse yellow flowers.

Pruning & Maintenance
Clip off dead flower stems and

leaves. Bulbs go dormant in winter. In periods of drought, plants die back to the ground but come back when moisture is supplied. Provide with good soil drainage.

Ziziphus jujuba
Chinese Date

Native to southeastern Europe to Asia
Deciduous
20 to 30 feet high, 15 to 20 feet wide
Full sun
Cold hardy as far north as New York
Moderate to high water use

Picturesque gnarled branches in weeping form support glossy, bright green leaves. Yellow flowers appear May through June. Edible, datelike fruit follow in fall, when leaves turn shades of gold. Grows slowly.

Pruning & Maintenance
Late-winter applications of fertilizer benefit growth. Prune in winter to direct growth or to remove branches that cross one other. Produces deep roots, so water deeply. Accepts saline or alkaline soils.

Ziziphus obtusifolia
Gray Thorn

Native to Arizona, Nevada, California,
    New Mexico, Texas and Oklahoma at
    1,000 to 5,000 feet
Deciduous
6 feet high, 8 feet wide
Full sun
Hardy to 15F
Low water use

Valued as a barrier-security plant and for attracting wildlife. Dense stems have thorns at tips. Small, blue-black fruit in fall contrasts nicely with gray leaves. Interweaving branches provide shelter and nesting sites for birds as they enjoy the fruit.

Pruning & Maintenance
Plants shape themselves rather well, reaching maturity with minimum pruning. Provide with well-draining soil. After plants have been growing for a year or two, they can survive on rainfall, except in hot low-elevation desert regions. A good alternative to *Celtis pallida*.

Public Gardens

Public botanical gardens and arboretums are excellent places to visit and learn about the native and adapted plants that will grow in your region.

ARIZONA GARDENS

Arizona-Sonora Desert Museum
2021 North Kinney Road
Tucson, AZ 85703
(520) 883-2702 for information
More than 15 developed acres, including natural habitat zoo and demo gardens.

Desert Botanical Garden
1201 North Galvin Parkway
Phoenix, AZ 85008
(602) 941-1225
145 acres of landscaped grounds of arid-land plants.

Boyce Thompson Southwestern Arboretum
37615 Highway 60
Superior, AZ 85273
(520) 689-2811
Over 35 acres and 2 miles of nature trails.

Tohono Chul Park
7366 North Paseo del Norte
Tucson, AZ 85704
(520) 575-8468 for recorded information
(520) 742-6455
Over 400 plant species on 48 acres of demonstration gardens and nature trails.

Tucson Botanical Gardens
2150 North Alvernon Way
Tucson, AZ 85712
(520) 326-9686
Over 5 acres of gardens including a Xeriscape demonstration garden.

CALIFORNIA GARDENS

Arboretum of Los Angeles County
301 North Baldwin Avenue
Arcadia, CA 91007-2697
(818) 821-3222 or (213) 821-3214
Over 127 acres of landscaped grounds and plant collections.

Univ. of California at Berkeley
Berkeley Botanical Garden
Centennial Drive at Strawberry Canyon
Berkeley, CA 94720
(510) 643-8040 or 642-3343 for recorded message
30 acres of gardens with over 12,000 plant species.

Rancho Santa Ana Botanic Garden
1500 North College Avenue
Claremont, CA 91711
(714) 625-8767
86 acres of native California plants, including more than 1,500 species.

Davis Arboretum
Univ. of California at Davis
Davis, CA 95616
(916) 752-2498
Over 100 acres of gardens. Emphasis given to California native plants.

Quail Botanical Gardens
230 Quail Gardens Drive
Encinitas, CA 92024
(619) 436-3036
Over 30 acres of landscaped grounds, with trails, gardens and pools.

Fullerton Arboretum
California State Univ., Fullerton
P. O. Box 34080
Fullerton, CA 92634-9480
(714) 773-3579
26 acres of gardens, with botanical collections from around the world.

Univ. of California at Irvine Arboretum
(North Campus)
Irvine, CA 92717
(714) 856-5833
10 acres of gardens, with emphasis on cacti and succulents, as well as flowering bulbs and corms.

Descanso Gardens
1418 Descanso Drive
La Canada, CA 91011
(818) 952-4400; (818) 952-4401
Over 165 acres, including 15 acres of California natives.

The Living Desert
47900 Portola Avenue
Palm Desert, CA 92260
(619) 346-5694
Over 1,200 acres, with 20 acres in natural desert gardens, desert animals and demonstration gardens.

South Coast Botanical Garden
26300 Crenshaw Boulevard
Palos Verdes Peninsula, CA 90274
(310) 544-1847
Over 87 acres of gardens, demonstration plots and natural landscapes.

Univ. of California at Riverside Botanic Garden
UCR Campus
Riverside, CA 92521
(909) 787-4650 for recorded message
39 acres of natural gardens, with over 3,000 plants arranged by plant community.

Strybing Arboretum & Botanical Gardens
Golden Gate Park
Ninth Avenue at Lincoln Way
San Francisco, CA 94122
(415) 753-7089
75 acres within Golden Gate Park. Many specialty gardens. Contains over 8,000 plant species.

The Huntington Library, Art Collections and Botanical Gardens
1151 Oxford Road
San Marino, CA 91108
(818) 405-2141
150 acres of gardens, organized by themes such as Desert, Japanese and Jungle.

Santa Barbara Botanic Garden
1212 Mission Canyon Road
Santa Barbara, CA 93105
(805) 682-4726
65 acres of preserve and displays of California natives.

The Theodore Payne Foundation for Wildflowers and Native Plants
10459 Tuxford Street
Sun Valley, CA 91352
(818) 768-1802 for message
Over 21 acres of California natives and wildflowers.

Filoli
Canada Road
Woodside, CA 94602
(415) 364-2880
16 acres of gardens organized by themes: Sunken Garden, Walled Garden, Woodland Garden and Panel Garden.

COLORADO GARDENS

Denver Botanic Gardens
1005 York Street
Denver, CO 80206
(303) 331-4000
(303) 331-4010 for information
(303) 370-8032 (TDD)
22 acres including a Plains Garden, Xeriscape Garden and Rock Alpine Garden.

Chatfield Arboretum
8500 Deer Creek Canyon Road
Littleton, CO 80123
(303) 973-3705
A 700-acre natural area. Includes grassland, wetland, and historic farmstead.

NEVADA GARDENS

Ethel M Botanical Garden
2 Cactus Garden Drive
Henderson, NV 89014
(702) 458-8864
2 acres of desert shrubs, trees and cacti.

Las Vegas Desert Demonstration Gardens
3701 West Alta Drive
Las Vegas, NV 89153
(702) 258-3205
A small water-conservation garden, containing over 160 plant species.

Univ. of Nevada, Las Vegas Arboretum
Box 451013
4505 Maryland Parkway
Las Vegas, NV 89154
(702) 895-3392
An on-campus arboretum on the grounds of UNLV.

NEW MEXICO GARDENS

Living Desert Zoo and Gardens State Park
1504 Skyline Drive
Carlsbad, NM 88220
(505) 887-5516
Animals and plants of the Chihuahuan Desert.

TEXAS GARDENS

Austin Area Garden Center
(in Zilker Park)
2220 Barton Springs Road
Austin, TX 78746
(512) 477-8672
Several theme gardens including Xeriscape Garden.

National Wildflower Resource Center
4801 La Crosse Ave.
Austin, TX 78739
(512) 292-4100
(512) 292-4200 Wildflower bloom information.
60 acres of grounds. Native plants and their conservation.

Dallas Arboretum and Botanical Society
8617 Garland Road
Dallas, TX 75218
(214) 327-8263
66 acres, including 25 acres of landscaped gardens.

Dallas Horticulture Center
(in Fair Park)
3601 M.L.K. Blvd.
Dallas, TX 75315
(214) 428-7476
8 acres of gardens, including the Benny J. Simpson Texas Native Plant Collection.

Fort Worth Botanic Garden
3220 Botanic Garden Drive North
Fort Worth, TX 76107
(817) 871-7686
114 acres, including many specialty gardens.

Houston Arboretum and Nature Center
4501 Woodway Drive
Houston, TX 77024
(713) 681-8433
155 acres, including 5 miles of trails and wildflower garden.

Mercer Arboretum and Botanic Gardens
22306 Aldine Westfield
Humble, TX 77338
(713) 443-8731
214 acres, including many specialty gardens.

San Antonio Botanic Garden
555 Funston Place
San Antonio, TX 78209
(512) 821-5115 or 821-5143 for recorded information
30 acres of gardens, half of which are dedicated to showcasing native Texas plants.

Index

Numbers in bold italics refer to pages where photographs or illustrations appear.